ASTROLOGY
REALLY
WORKS!

ABOUT THE COVER

The cover is printed with the astrological birth chart of the Declaration of Independence, which is also the birth chart of the United States of America. Until the publication of this book, astrologers never understood the real reasons why the United States was so powerful and blessed. In this book, you will learn why July 4, 1776 was one of the most propitious astrological days of all time. You will also learn that America's Founding Fathers used astrology to choose the day on which to sign the Declaration of Independence.

ASTROLOGY REALLY WORKS!

THE
MAGI  SOCIETY™ ₛₘ

Astro Room,
a Division of
Hay House, Inc.
Carson, CA

Published and distributed in the United States by:
Hay House, Inc.
1154 E. Dominguez St., P.O. Box 6204, Carson, CA 90749-6204
(800) 654-5126

Edited by: Jill Kramer
Designed by: Highpoint, Claremont, CA

Library of Congress Cataloging-in-Publication Data

Astrology really works! / the Magi Society.
    p.   cm.
ISBN 1-56170-134-3 (trade paper)
1. Astrology. I. Magi Society.
BF1708. 1A88 1995
133.5—dc20   95-7644
                                        CIP

ISBN 1-56170-134-3

99 98 97 96 95 ,   5 4 3 2 1
First Printing, July 1995

Printed in the United States of America

The Magi Society is a forward-looking group;
we dedicate this book to all who will in the future
help the world to attain spiritual growth in
the coming Age of Aquarius.

C O N T E N T S

Chapter:

INTRODUCTION: ASTROLOGY
IS FINALLY PROVABLE

The Magi Society has been looking forward to January of 1996. It is then that Uranus will fully enter Aquarius and will remain there until 2003. We look forward to this date because we believe in astrology, and astrology flourishes when Uranus is in Aquarius. Such was the case the last time Uranus was in Aquarius from 1912 to 1919. In those years, there was a worldwide resurgence of astrology, led by the United States and England. In fact, a number of books tell us that during that time, the great American astrologer Evangeline Adams was acquitted of a fortune-telling charge because Judge John H. Freschi decided that she had raised astrology to the dignity of an exact science; Evangeline Adams' clients included J.P. Morgan and King Edward VII.

In anticipation of the placement of Uranus in the sign of Aquarius, the Magi Society conducted an extensive investigation into the birth charts of the super-rich, the super-famous, the super-successful, and the super-powerful. Our goal was to prove the validity of astrology. After researching the birth charts of all of the most successful men and women in America, we found that astrology unquestionably works. But of course, we, of the Magi Society, knew that all along due to our extraordinary and unsurpassed knowledge of astrology, which we call Magi Astrology.

One of the many things we learned during our study is that although the odds were much higher than a million to one, the five richest men in the United States all have the same ASTROLOGICAL ASPECT.

(All terms printed in the upper case will have an entry in the Glossary at the back of the book.) An astrological aspect is a specific type of alignment of specific planets at the time of birth. And billionaire businessmen Bill Gates, Warren Buffett, John Kluge, Edward Johnson III, and John Van Andel were all born with the same unusual astrological aspect. This aspect is rare enough that after this book is published in 1995, people will have to wait three years before it occurs again. So, there can be no reasonable doubt about it: astrology can tell you if someone has a jump start on amassing a real fortune. Together, these five men are worth over $30 billion, according to *Forbes* magazine.

Standard astrological knowledge and theories could not have accomplished this feat. But by applying Magi Astrology, a new and greatly expanded knowledge of astrology, it was easy to discover this astrological aspect of super success and finally prove conclusively that astrology really works. We must point out here that we are not referring to proving the astrology of the street-parlor charlatans that have been sprouting up all over. We are talking about proving the astrology of Sir Isaac Newton, Johannes Kepler, and Benjamin Franklin. These three men were the greatest scientists of their respective times, and all three were great believers in astrology their whole lives. Skeptics could ask why these three geniuses could not prove that astrology really worked during their lifetimes. Well, the answer is simple. They simply did not have large enough telescopes. You see, they did not know about Uranus, Neptune, and Pluto. Uranus was not discovered until 1781, when Franklin was 75 and long after Newton and Kepler died. Neptune was discovered in 1846. And Pluto was discovered so recently that if you were born after its discovery, you are probably still working and have not yet retired. Trying to prove astrology without knowledge of these three planets is like trying to do mathematics without three of the ten digits. You know it works, but you cannot prove it because there are too many blanks. And it is important to emphasize here and now that nobody has ever disproved astrology, even though astrology was missing key planets.

As we continued our research of famous people, we found something even more interesting. We discovered that people whose birth charts have this same specific rare astrological aspect that the five billionaires had were also much more likely to achieve great success in any profession. For this reason, the Magi Society has named this aspect the SUPER SUCCESS ASPECT. The most successful entertainers were born with this aspect. They include Mick Jagger, Oprah Winfrey, Kevin Costner, Harrison Ford, Kim Basinger, Denzel Washington, Barbra Streisand, Sean Connery, Clint Eastwood, Bill Cosby, Kathleen Turner, Robert Redford, and Mel Gibson, to name just some of them. Also, many of our most successful athletes were born with this Super Success Aspect. Joe Montana and Terry Bradshaw in football, Wayne Gretzky and Mark Messier in hockey, and Chris Evert and Ivan Lendl in tennis, are examples. As we explored a broad spectrum of professions, we found that an extraordinarily high percentage of individuals that were at the top of almost all high-profile professions were born with this Super Success Aspect. Here are examples of just a few of the other individuals who were born with the Super Success Aspect:

- **Steven Spielberg**, the most successful producer/director in Hollywood
- **Donna Karan** and **Ralph Lauren**, two of America's most successful fashion designers
- **Arnold Palmer** and **Jack Nicklaus**, the great golfers
- **Luciano Pavoratti**, possibly the best opera singer of our time
- **Bill Russell** and **Wilt Chamberlain**, the basketball immortals
- **Willie Mays** and **Jackie Robinson**, the baseball legends
- Heads of state **Mikhail Gorbachev**, **Boris Yeltsin**, **Prime Minister John Major**, **Chancellor Helmut Kohl**, **Ronald Reagan**, **George Bush**, **John F. Kennedy** and **Jimmy Carter**
- First Ladies **Hillary Clinton**, **Jacqueline Onassis**, **Barbara Bush**, and **Nancy Reagan**
- Extraordinary ballet dancer **Mikhail Baryshnikov**
- **Pope John Paul II**

All of this information is thought-provoking, but it is not as meaningful as our next discovery. We discovered that the most successful businesses were also formed on days that had this same Super Success Aspect. General Electric, Procter and Gamble, Honda Motors, and Motorola are good examples. This fact means that you can become more successful by using astrology and, in essence, acquire the Super Success Aspect for your own business dealings to help you achieve great things in life.

Our research also revealed that astrology works on birth charts of weddings, contracts, and starting dates of employment. It means we can get engaged or married, buy a house, or start a job on days that are astrologically favorable and that greatly increase our chances of success. This is all called ELECTIONAL astrology, and it is this part of astrology that we believe to be the most useful.

The theory of electional astrology is that everything has a birth chart. For example, if you get married, the day you get married is the birth chart of your marriage. Or, if you start a new business or a new job, the birth chart of the day you begin is the astrological chart of your new business or your new job. The more astrologically favorable the birth chart, the more successful the wedding, business, or job. But if we begin something on an unfavorable astrological day, it will be inclined to fail. Our research provides conclusive evidence that this theory works. In fact, the evidence is so solid that it is irrefutable.

As we continued our extensive research, we found other astrological aspects that have very powerful beneficial influences. We found one astrological aspect that is particularly helpful to weddings and marriages. This aspect helps create long-lasting marriages.

The Magi Society also found certain astrological aspects that are so common among champion athletes that it makes sense to call them SPORTS CHAMPION ASPECTS. Almost all of the greatest baseball pitchers in history have this type of aspect. Included among these athletes are Nolan Ryan, Greg Maddux, Tom Seaver, Sandy Koufax, Cy Young, Warren Spahn, Steve Carlton, Jim Palmer, and many more. But the Sports Champion Aspect does not work only on baseball pitchers. This type of astrological aspect provides enormous amounts of energy and helps participants in all sports. That is why other champions have it. Good examples are: Michael Jordan, Charles Barkley,

Hakeem Olajuwon, Deion Sanders, Emmitt Smith, Joe Montana, Lawrence Taylor, Steve Young, Stan Humphries, Natrone Means, Martina Navratilova, and Jimmy Connors.

Astrology's capabilities are enormous. When you are knowledgeable enough, you can determine which young athletes are most likely to be the superstars of the next decade and which of them will be lucky enough to be on championship teams. You can determine which young thoroughbred racehorses possess the capacity to be champions in the future, and which ones could not possibly be a champion. You can even have an advantage in forecasting which young companies are most likely to become the business giants of the future, and which ones will not make it. Our book will explain how to do all of this.

Of course, there will probably be a huge amount of skepticism regarding our discoveries. We realize all too well that astrology is not exactly a pet project of the scientific community. For over a century, scientists have nearly universally condemned astrology as totally unfounded; they have branded astrology as being no more than superstition. After all, they say, we are in an era where we can constantly see the advancements in technology and science. However, we would like to point out this simple fact of life: **There is actually no so-called scientific evidence that refutes astrology.** Can you think of one law of science that actually contradicts astrology? There are none! Notwithstanding the scientists themselves, the actual laws of science are neutral with respect to astrology; they neither refute nor confirm its validity.

We believe that astrology can help scientists bridge some major gaps. Although science has had innumerable triumphs, there are also innumerable failures. We cannot cure the common cold or the uncommon cancer. We cannot grow hair or cure asthma. There is a food shortage in many countries. We have not been able to create anything better than naturally found cotton, silk, rubber, wool, leather, wood, and so on. We cannot even predict with certainty when a baby will be born.

Scientists tend to overlook the limitations of science and, instead, concentrate on criticizing anything that they view as a threat to its foundations. They have bitterly condemned astrology even though they know virtually nothing about it. In spite of the often-bitter condemnation of astrology by scientists, nearly half of Americans share a strong inner belief in astrology that is unshakable. This is why a poll, published in *USA Today* on August 9, 1994, found that 47 percent of Americans believe there are "some scientific truths" to astrology. Forty-seven percent! That figure represents a greater number of Americans than those who voted for either Bill Clinton or George Bush.

This book is written for the 47 percent.

If you are one of those who always knew in your heart and mind that there really is a science of astrology, then this book will finally vindicate your belief. **This book will teach you vast new dimensions in astrology.** This knowledge will help prove that astrology really works. You can be proud that you were right all along. And you will no longer have to be afraid to speak up on behalf of astrology. Now you have this book to back you up.

If you are one of those who is an agnostic with respect to astrology, or one who wants to read this book with an open mind, then we welcome you as a reader, and we hope that you will learn and benefit from this book. We also hope that we can open up a whole new and informative world to you.

Even if you are a staunch skeptic when it comes to astrology and are simply reading this book with the preconceived notion of putting holes in what we write, you are still welcome. We gladly take on all challengers. Besides, we have half of America on our side. And we have some challenges of our own to present to you, the skeptic, throughout this book. Please do not disappoint us by backing away from our challenges; we look forward to your reaction and response.

To everyone who will review our book, we thank you for taking the time to read it. If, by the end of this book, we have convinced you that astrology has validity, we will have accomplished one of our goals. If we have not convinced you, at the very least, please accept one of our challenges to skeptics before making any final judgments.

And to all mankind, we say: "Listen! Can't you hear it? It is the Angel Gabriel announcing the dawning of the Age of Aquarius! On January 12, 1996, Uranus enters the sign of Aquarius. Uranus is the planet of astrology, and Aquarius is the sign of astrology. When the Sun enters Aquarius nine days later, Uranus will conjunct the Sun in Aquarius for the first time since 1919. That day will be the birth of the Age of Aquarius.

The Age of Aquarius will last about 2,000 years. What will it mean? Some say that it will mean advancements in space travel. Others say it will mark a new age of humanity and understanding, an era of peace and harmony. We are not sure whether those predictions will come true, but we certainly hope it will be the case. What we are certain of is that **the Age of Aquarius will be the age of astrology**. It will be the age where the human race realizes that just as physics is the science of physical matter, astrology is the science of what is non-physical.

We know that astrology will not be accepted overnight. Nothing that is true ever is. But 47 percent of Americans have consistently believed that astrology contains scientific truths. There is something inside of us that will not let this concept go. NO! We are neither stupid nor superstitious, as condescending skeptics might judge us to be. We are wiser than that by a long shot. We just know. And now, finally, following the publication of this book, we will be able to debate astrology with the skeptics and WIN.

Some may ask: what is the significance of proving astrology? Well, proving astrology is the closest thing to proof of Providence. This is because we will learn that there is an intrinsic benevolence in the design of astrology that you will read about in this book. It will be obvious that astrology was designed to help mankind, and that can only be the case if it is designed by a Benevolent Providence. The world is not chaotic. There is order in this world. Astrology is one of the ways God maintains the order. This order assures that what is good **does** overcome the bad, and astrology is designed to help the good prevail. This book will provide the evidence for this assertion.

Furthermore, astrology was used by at least some of those who wrote the Old and New Testaments. Christ's coming was predicted in the Book of Numbers, and His tag is a "star." And the Saviour was found in a manger, by Magi, who we know were astrologers. And these astrologers were "wise men," according to the Book of

Matthew, and they followed the Star of Bethlehem. And, as you will learn in this book, because astrology works, it invalidates the basis of the theory that evolution is the origin of all species. Astrology, as you will see, is an ally of religion, especially Christianity and Judaism.

How will we prove astrology? We will do so not in just one way but in many ways, and from several angles. There can be no reasonable doubt after you have completed this book. And there is plenty more proof to come. After all, we are about to enter the Age of Aquarius... and the Age of Astrology!

SYMBOLISM: THE KEY TO ASTROLOGY

The Magi Society has always known that astrology really works. But knowing that astrology works is different from proving that it does. Before making the decision to prove astrology, we thought it would be a good idea if we subjected astrology to a few simple tests just to see if it would be worth our while to undertake the monumental task of proving it. Why spend 10,000 hours gathering data and then finding out that it is not provable, even though it does work? Ideally, we were hoping that there would be some simple tests we could perform that would very quickly give us a good idea of whether there is any chance at all of finding that astrology is provable. After much thought, we decided to first conduct a simple test on the very essence of astrology. We decided to first test the astrological principle of SYMBOLISM.

At the very heart and soul of astrology is the concept that the movement and alignment of the planets influence our lives on Earth, and that **different planets have different influences.**

That's right. Astrologers have always believed that different planets have different influences on our lives. Jupiter, for example, has always been considered a very favorable planet. It provided peace, good fortune, success, and the horn of plenty. Venus was also viewed as a benevolent planet, but it was not as powerful as Jupiter. For this reason, both planets were called BENEFICS. Jupiter was the Greater Benefic, and Venus the Lesser Benefic. On the flip side, astrologers have always believed that Saturn and Mars were both MALEFICS, which meant they were malevolent, or could cause problems to occur.

Saturn was the Greater Malefic, and Mars the Lesser Malefic. Astrologers call this difference between the effects of planets the SYMBOLISM of the planets. If you think about this, you will conclude, as we did, that it would be very easy to disprove this symbolism if it were not true. It is black and white; it is not vague at all. Jupiter was good, Saturn was not good. As such, we began to conduct some simple testing and research.

Astrology Passes Its First Test

At the end of some very simple testing, the symbolism of astrology was confirmed, and we knew right away that the results were not just coincidence. Astrology had passed its first test. After all, the odds were about 40,000 to one against our test results being just coincidence. Those are pretty hefty odds.

We began by analyzing the astrology charts of war and peace. The very first charts were those of each of the three days that we thought were the most significant days of peace in this century: the day World War I ended in Europe; the day World War II ended in Europe; and the day East Germany opened up the border to Czechoslovakia, which resulted in the fall of the Berlin Wall, the unification of Germany, and the end of the Cold War. All three of these days of peace occurred when Jupiter was almost exactly 120 degrees from the Sun. Astrologers measure the angle between two planets and have given names to the most important angles. The 120-degree angle is called a TRINE. Astrologers would refer to an angle of about 120 degrees between Jupiter and the Sun as "Jupiter TRINE Sun." Whenever Jupiter was exactly 120 degrees from another planet, it was exactly trine to the planet. It only occurs about once every 200 days.

For 4,000 years, astrologers have said that a day that has Jupiter trine Sun is a particularly good day and a likely day for peace; it is a day representing good fortune and success. As we explained previously, astrologers believe that different planets have different effects on us, and astrologers call the different effects SYMBOLISM. Another example of astrology's symbolism is that Mars represents war. If Mars was 120 degrees from the Sun—that is, trine the Sun, it was a day when war could start, which of course is the opposite of peace. But Mars was not trine the Sun on any of the three days of peace we are discussing.

In this book, at the end of each chapter, we will provide birth charts for each date we discuss in the chapter. Whether or not you are familiar with reading an astrological chart, **please first refer to the glossary at the back of this book and read the section entitled "birth chart."** We, of the Magi Society, do our birth charts differently from any other astrologers, and we are confident that the general public will find our method significantly better.

Please refer to charts 1, 2, and 3 at the end of this chapter, which correspond to those three important days of peace we mentioned on the previous page. As you can see, Jupiter was trine Sun during all three days. Of course, we know what skeptics of astrology will say: "Coincidence." Their favorite word. We went a little further to look for more such "coincidences."

We checked on two more dates of peace: the day the Republic of West Germany was proclaimed, and the day Mikhail Gorbachev was born. Our reasoning was that Gorbachev was a man of peace, and perhaps his birth chart revealed that. After all, he had more to do with the unification of Germany than any other single man, because as Russia's leader, he was the one who decided to pull out Russian troops and to no longer support East Germany's Communist party. This forced East Germany's Communist party leader to resign and his successors immediately opened up the East German borders, which resulted in the sudden and complete fall of the Berlin Wall. German unification came shortly after that, and this led directly to the end of the Cold War. Certainly there would have been no end to the Cold War if any of Gorbachev's predecessors were still in power. That is why Gorbachev was awarded the Nobel Prize for peace in 1990 and why we believe Gorbachev is a man of peace.

So what do you think we found in the two birth charts of West Germany and Gorbachev? (Please refer to charts 4 and 5.) Both had Jupiter 120 degrees from the Sun. Gorbachev was born with Jupiter trine Sun, and West Germany was founded on a day with Jupiter trine

Sun. Now, instead of three coincidences for skeptics to explain away, there were five. The odds became 35 million to one that all five dates would have Jupiter trine Sun. Think about it: a man, Gorbachev, born with Jupiter trine Sun, helps a country, West Germany (founded on a day Jupiter trined the Sun) to find peace with East Germany, its neighbor and previously sworn enemy, and this peace occurs on a Jupiter trine Sun day. Pretty interesting. Remember, Jupiter trines the Sun only once every 200 days or so.

All of these "coincidences" point strongly to the validity of the symbolism of astrology. Naturally, we had to do the flip side and check to see where the stars were on days of war. The most famous, or infamous, day of war that probably comes to everyone's mind is, of course, Pearl Harbor day: December 7, 1941. What would an astrologer expect to find? Probably Mars 120 degrees from the Sun on that day because Mars symbolizes war. How do we verify that that is what ancient astrologers believed? One confirmation is that in Roman and Greek mythology, Mars was the god of war; the Romans and Greeks were told this by their astrologers, who were often their priests. Anyway, what we found was that Mars was indeed 120 degrees from the Sun on December 7, 1941 (chart 6). That was another victory for the astrologers.

So far, the symbolism of astrology is doing fabulously well on matters of peace and war. This makes sense. You see, 4,000 years ago when the Babylonians first designed astrology, they were interested primarily in predicting war and peace, because by being able to do so, they were able to foretell that which was most important to their kings. If the kings' astrologers could not get these predictions right, they probably would have had their heads chopped off. Then there would have been no more astrologers. But astrology flourished. So they must have been able to predict war and peace enough times to keep their heads, literally. But that would also mean that there is at least some truth to astrology. After all, astrology is the only methodology of prediction that has actually survived 4,000 years. During the last 4,000 years, literally thousands of different methods of predicting the future have been tried and discarded; astrology is the only one that has survived. In a very real sense, astrology has withstood the test of time—4,000 years of time.

Ancient Aspects

The Babylonians were very interesting people. They invented the circle. Have you ever wondered why there are 360 degrees in a circle? It is, after all, an unusual number. The reason is that the *astrologers* of Babylonia invented the circle. As we all know, there are 12 astrological signs, and each sign has 30 degrees. The Babylonian astrologers designed it that way because there are about 30 days in a lunar month, and 12 lunar months in a year. The Babylonian astrologers created the degrees so that they could measure the angle between planets. (Astrologers include the Sun and Moon as planets, and we will refer to them as planets in this book, for ease of writing.)

Through probably a thousand years of observation, Babylonian astrologers concluded that on days when any two planets were aligned such that the angle between them was any multiple of 30 degrees, the days had special meaning, and such days were different from those that did not have such planetary alignments. This meant that if Mars is 30 or 60 or 90 or 120 or 150 or 180 or 0 degrees from any other planet, it was meaningful, and they would refer to such an occurrence by saying that Mars was IN ASPECT to that other planet. Or, the two planets were in aspect to each other.

To put it another way, whenever two planets are in the same degree of any of the 12 astrological signs, they were in aspect to each other because they were separated by an angle that is a multiple of 30 degrees. This is one of the rationales for the division of the zodiac into 12 signs, as opposed to any other number of signs.

Ancient astrologers always believed that some aspects were good and some aspects were not so good. And they gave names to all of the possible aspects and evaluated them as good or not so good. If you have not studied astrology before, do not get bogged down in trying to remember the details of what was a good or bad aspect. At this stage, it is only important to know what aspects actually are. But this is what the ancient astrologers concluded:

Conjunction	0 degrees	sometimes good, sometimes bad
Semi-sextile	30 degrees	mildly negative
Sextile	60 degrees	beneficial
Square	90 degrees	very negative
Trine	120 degrees	very beneficial
Quincunx	150 degrees	negative
Opposition	180 degrees	very negative

(It is obvious that ancient astrologers thought that there were more negative aspects than positive ones. In this regard, the Magi Society believes that the ancient astrologers made a mistake. But we will deal with this point in a later chapter.)

When measuring the angle between two planets in a circle, there are always two possible angles; the sum of both of these angles always equals 360 degrees. Astrologers always use the smaller angle. Therefore, there is never an aspect greater than 180 degrees because astrologers always use the smaller angle.

The Ancient Symbolisms

As we were saying, whenever two planets were in aspect to each other, the ancient astrologers learned that such an occurrence could have special meaning, and this was different from times when the two planets were not in aspect to each other. To determine the full meaning of an aspect between two planets, astrologers used symbolism. Different planets had different symbolisms, or representations, or meanings. It was the combined symbolism of the two planets that created the aspect that determined the meaning of the aspect. Since there were many more ideas and symbolisms to represent than there were planets, each planet had to have many different symbolisms. Ancient astrologers, after thousands of years of observation, had decided that different planets had different symbolisms, and the symbolisms of the seven planets they were aware of were as follows:

- **Venus** symbolized love and marriage, beauty, and the woman.
- **Mars** represented war, the soldier, and the man.

- **Saturn** was the planet that could crystallize problems; it symbolized obstruction, shortages, losses, mistakes, and bad luck.
- **Jupiter**, as we already know, symbolized good fortune, success, peace, and life.
- The **Moon** had the symbolism of crops and food, the ocean and water, the Queen, and everything found in the ground, such as gold.
- **Mercury** represented the messenger and speed of foot, communication, the mind, and intelligence.
- The **Sun** was the ruler, the King. It also represents the day itself, as was the case in the examples of days of war or peace that we have used so far. The Sun also represents the very person who is the subject of the birth chart, such as Gorbachev, meaning that on a day when the Sun is 120 degrees from Jupiter, the person born on that day, and represented by the Sun, is a person of good fortune and peace. A day with Mars square the Sun could represent a soldier, but because the aspect is a square, the person would not be able to wage war successfully.

In order to determine how astrologers interpreted the aspects, we simply combine the symbolisms of the planets that are in aspect to each other. For example, if Jupiter was in trine to Venus, the aspect symbolized something about success and good fortune (represented by Jupiter) in love and marriage (represented by Venus). The fact that the trine aspect is always good meant that a day when Jupiter trines Venus was an excellent day for getting married.

This was the way the ancients read astrology and how astrologers interpreted the days. A day that has the Sun in conjunction to Saturn was a day of losses and shortages because Saturn symbolizes losses and crystallization, or culmination, of problems. A day that had Venus conjunct the Sun was a day for affairs of love and weddings because Venus was conjunct the Sun, and Venus symbolizes love and weddings.

In modern times, there are ten planets that can make aspects. But even in the old days, when there were only seven such planets, there were more than enough planets so that there were usually several aspects on any given day. For example, on a particular day, Jupiter and Saturn could be 180 degrees apart, and at the same time, Mars and Venus could be 30 degrees apart. And at the same time, the Moon and the Sun could be 90 degrees apart. This would mean that there were three aspects for that day. Astrologers have always believed that the correct interpretation of any given day is to blend into the interpretation the totality of all the aspects of the day. In this book, we will refer to this process of blending ALL aspects in a day to interpret a day as ASPECT INTEGRATION.

Another concept to understand is what astrologers call an ORB. It was determined that when two planets were not precisely and exactly in aspect, but were close to being in exact aspect, they still had an effect. In other words, even though the square aspect is 90 degrees, planets that were 87 or 88 or 89 degrees apart still had an effect on each other, and the effect was very similar to the effect of an exact square between the two planets. The planets' influences were strongest when they were in exact aspect. But planets that were close to exact aspect still had an influence. The maximum number of degrees that a planet can be away from an exact aspect, and yet still have influence, is called the ORB of the aspect. Traditional astrology usually allowed fairly wide orbs ranging from 5 to 8 degrees. But we will use a much tighter orb. In this book, two planets must be within about 3 degrees to be in aspect, depending on the actual aspect and the planets in question. We will give you more details about orbs later.

Examples of How Astrologers Assign Symbolisms

It would be helpful and instructive to give some examples of how astrologers assign symbolisms to a planet. Let us use Uranus and Pluto as examples, since they were not known to the ancients.

Uranus was not discovered until 1781, so it is one of the three planets that great astrologers such as Sir Isaac Newton and Johannes Kepler were not able to work with. To astrologers, the symbolisms of Uranus include inventions and inventors and manmade machines, among other things. But the reason that Uranus symbolizes inventions, inventors, and manmade machines is the history of Uranus. In the year

Uranus was discovered, James Watt invented the first steam engine that could convert steam power to rotary power. The Industrial Revolution began with this invention. Prior to Watts' engine, people were essentially limited to using animals or their own muscles for power in virtually all of their daily needs. Because the steam engine so closely coincided with the discovery of Uranus, astrologers have always associated Uranus with inventions and inventors and manmade machines. In fact, astrologers believe that the discovery of Uranus by human beings, and the influence of Uranus on such, was the actual impetus for the Industrial Revolution.

Uranus also has other symbolisms. 1781 was a very important year in history. The Thirteen Colonies won their independence from England in 1781, and the French Revolution soon followed. For these reasons, and others, astrologers have also assigned to Uranus the symbolism of revolutions, mass changes, and the general public. And by revolutions, astrologers are not just referring to revolts, but any broadbased change that affects an entire population. The revolution can be industrial, political, or scientific, or a revolution of ideas. Because revolutions also result in change, another symbolism of Uranus is change.

Also, shortly after the discovery of Uranus, some Frenchmen successfully completed the first manned balloon flight on June 5, 1783. This meant that human beings could finally get off the ground. For these reasons, astrologers have also used Uranus to symbolize flying and space travel.

We find the assignment of symbolisms interesting when it is tied into history. Don't you?

Let us now deal with the symbolisms of a planet that has a greater effect on our well-being—that of Pluto. Pluto is the newest planet in that it was discovered only 65 years ago in 1930. This would mean that if you are entitled to Social Security, you were born before Pluto was discovered. That is pretty recent because it means that we all know many persons who were born before Pluto was discovered. These people lived part of their lives believing that there were only eight planets.

During the few years just before and after Pluto's discovery, scientists resolved some of their differences in their theories on the structure of the atom, and the first controlled atomic chain reaction occurred. For this reason, astrologers associate Pluto with atomic energy and the nuclear bomb. Astrologers have also linked Pluto to beginnings and endings of eras and major milestones in a person's life. But the most important symbolism of Pluto is that of power. Pluto symbolizes power and the will to exercise that power. For this reason, it is Pluto that now represents kings and rulers, politicians, dictators, and people involved in big business—that is, people of power. Such individuals love to compete. Competitiveness is the common denominator of politicians and business people. For this reason, Pluto also represents competition, including competitive sports and men and women who participate in competitive sports—professional athletes, for example. You can see that if astrologers are correct about these symbolisms, Pluto is a very powerful and key planet. We will see throughout the rest of this book that Pluto is indeed the key planet of power and competition; Pluto is the key planet of the rich and powerful.

But first let us see some charts that will help us understand why we believe Pluto also symbolizes debt, the economy in general, and big business. Charts 7 and 8 represent the astrological charts of two very critical days in the history of American business. Chart 7 is for March 6, 1933, which was a date occurring within the Great Depression and was the beginning of a banking moratorium; the banks in the U.S. were closed from that date until March 15. The banks were closed. Closed.

If you had stock investments during the stock market crash of 1987 and thought that was terrible, think about how bad you would have felt if you had gone to your bank the next day and it was closed. Especially if you had gone to make a withdrawal. During that fateful banking moratorium in 1933, we noticed that Uranus was virtually exactly SQUARE to Pluto. Now this is a very, very rare aspect. Uranus squared Pluto two more times within a year of the bank closings. But there has not been another square of Uranus and Pluto since then. The next one is not due until April of 2014. As we said, this was a very rare aspect that occurred. We have found a very good general rule of thumb for astrology: the more unusual and rare an aspect, the greater the effect on the world.

We concluded that the Uranus square Pluto aspect caused the banks to close. This occurred not only in the United States, but in other parts of the world as well. Therefore, either Pluto or Uranus symbolized something very close to banking and big business. We did not think it was Uranus, because of chart 8, which is the chart of March 13, 1907, the day of the financial panic that started the Depression of 1907. Historians tell us that the 1907 Depression was every bit as bad as the 1930s Depression. It was just longer ago, so we do not talk about it as much. Anyway, the chart of March 13, 1907 shows a Saturn conjunct the Sun, and both planets were square Pluto. That makes Pluto the prime suspect, as the planet that symbolizes the economy, big business, and free enterprise.

You now understand better how astrologers do detective work on symbolism. We look at major events and isolate the planets and aspects that we believe caused it, and assign the planets symbolisms that represent the events.

The third chart (chart 9) that we want to use to demonstrate the symbolism of Pluto is that of December 2, 1942. That is the date of the first controlled atomic chain reaction.

Since Pluto symbolizes atomic energy and the nuclear bomb, we would expect strong aspects to Pluto. In examining the birth chart of that day of destiny, we find that the planets we would expect to be in aspect are indeed in aspect. But the actual aspects seem less predictable. We would definitely expect that there would be aspects between the Sun, Pluto, and Saturn. And we do have them. Saturn opposes the Sun, Pluto trines the Sun, and is in sextile to Saturn at the same time. In addition, Uranus and Neptune are in very close trine to each other. This day was obviously a very, very fateful day with very strong aspects that are hard to interpret. We can tell you this, though: Saturn, Uranus, Neptune, and Pluto are the four farthest planets from the Sun and therefore the slowest moving ones. They are referred to as the OUTERMOST PLANETS. It is extraordinarily rare that all four of them are somehow aspected to at least one of the other outermost planets. But that was exactly the case on that day. The interpretation of the aspect integration of this day will become clearer when we learn some more about astrology in a later chapter, and we will come back to interpret this chart at that time.

The Magi Society's Symbolisms of the Planets

Similar detective work by astrologers has revealed that every part of the human body is symbolized, or RULED, by one of the planets. The same is the case for professions; each profession is ruled by a planet.

Modern-day astrologers believe that they know some of the important symbolisms of all of the planets. Through monumental amounts of detective work and observation, astrologers believe that although they do not know all the symbolisms of the planets, the ones they do agree on are correct. The listing below represents the symbolisms that the Magi Society have found to be accurate. To some planets, we have also added symbolisms that we know are correct, but which no other astrologers are aware of.

- **Sun:** the actual person of the birth chart, often referred to as the NATIVE; the actual day represented by the astrological chart; the will to live; vitality and the heart; the circulation system; authority; gold; the ruler;
- **Moon:** the emotions, fluctuating moods; the subconscious; sympathy; the psyche; capriciousness; the nonsexual maternal instinct; fear and greed; emotional stability or lack thereof; uncontrollable urges;
- **Mercury:** the mind, the intellect, and the respiration system and lungs; the eyes and eyesight; the reflexes; intelligence; the ability to communicate and the act of communication; the nervous system; transportation and vehicles of transportation such as cars, bicycles, and motorcycles, trains and commercial airplanes; photography; lens and optical equipment.
- **Venus:** beauty; physical and sexual attraction; affections but not love; victory in war; partnerships and weddings; money and pos-

sessions of a movable nature; sense of humor; clothing and fashion; success and increases (the lesser benefic).

• **Mars:** energy and energization; sexual energy and sexual bonds; the sex drive; initiative and the desire to take action; enthusiasm; aggression; war and the soldier; weapons of war. Mars is the planet that has anything to do with war. Mars rules our muscles and stamina.

• **Jupiter:** fulfillment; prayers and wishes coming true; peace; the principle of expansion; success and increases (the greater benefic); good fortune; knowledge and the publishing of knowledge; Christianity; lenders and banks; optimism and hope; morality; forgiveness; the selfless servant; wisdom and good judgment; reasonableness and the ability to be responsible; the ability to overcome obstacles; good luck in competitive matters as well as life in general; positive public image; the horn of plenty; faith, hope, and charity; compassion; friendship; the principle of order; common sense; judges and the law; the higher order; Providence; power in the benevolent sense; generosity; true genius; rewards; true love.

• **Saturn:** the culmination of problems and the crystallization of mistakes; contraction and losses; too much or too little; dissolution; limitation, obstruction, hindrance, and failure; pessimism, bad judgment and selfishness; the will to do harm; susceptibility to immorality; confusion and recklessness; death and tragedy; carelessness and harmful behavior; negative public image; hatred and malice; concentration and focus; emotional depression; emphasis on the personal ego; coldness, heartlessness; stubbornness, and narrow-mindedness; undesirability.

(Since the world is not always rosy, it's logical that there would be at least one planet associated with problems, and Saturn is the one that astrologers have learned to associate with problems of all kinds. But if you make no mistakes and live perfectly, Saturn has no problems to crystallize in your life.)

- **Uranus:** the public, general population and the masses; the principle of fame and public acclaim; popularity, success with the public and the voters; universality; revolutions of all kinds, change on a national or worldwide scale, political or scientific or economic; broadcasting and telecommunications, the business of public entertainment; the film, radio, and television businesses; men and women who move the masses; mass merchandising; space travel and flying; technology, inventors and manmade things; astrology and technology; chess; involvement of the public; models and modeling; oratory and the ability to project a pleasing image; the principle of independence; unconventionality; change, the desire for change and the urge to revolt. Uranus is the planet that has anything to do with the public. In our bodies, Uranus rules coordination and balance.

- **Neptune:** the principle of healing and regeneration; longevity and things that are long-lasting; artistic talents of all kinds; drugs and medicine; financial security from sources of a long-term nature such as real estate, stocks, patents, copyrights, inheritances in the form of long-term trusts; minerals and anything that is found in the ground, including oil, gold, and silver; photographic film containing silver; food and anything that grows from the ground; electricity, electrical devices of all kinds including computers; the ability to heal quickly and completely; the fountain of youth, being forever young in mind and body; impressionability; bliss; submission and being easily satisfied; the Catholic Church, religions and spirituality; real estate and land, mining properties and oil wells; romanticism and true long-lasting love. Neptune is the planet of everything that is long-term.

- **Pluto:** the principle of power; power of all kinds, financial, political, and all other forms of power; power over others and the will to exercise that power; men and women of power including politicians, film stars, famous athletes and businessmen; the desire to win; entrepreneurs and big business; debt and bonds; investments and profits from investments; competition of all kinds, including professional sports and business; professional athletes, the competitive spirit and the will to win; aggressiveness; never being satisfied; beginnings and endings; the organs of regeneration; obsessions; the atomic bomb and nuclear energy; gambling; new beginnings and endings of dramatic scale, both personal and national or international. Pluto is the planet of power and everything that can enhance power.

Those of you who are familiar with symbolism will notice that there are a number of symbolisms that you have not seen before. We had informed you that this is because we, of the Magi Society, have added some of our own, and by the end of this book, you will know the reasons for them. Also, some of our symbolisms differ from those normally used by astrologers. For example, we believe computers are symbolized by Neptune, but technology and inventions remain the symbolism of Uranus. The astrology of the Magi Society is the most accurate and complete astrology in the world, and by the time you finish this book, you will agree.

The Symbolism of Astrology Passes More Tests

Now that you know so much about symbolism, we can go on and continue to test the symbolisms of astrology.

As the Magi Society continued to test the symbolisms of astrology, we found that one of the problems that astrologers faced was that they would be only half right a lot. By this we mean that they would know what particular planets should be in aspect on a specific type of day, but astrologers could not predict the actual aspect that would exist. For example, the day that North Korea invaded South Korea did not have Mars trine the Sun, which was the case on the day the Japanese bombed Pearl Harbor. But Mars was in a different aspect to the Sun the day the invasion began. Mars was 90 degrees from the Sun; Mars was SQUARE the Sun. So that day did have something to do with Mars and what it symbolized. The astrologers were half right. Mars was in aspect to the Sun on that day, but it was not the aspect astrologers expected. We think it is these half-right predictions that prevented astrology from gaining greater acceptance. But it also kept astrology going because it was not all wrong either. The symbolism of astrology worked, but the expected aspect was harder to predict.

In our research, there were many cases where astrology's symbolism worked, but the actual aspects were less predictable.

Space travel is a great example. We certainly thought that the day man first landed on the moon was a momentous enough event, such that the day would be a good test of astrology. Another good test was the day that a satellite first orbited around the earth, and also the day a living human first orbited the earth. We also checked the day when man first flew on a plane. What planet do astrologers believe symbolizes flying and space travel? As we learned just a few pages ago, it is Uranus. We are now ready to determine whether this symbolism worked on the critical historic dates corresponding to flying and space travel. All the days should have significant aspects to Uranus, but we will probably be surprised to see what the actual aspect is.

- **First non-manpowered flight:** Wright brothers at Kitty Hawk, December 17, 1903. Uranus was zero degrees from the Sun. This is a conjunction; therefore, it is a Uranus day and astrologers are correct (chart 10).
- **First orbital flight of unmanned satellite:** Sputnik I, October 4, 1957. Uranus was 60 degrees from the Sun. This is a sextile; therefore, there is another aspect of Uranus to the Sun. Astrology worked again (chart 11).
- **First manned orbital flight around the earth:** April 12, 1961. Uranus was 120 degrees from the Sun. The Sun of this day was also aspected by Uranus by a trine. The symbolism of astrology was again correct (chart 12).

All three days represented a first in flying, and on all three days, the Sun was aspected by Uranus, which is what astrologers would expect. And what about the day man first stepped on the Moon (chart 13)? There were no aspects by Uranus to the Sun on that day. However, there was an exact CONJUNCTION of Jupiter and Uranus. Such a conjunction, as exact as it was, did not occur again for 14 years. And using the consistent symbolism we have already discussed, a Jupiter conjunction to Uranus means good fortune and success (Jupiter) in flying (Uranus). What could be more successful in flying than successfully landing on the moon? Shall we give astrology another "A"?

We also noticed that on the day that the Russians successfully launched Sputnik I, Uranus was not the only planet to make an aspect to the Sun. At the same time, Jupiter also did so. Jupiter was less than one degree from the Sun; so astrologers would say that Jupiter was CONJUNCT the Sun. You often have more than one aspect to the Sun because there are nine planets that can make an aspect to the Sun at any given time. Therefore, theoretically, it is possible for there to be nine different aspects to the Sun at the same time. Usually, there are one or two aspects on any given day. Sometimes there are none. Using the language of the symbolism of astrology, and using aspect integration, what the two aspects would mean is that on that day, there would be good fortune and peace (Jupiter conjunct the Sun), and it was a good day for flying (Uranus sextile the Sun). This happens to have been the case. The launch was successful, and space has never been used for military purposes. Again, astrology was correct.

So far, except for Pearl Harbor and the invasion of South Korea, the dates we have dealt with have been positive times in history, and the symbolism of astrology has worked remarkably well. But what would we expect on not-so-positive dates? Astrologers have singled out Saturn as the planet that symbolizes the crystallization of problems, as well as losses, failure, and tragedy. On tragic days, we would expect to see Saturn make aspects to the Sun or other planets. Since we have looked at days when flying and space travel have occurred, we should check on the two tragic days of space travel: the day the Challenger space shuttle blew up, and the day that the Apollo fire killed three astronauts (see charts 14 and 15).

The day the space shuttle blew up, Saturn made a 60-degree aspect to the Sun. It also made a 30-degree aspect to Pluto. Remember, Saturn is the planet that symbolizes problems, losses, hindrance, failure, and tragedy. Pluto symbolizes beginnings and endings, among other things. The astrological interpretation of that day's Saturn aspects would be: a day (the Sun) that a problem (Saturn) could occur, and a time for a tragic (Saturn) beginning or end (Pluto). So tragedy for the day could have been expected.

On the day of the Apollo fire that killed three astronauts and burned up an Apollo spacecraft, Saturn did not make an aspect to the Sun. But it was in aspect to a total of five other planets. Saturn was within 2.5 degrees of an exact aspect to five planets. We think that the most important aspect is the Saturn opposition (178 degrees in this case) to Uranus, which we can interpret as tragedy and losses (Saturn) to space travel (Uranus).

Again, astrology receives an "A."

Proving Astrology Requires More Than Historic Dates

So far, we have tested and examined some of the most important dates in the history of this century. We have found that the symbolism of astrology worked on these dates. Symbolism is the most important principle of astrology, and it worked. And some of this symbolism was handed down to us from the ancient astrologers of 4,000 years ago.

This is certainly encouraging to those of us who believe in the validity of astrology. But we have not yet proven the validity of astrology. To actually prove astrology requires many, many more examples. We have not done enough charts of momentous historic dates to have proven astrology because statistical validity requires hundreds of such symbolic dates. However, even if we do that, we will always be faced with skeptics who will say that we selected certain dates and left out others. For instance, we of the Magi Society believe that we used the most important dates of peace, but the skeptic will find some dates when peace treaties were signed in countries we never heard of, and these treaties concluded wars most of us were never aware of. The skeptics will say that we should include them in our analysis. Then, instead of arguing about astrology, we would be arguing about history, which in many ways is subjective.

Subjectivity is the big problem when dealing with astrology and historical dates. Take, for example, the assassination of Dr. Martin Luther King, Jr. Saturn was within one degree of the Sun on that terrible day.

Using the symbolism of astrology, this would be expected because it was a tragic day, and most people would agree with such an interpretation. But there can usually be some degree of subjectivity over whether an assassination was a loss or gain for the world. Almost everyone would agree that King's assassination was a tragedy. But it is not the case with many other assassinations. For example, Anwar Sadat, the Egyptian leader who made peace with Israel, was assassinated on a day similar to Dr. King's assassination. Saturn was conjunct the Sun on both of these assassination days. But there are many people in the Middle East who would be very upset with you if you say it was a tragic day. They believe Sadat was selling out Islamic claims to the land that is now called Israel; they regard his assassination day as reason for celebration.

The dates used earlier in this chapter are pretty much interpreted universally in the same light. But there are not enough of them. When President Lincoln was assassinated, most of the people in the South thought that this was a positive occurrence.

In other words, our inspection of symbolism has given us a green light on astrology. But we cannot prove astrology in this way. There are simply not enough dates of historic proportions to perform any valid statistical tests.

And some of the dates are subjectively interpreted. If we want to truly prove that astrology works, we have to do it another way. And we will. But it is nice to know that the symbolisms of astrology work on days of historic importance. You prove one little part of astrology, and the flood gates break open!

☄ ☄ ☄

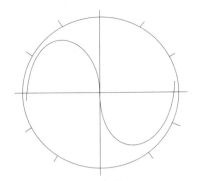

♈ ARIES	♎ LIBRA	☉ SUN	♄ SATURN
♉ TAURUS	♏ SCORPIO	☿ MERCURY	♅ URANUS
♊ GEMINI	♐ SAGITARIUS	♀ VENUS	♆ NEPTUNE
♋ CANCER	♑ CAPRICORN	♂ MARS	♇ PLUTO
♌ LEO	♒ AQUARIUS	♃ JUPITER	
♍ VIRGO	♓ PISCES		

Chart 1: November 11, 1918
World War I Ended

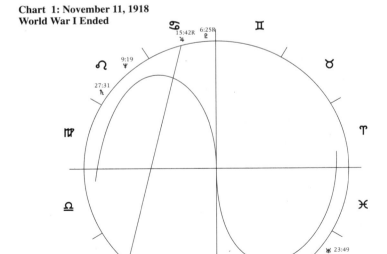

**Chart 2: May 7, 1945
Germany surrenders,
victory in Europe,
end of World
War II in
Europe**

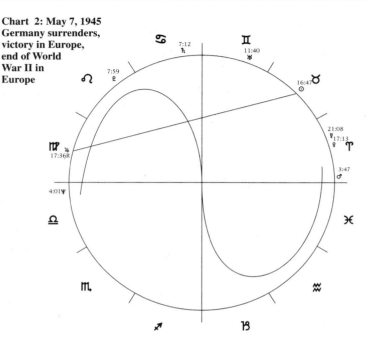

**Chart 3: November 4, 1989
East Germany opens up its
borders to Czechoslovakia—
this leads to fall of
Berlin Wall**

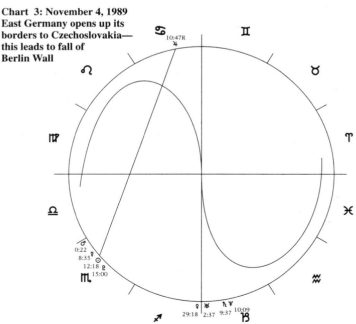

Chart 4: March 2, 1931
Birth of Mikhail Gorbachev

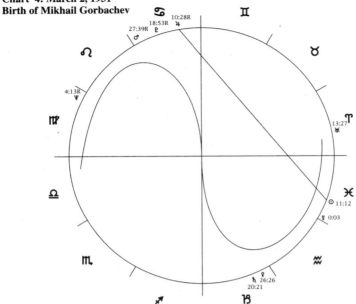

Chart 5: May 23, 1949
Birth chart of West Germany

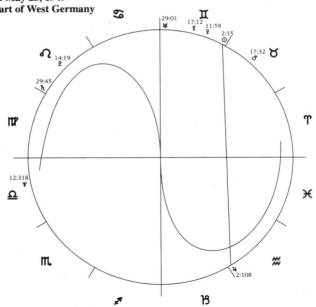

Chart 6: December 7, 1941
Japan attacks Pearl Harbor

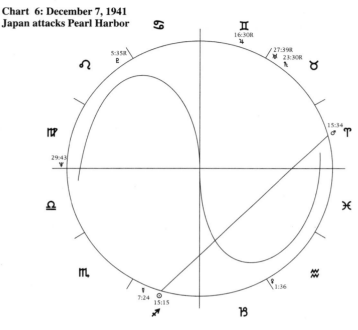

Chart 7: March 6, 1933
Banking moratorium begins—
banks closed

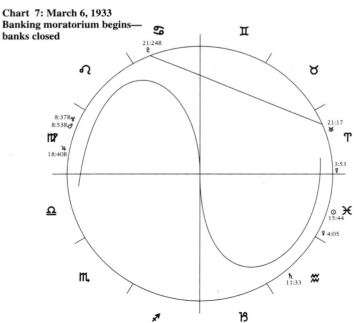

Chart 8: March 13, 1907
Financial panic of 1907;
beginning of Depression

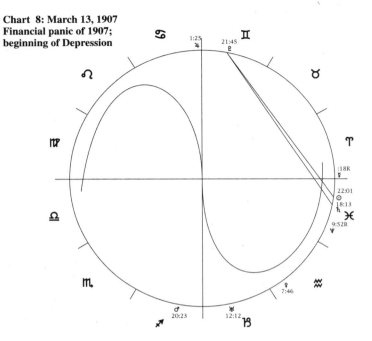

Chart 9: December 2, 1942
First controlled atomic
chain reaction

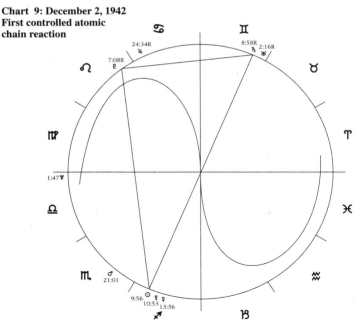

**Chart 10: December 17, 1903
First motorized flight,
Kitty Hawk, Wright
Brothers**

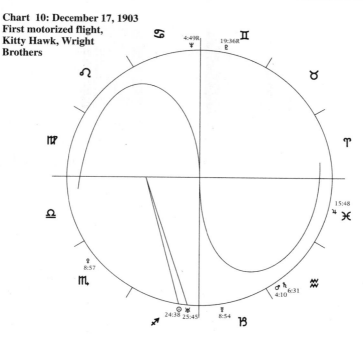

**Chart 11: October 4, 1957
First manmade satellite to
orbit Earth: SPUTNIK I**

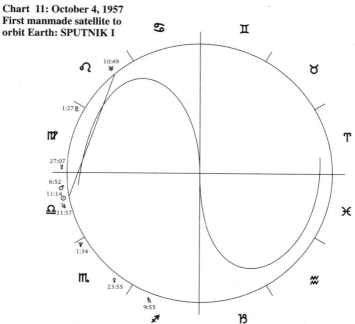

**Chart 12: April 12, 1961
First manned orbital flight,
by Yuri Gagarin**

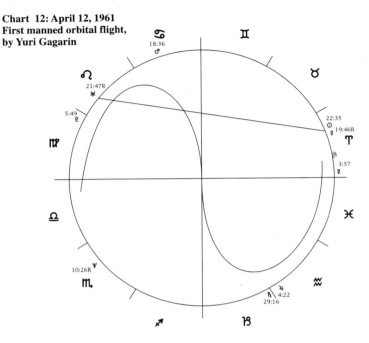

**Chart 13: July 21, 1969
First manned lunar landing,
Neil Armstrong, et al.**

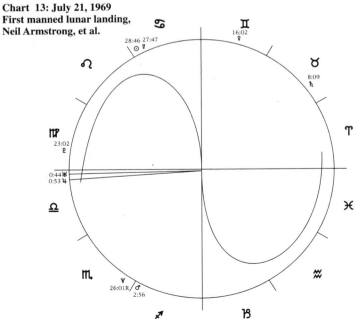

Chart 14: January 27, 1986
Space shuttle Challenger
blows up

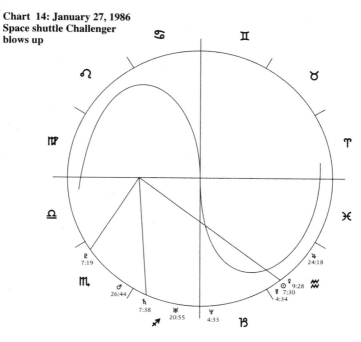

Chart 15: January 27, 1967
Apollo fire disaster

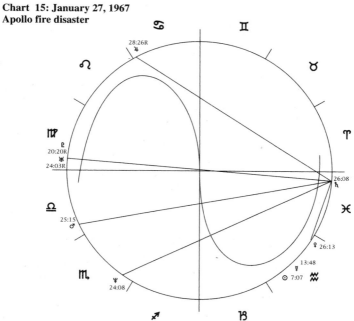

HOW WE WILL PROVE ASTROLOGY

F rom the charts and examples used in the last chapter, we can
conclude that there is a very good chance that there is at least
some truth to astrology because there is strong evidence that the
symbolism of astrology works. Although this fact alone does not yet
prove that astrology works, we have taken a first step, and the results
encourage us to investigate further.

Our next step is to devise a method of truly proving whether astrology actually works. In order for us to be better able to choose a methodology for proving astrology, it is a good idea to learn what methods have
been used in the past to attempt to prove astrology. Since all previous
efforts have failed, we do no want to make the same mistakes.

How People Have Tried to Prove Astrology in the Past

Astrologers and others have made many failed attempts to prove
that astrology works. But they have focused their efforts on trying to
prove the validity of the 12 signs of the zodiac. For a very long time,
astrologers believed that people born with their Sun in certain signs
were more prone to engage in certain professional activities. For example, many of us have heard of the familiar astrological idea that
Leos are good actors or actresses. And, supposedly, a female Virgoan
makes a good secretary. Many astrologers have done massive statistical studies on such so-called astrological relationships between the
Sun sign of an individual and the professions. Guess what? None of
the relationships were STATISTICALLY VALID, meaning that
none of the relationships were proven when subjected to statistical

tests generally used by scientists. What this means to us is that either the relationships are not valid, or that it is virtually impossible to prove anything based on the 12 signs of the zodiac.

Astrologers divide the birth chart into 12 divisions, which they call HOUSES. Astrologers have made many failed attempts to prove the validity of these houses. Just as each planet has different symbolisms, each house is believed to rule or symbolize different things. On any given day, the planets will move through all 12 houses just as the Sun and the other planets move across the sky. In one day, each planet moves through each of the 12 houses once. (Please see the diagram in the glossary under "houses.") Which house a planet is in at any given time of day depends on the time of day and the location of the observer on the Earth. In spite of many attempts, astrologers have failed to prove any correlation between the 12 houses and the placement of a planet in any of these houses in the birth chart. For example, it is generally agreed among astrologers that the second house is the house of money and possessions. Therefore, astrologers usually concur that a person who is born with Jupiter in the second house should succeed in making money and accumulating possessions since Jupiter symbolizes success and expansion. On the other hand, astrologers believe that the placement of Saturn in the second house would significantly limit that person's ability to make a great deal of money because Saturn symbolizes shortages. However, no astrologer has been able to show that any such house relationships are statistically valid.

Astrologers have also attempted to prove that the placement at birth of certain planets in certain SECTORS of the birth chart is related to the professions chosen by the individual of the chart (referred to as the NATIVE by astrologers). A sector is defined as a contiguous group of houses, such as the 10th through 12th houses. Many astrologers believe that Mars placed in the 10th through 12th houses gives the native above-average athletic ability and therefore makes the native more likely to become a professional athlete. Although there is a great dispute between astrologers and scientists about whether or not such relationships have been statistically validated, such relationships have either not been provable at all or not provable conclusively enough to have any real bearing on the skeptical scientists' strong negative perception of astrology.

There have also been many attempts by astrologers to try to prove that the ASCENDANT or MIDHEAVEN of a birth chart has an influence on the native's profession, or personality traits and characteristics. The ascendant and midheaven are part of what are called CALCULATED POINTS. They are called such because they require calculations. Whereas the position of a planet is discernible and locatable by the eye, the position of calculated points such as the ascendant and midheaven must be calculated. The ascendant is the degree of the zodiac that is just rising on the eastern horizon at the time and place for which the birth chart is cast. The midheaven is the most elevated degree of the zodiac at the time and place for which the birth chart is cast. All attempts to prove astrology using these calculated points have also failed.

The conclusion that the Magi Society drew from all of this is twofold.

A. First, astrology was probably not provable in any of the ways that have been previously attempted so many times in the past.

B. Second, perhaps there needed to be some improvements in astrological theory and expansion of astrological knowledge before astrology could be provable.

We decided that astrology, as it was generally practiced and understood by the average astrologer in 1994, was not yet solid enough to be proven. In other words, perhaps just as physics needed Isaac Newton to make a monumental breakthrough when he developed his laws of gravity, astrology needed a monumental breakthrough of a similar nature before it could be proven and accepted by most of its critics.

In the next chapter, we will take astrology the necessary monumental giant leap ahead by adding a whole new dimension to it; by doing so, astrology becomes provable.

In the rest of this chapter, we will discuss the areas of astrology we will prove, and the methodology we will use to do so.

We Do Not Need an Exact Time of Birth

Having analyzed the reasons for the past failures of astrologers in attempting to validate their beliefs, we decided that we needed an entirely new approach if we were to avoid joining these astrologers in their mistakes.

Most previous attempts to prove astrology depended on knowing the locations of certain calculated points. There are a number of cogent reasons that support trying to prove astrology without having to use any of these calculated points. If we want to prove astrology using calculated points, we need to know the exact time of birth because it is not possible to know the location of any calculated point without the exact time of birth. But it is very difficult to know the exact time of birth of any individual. Even birth certificates that have exact times are almost always wrong. This is because the doctors and nurses are much more concerned about delivering the baby than they are about noting down the exact time of birth. This is the way it should be; the primary responsibility of the delivery team is the safety of the baby and the mother. For this reason, the time of birth written on a birth certificate is almost always an estimate made by a nurse or doctor, almost as an afterthought. Some birth certificates do not have any time at all; they just have the date.

If we cannot obtain exact times of birth, how can we prove astrology using methods that require the exact birth time? The fact is, we cannot. And it would be a waste of time to try. This reason alone is enough for us to decide to not use midheavens, ascendants, and the houses when trying to prove astrology. These calculated points require the exact time of birth and are very sensitive to changes in birth time. A four-minute change in the exact time of birth creates a one-degree change in the ascendant and similar changes in the midheaven and locations of the houses.

This means that we must try to prove astrology by using only the date of birth, without needing the time of birth. There are other good reasons for using only the date of birth and not the time of birth in our research. The best of these reasons is that birth dates are easily verifiable; therefore, skeptics cannot question our data. If we were to prove astrology based on the time of birth, skeptics will claim that we fudged our data. But skeptics cannot claim we fudged birth date data. And the general public will have much more confidence in our research. They can verify our research by themselves. This is very, very important.

For the above reasons, we will not be using any calculated points in this book. We will use only the birth dates.

At this point, some of you might be wondering how well we can prove astrology without using the calculated points. The answer is: the Magi Society will conclusively prove that astrology really works by using only symbolism and the aspects. But we will have to take the giant step of expanding astrological knowledge in the next chapter in order to prove astrology. Before we do that, let us first take a closer look at aspects.

The Importance of Aspects

The Magi Society has found that aspects are the most important part of a birth chart. Strangely enough, aspects represent the one area of natal charts that is emphasized least by astrologers. Virtually all astrology books we have seen concentrate on the 12 signs and the calculated points. They do not discuss the aspects as much as they should. In fact, many astrologers are uncomfortable talking about aspects. They actually try to avoid them in their interpretation of a chart.

Because most astrologers place little value on the aspects, the general public has been conditioned to disregard the aspects. One of the founders of the Magi Society vividly remembers being at a party where he met a woman named Joyce who told him that she was a Capricorn, with Moon in Leo and Scorpio rising. She informed our founding member that her husband, George, was a Taurus, with Moon in Aries and Pisces rising. She wanted to know if her astrologer was correct in assessing that this was a good match. The Magi told her that he would have to analyze both charts carefully before giving her an answer. But the Magi wanted to know what the important aspects were in both charts and asked Joyce for them. Joyce did not know. This is because her astrologer, like almost all other astrologers, did not focus on aspects. When is the last time anyone told you what their aspects were? Or asked you what your aspects were? Probably never. But it is very common for someone to ask you what your sign is—that's for sure!

Remember all those charts from the last chapter? The similarities between the charts corresponding to certain dates were not determined by the signs that the planets were in. The similarity lay in the types of aspects each day had.

Now as it turns out, Joyce, the lady at the party, was born with Neptune conjunct her Sun. To a Magi, that is very meaningful. For one thing, in our research and studies of astrology, we have learned that Neptune is the fountain of youth. Honest. Anyone whose Sun is conjunct to Neptune, or trined by Neptune, looks much younger than anyone else their age. They are also less prone to injuries and recover faster if they are injured. And they are gentle individuals, generally letting things slide off their shoulders; therefore, they are rarely aggressive. They are trusting and make great friends, love to party, and will imbibe. They do not resist you if you pour them a drink; in fact, they do not resist you if you pour them ten drinks. And charm! People with this aspect are the most charming people you can possibly hope to meet.

You can figure all of this out from one aspect, the knowledge that a person has Neptune trine or conjunct his or her Sun at birth. And it does not matter at all what sign the Sun is in.

One significant astrological aspect says a lot about someone. Now we agree that the Sun in Capricorn does give us a great deal of information about the native. For example, two of Capricorn's KEY WORDS are *aspiringly* and *calculatedly*. But there is a big difference between being aspiring as opposed to being calculated. Ambition is a positive attribute; it's a necessity for anyone who wants to attain lofty goals and realize their dreams. But being calculated is a two-edged sword. A calculated person is often not trustworthy, especially where his or her own interests conflict with yours. In our experience, it is possible to know which of these two characteristics people have by knowing the aspects to their Sun. If they have positive aspects to their NATAL Sun, then they will have the good qualities of the Sun's sign. If they have stressful aspects to their Sun, they generally will have some of the negative characteristics of the Sun's sign. For this reason, it is paramount to know the aspects.

In addition, most major aspects have key words of their own, regardless of the sign that the aspect is in. For example, a Pluto conjunction to the Sun is very powerful. The conjunction's astrological description is: the desire for power, and the ability to obtain it. This conjunction acts the same in all signs and can occur in any sign, and the individuals will all be essentially the same, but the sign will add its own little spin to it. A Capricorn with the Sun conjuncted by Pluto will have the greatest desire for power and the greatest ability to achieve it. The possession of power can become an obsession with such people. On the other hand, individuals with this aspect at birth who are Aquarians will have a much tamer desire for power. They will still desire it and will still have the ability to achieve it, but the desire will not become obsessive.

All aspects are important, but the aspects to the Sun are the most crucial; they determine the kind of day it really is and therefore the primary inner desires of the person born on that day. The aspects by Jupiter or by Saturn to any of the major planets are the second most important. But aspects between planets other than the Sun are never as significant as an aspect involving the Sun. For example, it is generally agreed that the Saturn square Pluto aspect is a negative aspect. And this is true, in general. However, Saturn and Pluto move so slowly that this aspect could occur for several weeks in a row. If all of the days that had this aspect were automatically considered negative because of this one aspect, we would be in for some really long-lasting tough times. But this is not the case, because in our research we have found that a day with such an aspect is not bad unless the aspects to the Sun are also problematic. This is another example of aspect integration and how we always need to take into consideration all of the aspects of a birth chart.

Equal-Degree Aspects

We discussed aspects in the last chapter and learned that whenever two planets are in the same degree of any sign, they are in aspect to each other. We will call such aspects EQUAL-DEGREE ASPECTS for obvious reasons. There are other angular relationships between planets that cause them to be in aspect to each other, and yet the two planets are not in equal degrees of signs. For example, if two planets are 72 degrees apart, they are in aspect to each other. Such an aspect is called a *quintile*. But in this book we will not study any aspect that is not an equal-degree aspect. Equal-degree aspects are by far the most important type of aspects. These are the ones that we will use to prove astrology. Other types of aspects are not necessary to prove astrology. We will learn, beyond any reasonable doubt, that when planets are in equal-degree aspect to each other, it is very meaningful and entirely different from situations where the two planets are not in aspect to each other, or are in UNEQUAL-DEGREE ASPECT to each other.

It is the equal-degree aspects that the Magi Society will use in this book to prove conclusively that astrology really works.

The next step is to decide on the methodology that we will use to prove astrology.

How We Will Prove Astrology

There are a number of different scientifically valid methods that can be used to prove that astrology works. The most common method is to do an analysis of a massive number of birth charts and subject the results to a statistical analysis. For example, we could conduct a study of 10,000 randomly chosen individuals, and we could test for an astrological effect such as the Jupiter effect. The Jupiter effect refers to the astrological principle that persons born with Jupiter trine the Sun, or Jupiter conjunct the Sun, are usually more successful than the norm. But if we did such an analysis and found out that there is indeed a Jupiter effect, skeptics would attack our methods from many angles. They would say that our sampling of 10,000 individuals was not random, implying that we skewed the data and added more successful people with the Jupiter effect than was actually normal. You see, it is virtually impossible to verify randomness. Skeptics would insist that we do it all over again, under their scrutiny and supervision. And we could fight about the sampling methodology forever. Then the skeptics could also contest our yardsticks for measuring success. Was it money or happiness or achievement or good health? Because of these problems, after much consideration, we decided not to do any massive statistical analyses to prove astrology.

We know that astrology works; therefore, the birth charts of men and women who have been at the very top of their professions for the long term must contain a number of rare astrological aspects that they share in common. So, if we examine the birth charts of the super-successful in a particular profession, there should be a similarity of astrological aspects, and these similar aspects should occur at least several times more often in the birth charts of these super-successful persons than they occur normally.

This would be a very valid scientific methodology. It is very similar to the way geneticists conduct some of their research into genes. Recently, geneticists have announced what they consider to be a major breakthrough in genetic research. They announced that they believe the tendency towards being homosexual is genetically inherited. They have identified a gene that they say acts in such a way that a person born with that gene is twice as likely to become homosexual. Geneticists have made similar findings with alcoholism, as well as drug addiction.

The methodology that the geneticists used was one of testing the genes of a small segment of the population that had a characteristic different from the norm, and looking for a gene that was more prevalent in the unusual group than in the general population. We decided to use this same methodology since astrological aspects, like genes, are something someone is born with.

Similarly, we will analyze the birth charts of the super-successful and find out how the astrological aspects of their natal charts differ from those of normal people. We will not do the birth charts of any short-lived successes. There are 100 times as many one-year wunderkinds than there are long-term success stories. It is the lasting ones that have the special astrological birth charts. Therefore, we will only include the birth charts of the very long-term super-rich and super-successful. We will include the true superstars of professional sports of the present and the past. We will analyze the birth charts of the powerful men and women in Washington who have influenced our lives and those of the entire world population. We will analyze the birth charts of the long-term success stories of Wall Street and Hollywood. And by studying these charts, we will come to understand which astrological aspects helped these men and women to be so successful.

Then, we will reveal the birth charts of this country's most powerful and enduring corporations, showing that they also have these aspects of success. This information tells us that we can probably take advantage of astrology and be more successful by using our knowledge to select days with favorable astrological aspects to start up or purchase new businesses, or invest in buying a home. We will also analyze the birth charts of famous marriages, and we will see that astrology is applicable there, also. This fact is significant, as it means that choosing an astrologically favorable day to get married can have a strong influence on the success of your marriage.

By focusing our research on the astrological charts of the birth dates of the long-term rich and famous, we will avoid a number of problems. There will never be any doubt about the validity of the birth dates. No one can say we fudged them. They are a matter of public record and easily accessible to anyone who cares to check. Another problem we will be able to bypass is the issue of randomness in our samplings. That is because we will not be sampling a small percentage of the available birth charts; we will be doing all the birth charts of the most successful and famous. All of them. And we will learn that they virtually all share the same astrological aspects of success. Astrology will be proven beyond any reasonable doubt.

In addition, as another proof of astrology, we will show that the aspects that are common denominators of the super-successful are also consistent with the symbolism of astrology. In other words, for example, the aspects that are common denominators of the super-successful business people involve Pluto, because it rules big business, investing and debt, and power. These aspects also involve Jupiter or Venus because they rule success and money. This is what it should be according to the symbolism of astrology, and this is what we find to be the case in our research.

But before we embark on the proof, we mentioned earlier that we will have to greatly increase our knowledge of astrology. That is what we will do in the next chapter.

✦ ✦ ✦

DECLINATIONS: AN INDISPENSABLE DIMENSION OF ASTROLOGY

J ust as astrologers in the past have erred by concentrating too much on the calculated points and the 12 signs, they have also been wrong in ignoring the DECLINATIONS. Without declinations, you are missing a whole powerful dimension in astrology. With them, you can prove astrology and be more than twice as accurate in your forecasts.

Virtually all astrologers only work with LONGITUDES, which involve the dimension that includes the 12 signs of the zodiac. The Magi Society has been using two additional dimensions of astrology, the DECLINATIONS and the DIAGONALS. If that is a mouthful, don't worry. For the purposes of this book, you only need to learn about declinations, which is a very simple concept and which will more than double your knowledge of astrology. (See the Glossary at the back of this book for a brief definition of *diagonals,* which comprise a totally new and very complicated dimension in astrology and need only concern the serious astrologer.)

Learning About Declinations

In order to understand declinations, we should think about how we can locate the position of a planet in the sky. We do it in the same way that we would locate a city on a map. There are two coordinates on a map, the horizontal and the vertical. It is the same with a planet in the sky. To locate a planet, we need two coordinates, a horizontal and a vertical. The horizontal coordinates are called the LONGITUDES.

The vertical coordinates are called the DECLINATIONS. If you know anything at all about astrology, you are already familiar with longitudes. If a woman says her Sun is in Leo, she really means that the longitude of her natal Sun is in Leo. Whenever anyone refers to any of the 12 signs, they are referring to the longitude of a planet. It is just that they do not include the word *longitude*.

Obviously, the planets are constantly in motion. We all know that if we look up at the sky at night, the locations of the planets will change and that these changes are caused by the fact that the Earth and the other planets revolve around the Sun. What some of us do not realize is that astrologers measure these changes in the planets' positions in the sky, and it is these changes that determine which of the 12 astrological signs a planet is in, and which degree of a sign a planet is in. The longitudes measure the horizontal movement of a planet and are measured in degrees. **But all of the planets also move vertically in the sky**. This vertical movement is also measured in degrees and are called the declinations. So, just as the movement of a planet and the Earth causes its longitude to change, so, too, the movement of the planet and the Earth will cause its declination to change. And just as changes in the horizontal location of a planet have astrological significance, all changes in the vertical locations (the declinations) also have astrological significance.

Declinations are very easy to understand. We all know that the Sun reaches its highest point in the sky on the date of the Summer Solstice, around June 21 each year. And six months later, the day is shortest and the night is longest because the Sun rises to its lowest maximum height in the sky. This occurs on the date of the Winter Solstice, around December 22. Now just as the Sun's daily highest point in the sky will vary from day to day, so does the daily highest point in the sky of each of the other planets (please keep in mind that in this book we refer to the Sun and Moon as planets for simplicity). This is caused by the fact that the Earth is tilted about 23-and-a-half degrees on its axis as it revolves around the Sun. The difference in the Sun's peak elevation between the Summer Solstice and the Winter Solstice is about 47 degrees, or twice the angle of the tilt of the earth. Astrologers and astronomers have used the midpoint of this 47-degree range as the zero point, and they call it the CELESTIAL EQUATOR. They measure the declinations of planets as either north or south of this celestial equator. **In other words, the declination of a planet is the vertical dimension of a planet's position.** On June 21, the Sun is in 23.4 degrees north declination. At the same time, it is in 0 degrees Gemini. These two coordinates are used like a map reading, which always has both a vertical and horizontal coordinate. Astronomers use the declinations and longitudes in order to locate stars as well as planets.

To summarize, the longitudes measure the horizontal position of a planet, and the declinations measure the vertical position of a planet. The longitudes are what we are familiar with because that is what is used when astrologers tell us that a planet is in one of the 12 astrological signs. Since astrologers believe that we are influenced by the movement of the planets, it has always puzzled us that they have not paid more attention to the declinations, which measure the vertical movement of planets. In our opinion, it would make no sense to think that only the horizontal movement of the planets can influence us, but that any vertical movement does not. We, of the Magi Society, know that both types of movement have profound influences on our lives. Therefore, the declinations are an entirely separate dimension of astrology, and they are just as valid as the longitudes.

Declinational Aspects

Just as there are aspects in the longitudes, there are also aspects between two planets in the declinations. But there are only two circumstances that cause two planets to be in aspect to each other in the declinations. When two planets have the same declination on the same side of the celestial equator, astrologers say that these two planets are PARALLEL. This is similar to a conjunction in the longitudes. If two planets are in the same degree declination, but one is north of the celestial equator and the other is south, astrologers refer to this as a CONTRA-PARALLEL. The few astrologers who have experimented with the use of the declinations consider a parallel the same as a conjunction, and the contra-parallel the same as an opposition. However, we will learn in this book that the contra-parallel is actually exactly like a conjunction, and it is absolutely nothing like an opposition. Both the contra-parallel and the parallel aspects are helpful positive aspects.

Conjunctions, parallels, and contra-parallels are essentially the same because they create the same influence. Since it's more convenient to refer to any of them with just one term, we have chosen the term CONJOIN to refer to the action of any of these three aspects. So if we write that Jupiter conjoins the Sun, we mean that Jupiter could be conjunct the Sun or parallel the Sun or contra-parallel the Sun.

It is also important to define the meaning of ENHANCEMENT, which is another new term. An enhancement is any aspect that is strongly positive. This means that if we write that a birth chart has a Jupiter enhancement of Venus, it means that Jupiter is in a strongly positive aspect to Venus, and the aspect can be any of the three conjoining aspects we discussed above (conjunctions, parallels, or contra-parallels). In addition, it could mean that Jupiter is trine to Venus, which is another strongly positive aspect. A sextile is also a positive aspect, but it is weaker than any of the other four so we will not include sextiles as enhancements.

Planetary Eclipses

Now, getting back to declinations, when there is an eclipse of the Sun by the Moon, it means that both the longitudes and the declinations of the two planets are the same. In other words, the Sun and Moon are in conjunction in longitude, and in parallel in declination. This is the only way the Sun or Moon can be blocked from our view by the other. The fact that both of these dimensions have to be the same for an eclipse to occur tells us that, in our opinion, all of the ancient astrologers must have had knowledge of declinations. Otherwise, they would not have been able to predict eclipses. If the Sun and Moon were in conjunction, but not in parallel, there would be no eclipse, because the Sun and Moon would be vertically stacked one above the other in the same longitude but not the same declination.

Eclipses are very meaningful astrologically. But astrologers have overlooked an entire range of them.

The term *eclipse* is used only when referring to the Sun and Moon. But from time to time, other planets align in a way similar to the alignment of a solar or lunar eclipse. When any planet is in the same longitude and declination as the Moon, that planet will be eclipsed by the Moon. Astronomers call this an OCCULTATION, but the Magi Society does not like that term because it connotes the occult. We do not believe that anything to do with the occult should be associated with astrology—not even terminology. Therefore, in this book, we will refer to an eclipse of a planet by the Moon or by any other planet as a PLANETARY ECLIPSE. For example, if Jupiter and Venus form an alignment such that Venus eclipses Jupiter, we will call this event a Venus-Jupiter planetary eclipse.

We will learn in this book that planetary eclipses are unbelievably strong aspects. They are caused by a conjunction of two planets, which at the same time are in parallel—essentially having the power of two aspects. But there seems to be a multiplier effect. A planetary eclipse of major planets is much more powerful than just the combination of a conjunction and parallel.

***

For those of you who really want to learn all you can about astrology, it is imperative that you obtain a special book that presents the positions of the planets on a day-to-day basis. A book with such information is called an EPHEMERIS. But make sure that you obtain an ephemeris that has the declinations. Hay House, Inc., the publisher of this book, also publishes The Magi Society's ephemeris, which not only provides the declinations, but also highlights all planetary eclipses and offers all the other special astrological information you will learn about later in this book. (Hay House's publication of our ephemeris is copyrighted, so no other ephemeris contains all this information.)

***

More Information About the Declinations

We admit that we are not anywhere close to being the first astrologers to use the declinations. The ancient Babylonians used them. So did the Greek and Chinese astrologers. But as we explained in the last chapter, we have a basic disagreement with standard astrological interpretation. Standard astrology teaches that the primary characteristics of an individual depend upon the signs that his or her natal planets are in, the houses that these natal planets are in, and the ascendant and midheaven locations. Although we agree that all of these factors do have very significant influences on the character and personality of an individual, the Magi Society's own research shows that such factors hold little weight in determining the probable success of the native. The fact is that we have found that the astrological aspects, particularly declinational ones, most strongly determine whether an individual has a good chance of super-success in any field of endeavor.

One reason that astrologers have not used the declinations much in recent times is that the declinations are not divided into different signs or houses. Virtually all astrologers concentrate their interpretations on the houses and the sign placements of the planets. We believe that they should have included declinations, because after you are finished with this book, you will wonder how anyone could have performed an accurate astrological interpretation without them. Besides, in a subsequent book, we will reveal how to divide the declinations into divisions that resemble houses and signs.

Since astrologers have not been using declinations in their interpretations, they have also left out the declinations in the natal charts. For this reason, we have designed a way of including declinations in a natal chart. Please look at the first chart at the end of this chapter. You will immediately realize that it looks like no other natal chart you have seen in any other publication because there are two full sets of planet symbols in a single chart. The planetary symbols inside the circle represent the declinations of the planets. All of the birth charts in the rest of this book will be represented in this way. Chart 16 is the Magi Society's method of visually representing the planetary alignments and planetary locations in longitudes and declinations for December 2,

1942, the date of the first controlled atomic chain reaction. We call such a birth chart a MAGI ASTROCHART (see entry in Glossary).

Notice that this chart is exactly the same as chart 9 except that it has a whole new set of planets drawn inside the circle. We always exclude the Moon in this book, but the other nine planets are drawn along the roller coaster-like sideways *S* shape inside of the circle. Planets that are in north declination are drawn on the left half of the roller coaster; planets in south declination are in the right half.

Going from left to right on the roller coaster, and referring to planets that are in north declination, a planet that is rising in declination (going to higher degrees of north declination) is placed on that part of the curve that is rising as one goes from left to right. On the other hand, if a planet is moving towards the extreme south declination, we draw the planet's location on the part of the curve that is falling. This is the middle part of the curve, between the highest point of the curve and the lowest point of the curve. Finally, if a planet is rising in declination and is in south declination, we draw the planet on the last quarter of the curve, which is the one-quarter section to the right of the lowest point of the curve. This method of drawing up the planets in the declinations allows you to visually determine if a planet is rising or falling in declination at the time of birth. In chapter 7, you will understand why it is beneficial to be able to visually tell if a planet is rising or falling in the declinations.

When we look at chart 16, we are looking at two dimensions of astrology rather than just one. And in this chart, notice that Jupiter and the Sun are in the same degree of declinations. The Sun is in 21 degrees south declination, and Jupiter is in the same degree in north declination. This is a contra-parallel aspect, and as we said earlier, we regard this to have the same effect as a conjunction of the Sun and Jupiter. This would mean that on that fateful day of the first controlled atomic chain reaction, there were contradictory symbolisms for the day. The Sun was opposed by Saturn, which means a problematic day, possible tragedy, and bad luck and losses. At the same time, we have in the declinations an aspect of the Sun contra-parallel Jupiter, which is the same as the Sun-Jupiter conjunction. And this would symbolize that it was a day of peace, success, and good fortune. You might say that the aspects are contradictory. But when you think about it, we believe that you will agree that this mixed pair of symbolisms is very accurate. Atomic energy and the nuclear bomb have been both a scourge that humankind has feared, and a blessing, all at the same time. The two bombs dropped on Japan in 1945 effected peace, but it did so through fear and tragedy. Since that time, atomic bombs have never been used in war. Some say that the threat of nuclear war is what has kept the peace. But always, the threat of nuclear destruction and tragedy weighs heavily on the human race. Thus both symbolisms have been reflected at the same time. Isn't astrology interesting? The more you learn about this astrology, the more impressed you will be with it.

The natal chart with the two dimensions, and the inclusion of declinational aspects, is entirely new, and we have named all of this "Magi Astrology."

An Overview of the Movement of the Planets

It is helpful to understand how the regular motions of the planets effect changes in the planets' positions in both the longitudes and the declinations.

As we know, nine planets revolve around the Sun, and their paths follow Kepler's laws.(Serious students of astrology can obtain an understanding of Kepler's laws from books on physics or astronomy.) Except for Pluto, the eight planets revolve around the Sun on approximately the same PLANE. Pluto's orbit is more elliptical than the orbit of the other planets, and the plane of its orbit is tilted at a slight angle to the REFERENCE PLANE of the solar system. Most people do not know that Pluto's orbit is so irregular that there are times when Pluto, the ninth planet, is actually closer to the Sun than Neptune, the eighth planet. In fact, that is the case now. Pluto is closer to the Earth than Neptune until 1999, after which time Pluto's highly elliptical and somewhat irregular orbit will again take the planet beyond Neptune and make it the farthest planet from the Sun.

With regard to the longitude of a planet, it is a useful approximation to say that each planet spends an equal amount of time in each of the 12 signs. This is not the case with the declinations. The planets do not move through the different declinational degrees at the same pace. The planets move slowest through the highest degrees of declination, and move fastest through the smaller degrees. This fact has a very strong bearing on Magi Astrology. Keep in mind that in general, the highest or EXTREME DEGREES of declination are about 21 degrees or greater, either north or south declination. The planets spend more time between 21 degrees and 23:3 degrees declination on either side of the celestial equator than they do at any of the other degrees of declination. Changes in the declinations are primarily caused by the tilt of the Earth's axis and APPARENT changes of a planet's position in the sky as the Earth revolves around the Sun.

Please do not worry if you do not understand most of this. It is not necessary to comprehend all of this information in order to understand and appreciate astrology. Unless your goal is to be a serious astrologer, it is only important to know that the movement of the planets in the solar system are such that the planets move through the individual degrees of the declinations at varying rates of speed; the planets move fastest through the degrees that are closest to the zero degree declination, and slow down as they move farther and farther away from the zero degree declination on either side of the celestial equator. The reason this is meaningful, astrologically speaking, is that there are more chances of parallels and contra-parallels in the highest degrees of declination because the planets are there for a longer period of time. This means that there are more aspects formed by planets between 21 and 23:3 degrees north or south declination than any other degrees of declination. It is this non-uniform formation of aspects that has significant astrological bearing.

In the case of the longitudes, all of the 360 degrees have an equal chance of aspect formation. But, unlike the longitudes, the declinations of planets are such that there is significant unequal distribution of aspects depending on the degrees of declination. Using an orb of one degree, a parallel of Mars to the Sun may last as little as three days in the zero degree declination area, but could last more than a month at 22:3 degrees north or south declination. We will learn that this asymmetry makes astrological interpretation very interesting. We want to be able to refer to this concept regularly in this book, so let us call it DECLI-NATIONAL BIAS. There are more persons born with Mars-Sun parallel at the 22:3 to 23:3 degrees declination than any other degrees because of declinational bias.

We are now ready to use our new knowledge of the declinations and apply it in ways that are new to astrology. The first step is for us to become more familiar with the declinations and learn how very important they really are, and how it is impossible to fully interpret birth charts without them. We will, at the same time, provide you with our first proof of astrology because we will prove one of the symbolisms of astrology.

Our First Proof of Astrology

From time to time, we all tend to meet one of those very rare individuals who looks much younger than he or she really is. Many people attribute the good fortune of those individuals to genes, chromosomes, and stress-free lifestyles. This explanation has never made much sense to the Magi Society. So we did some astrological research on this matter and discovered that persons blessed enough to be born with a Neptune ENHANCEMENT of their Sun will look and feel much younger than they actually are.

An enhancement, as we explained earlier, is one of our new astrological terms. A Neptune enhancement of the Sun could mean that Neptune is trine the Sun, or Neptune is parallel the Sun, or Neptune is contra-parallel the Sun, or Neptune is conjunct the Sun. These four types of aspects are all enhancements. And anyone who has a Neptune-Sun enhancement in his or her birth chart will look and feel much younger than they actually are for their entire life, and they will live longer than the average person. In addition, the Neptune enhancement of the Sun gives natives the athletic ability that makes them much more durable than other athletes.

It is easy to prove this Neptune enhancement effect, and it will be one of the ways in which we will prove astrology in this book.

The Magi Society analyzed the astrological charts of famous people who fit the fountain-of-youth criteria, and the majority of them have the Neptune enhancement aspect. The astrological charts of five of these people appear at the end of this chapter. Below is a listing of some of the people who are renowned for their longevity and/or youthful appearance.

Cheryl Tiegs was the first "Supermodel" to be able to continue modeling past the age of 30. In fact, now in her mid-40s, she recently appeared in *Sports Illustrated's* annual swimsuit issue. Before Cheryl, Supermodels stopped modeling in their mid-twenties. Cheryl was the oldest "Cover girl make-up" model. She was born with Neptune parallel her Sun. The orb we are using for declinational aspects will be 2:2 degrees. The orb for longitudinal aspects will be 3 degrees.

We all love Bob Hope, who has lived a long and healthy life. He was born on May 29, 1903. He was emceeing the Oscars into his seventies, and he looked (and still looks) great. He was born with Neptune parallel the Sun.

George Burns, one of the most famous nonagenarians in the world, is known for his agile mind and body. He was born January 20, 1896. We all hope he will celebrate his centennial next year. George Burns was born with Neptune contra-parallel Sun.

By this time, we are sure that some of you are wondering how often Neptune is either parallel or contra-parallel the Sun. It occurs about two weeks a year. Which is not often.

Ginger Rogers was famous for having been able to extend her career as a dancer longer than any other woman. And she has Neptune parallel the Sun. She also has Neptune conjunct her Sun. We learned earlier in this chapter that when both the parallel and the conjunction occur at the same time, it is a planetary eclipse and is more powerful than the sum of the two aspects separately.

Remember how great John Forsythe looked in the television series "Dynasty"? He was born January 29, 1918. He was in his mid-sixties when "Dynasty" was the rage and he looked forty. His birth chart also has Neptune parallel the Sun.

Skeptics might now be thinking that all of the above does not mean anything because physical appearance could be orchestrated by Hollywood make-up artists and plastic surgeons. Although this is obviously not what we are talking about here, let us overcome this criticism by talking about certain athletes who are famous for having unusually long careers playing their respective sports at the superstar level. They are:

- **Martina Navratilova**, tennis's most durable female superstar, who retired in 1994 after a career spanning 19 years. She has won more tournaments than anyone else, male or female, and has had the longest career of any female tennis player. She was born with Neptune parallel her Sun.

- **Jimmy Connors**, the tennis superstar whose career was even longer than that of Martina's. In 1992, Jimmy became the oldest player to ever reach the semifinals in the U.S. Open at the age of 40. Connors has won more tennis tournaments than any other male tennis player. He was born with Neptune contra-parallel the Sun.

- **Edwin Moses**, the track star who won 122 consecutive races and whose Olympic career spanned 16 years, the longest of any successful Olympian track-and-field athlete. He won a medal in each of the Olympics that he competed in. He was born with Neptune parallel the Sun.

- **Nolan Ryan**, the baseball pitcher who pitched no-hitters in his forties, the oldest man to do so. His Sun was trined by Neptune at birth.

- **Gaylord Perry**, the baseball pitcher who won the Cy Young award as the best pitcher in his league when he was 40 years old, the oldest man to do so. He was born during a Sun-Neptune planetary eclipse, which means Neptune was conjunct his Sun and parallel his Sun.

- **Cy Young**, who had a baseball career spanning 22 years and won more games than anyone else. He was also born during a the Sun-Neptune planetary eclipse.

All of these famous athletes had Neptune enhancement of the Sun in their birth charts. They include the longest-lasting male and female superstars of tennis and the three baseball superstar pitchers who have had the longest careers.

***

FIRST CHALLENGE TO SKEPTICS

A Neptune enhancement of the Sun occurs within the orbs we are using about one out of ten days. Therefore, if the Neptune-Sun enhancement is not the reason for the longevity and success of the athletes we have listed, then skeptics should be able to find ten times as many athletes without any Neptune-Sun enhancements, but who have nonetheless had careers that are equally successful and lengthy. In order for skeptics to prove that the Neptune-Sun enhancement is not the cause of these athletes' longevity, they must list ten times as many athletes who do not have a Neptune-Sun enhancement, but who have had careers just as long and just as successful. We challenge skeptics to do so.

HOW TO CONTACT THE MAGI SOCIETY: Friends and skeptics of astrology can contact the Magi Society by telephone. Our telephone number is (212) 867-2905. If this number changes, we will always be listed in the Manhattan telephone directory (area code 212); we will be happy to hear from you.

***

Unless the skeptics can meet this challenge, astrology is proven in this limited way. But even limited proof of astrology opens the flood gates.

It is important at this time to point out that Neptune enhancement of the Sun is not the only astrological aspect that increases longevity. But it is the most powerful one and increases longevity to the greatest extent.

Using the symbolism of astrology, one would expect that Jupiter enhancement of Neptune will also increase longevity, and it does. Jupiter enhancement of Neptune is interpreted as expansion and increase

(Jupiter) of longevity (Neptune). An example of this phenomenon is Robert Parrish, who is, at the writing of this book, the oldest active player in professional basketball. Parrish has Jupiter trine Neptune.

The symbolism of astrology also tells us that Jupiter enhancement of the Sun will improve the native's longevity. Jupiter-Sun enhancement is interpreted as a person (the Sun) of good fortune and success (Jupiter). Some of this good luck has to overflow into looking young and feeling young. Dick Clark has a Jupiter-Sun enhancement.

There are other aspects that also increase longevity. Another example would be Mars enhancement of the Sun. Occasionally, an individual is fortunate enough to have a combination of such aspects at birth and will therefore have an excellent chance of leading a very long life. But there is no question that the single most important astrological aspect that provides the native with the gift of prolonging youth and vitality is the Neptune-Sun enhancement.

Before we go on to the next chapter, let us look back at the natal chart of the first manned lunar landing (see chapter 2). Remember that we had a Jupiter conjunction to Uranus on that day, and this aspect represents success in flying. On the day the lunar mission was launched on July 19, 1969, Neptune was trine the Sun. By using aspect integration, we can interpret the two aspects to mean the longest-lasting (Neptune trine Sun) successful flight (Jupiter conjunct Uranus). What could be longer lasting than man's first flight to the Moon? And back!

With the declinations, we learned that Neptune rules longevity. We applied this knowledge to the longitudes, and we used it to more fully understand a critical day in history. The more we learn about astrology, the more valid it is.

Chart 16: December 2, 1942
with declinations
First controlled atomic
chain reaction

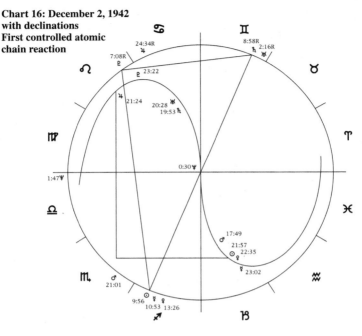

Chart 17: September 27, 1947
Birth date of Cheryl Tiegs

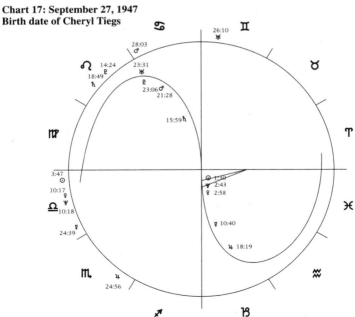

Chart 18: May 29, 1903
Birth date of Bob Hope

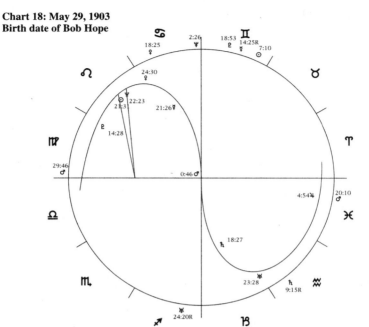

Chart 19: January 20, 1896
Birth date of George Burns

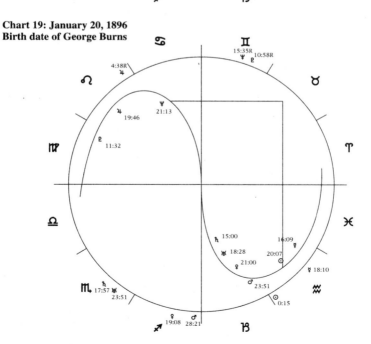

Chart 20: September 2, 1952
Birth date of Jimmy Connors

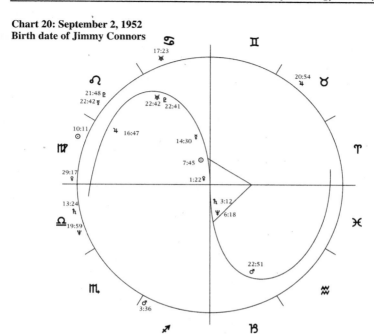

Chart 21: March 29, 1967
Birth date of Cy Young

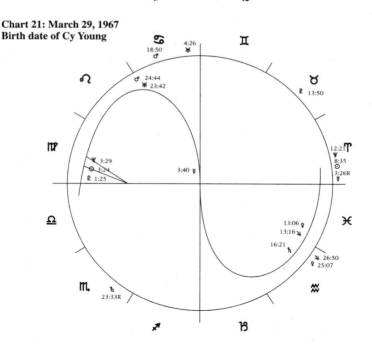

THE ASTROLOGY OF FAME AND FORTUNE

Astrologers have been looking for the astrological common denominators of power, fame, and fortune for centuries and have not found them. But they did not use the declinations, and they were not emphasizing the aspects. We will use the declinations and emphasize the aspects and prove that it is much easier to achieve lasting power, fame, and fortune if you have the advantage of being born with certain astrological aspects.

After conducting thorough and extensive investigations into the birth charts of virtually all of the famous Americans who have achieved the greatest long-lasting success, it was obvious to the Magi Society that astrology was indeed provable. These Americans almost always have at least one, and on the average, two to three, astrological aspects that we would expect to be helpful to them in becoming so successful. And generally, the more of these aspects they have, the more successful they are. The aspects that represent the common denominators are the ones we would expect. They are consistent with the symbolism of astrology; in fact, they confirm the symbolism of astrology.

The 12 Super Aspects

The Magi Society has established that there are 12 astrological aspects that are so powerful that anyone who possesses even one of these aspects has a jump start on achieving great success. We call them the 12 SUPER ASPECTS.

We list below these 12 Super Aspects and provide the astrological rationale for their power.

1) Jupiter enhancement of Pluto
2) Venus enhancement of Pluto
3) Pluto enhancement of the Sun
4) Uranus enhancement of Pluto
5) Jupiter enhancement of the Sun
6) Jupiter enhancement of Venus
7) Jupiter enhancement of Uranus
8) Jupiter enhancement of Neptune
9) Uranus enhancement of Venus
10) Neptune enhancement of Venus
11) Uranus enhancement of the Sun
12) Neptune enhancement of the Sun

The fact that we found these 12 particular enhancements to be the most important ones makes perfect astrological sense and confirms the symbolism of astrology. Below are some of the reasons why we would expect the above 12 Super Aspects to help the NATIVE (the actual person represented by the birth chart) achieve super-success.

Pluto is the most important planet for attaining power, fame, and fortune because it symbolizes competition and big business. Pluto also represents the entrepreneur, politicians, film stars, and the professional athlete. Since the super-rich and super-famous are usually involved in big business, Hollywood, politics, or professional sports, there should be more enhancement aspects involving Pluto in the birth charts of rich and famous people than any other types of aspects.

In chapter 2, we learned that Jupiter is the greater benefic, and Venus is the lesser benefic. It would therefore make astrological sense that many of the super-rich and famous would have Jupiter enhancement of Pluto, or Venus enhancement of Pluto. An enhancement, as we learned in the last chapter, is a trine, conjunction, parallel, or contra-parallel. Using the symbolism of astrology, we would interpret an enhancement of Jupiter to Pluto to mean success and good fortune (Jupiter) in big business (Pluto), in competition (Pluto), and in obtaining power (Pluto). We can also use the same symbolism to interpret the Jupiter-Pluto enhancement as having good fortune and success (Jupiter) from big business, power, and competition (Pluto). Obviously, from the symbolism of astrology, the Jupiter-Pluto enhancement would be expected to be the single most powerful aspect for lasting success. And as we will learn over and over again in this book, this is precisely the case. And this proves astrology works.

Since the astrological influences of Jupiter and Venus are very similar (they are the two planets that are the benefics), we can assume that the Venus-Pluto enhancement acts much the same as the Jupiter-Pluto enhancement, but it would be expected to be a little less powerful. Our research has found that this is the case, and therefore astrology is again proven.

We can also expect many Sun-Pluto enhancements among the super-successful. The Sun symbolizes the actual person. The Sun-Pluto enhancement means that people born on such a day are men and women of power, of big business, and of competition.

And finally, the symbolism of Magi Astrology would lead us to expect Uranus-Pluto enhancements to be Super Aspects because Uranus is the third benefic in Magi Astrology. Uranus-Pluto enhancements mean bringing big business, politics, acting, and professional sports (Pluto) to the masses (Uranus) and being successful at it (because the aspect is an enhancement aspect).

To summarize, by utilizing the symbolism of astrology, we would expect to find enhancements of Pluto by Jupiter, Venus, the Sun, or Uranus in the birth charts of the super-rich, the super-powerful and super-famous. All four such aspects are part of the 12 Super Aspects. The common denominator of all of the above four aspects is that they all involve Pluto, the planet that was not discovered until 1930. Pluto's discovery 5,000 years after the rudiments of astrology was formulated finally allows astrology to be provable, when you include the declinations. It can be proven that these four special enhancements of Pluto give a person a jump start on fame and fortune.

Of these four aspects involving Pluto, the Uranus-Pluto enhancement sometimes does not occur for decades. This is because Uranus and Pluto both move so slowly. The Sun-Pluto enhancement and the Venus-Pluto enhancement each occur in exact aspect about seven days a year. The Jupiter-Pluto enhancement is three times as rare. These four enhancements of Pluto are the four most powerful aspects of success in the business world, sports, politics, and entertainment. From time to time in this book, we will refer to them collectively as the FOUR STRONGEST PLUTO ENHANCEMENTS.

Besides Pluto, the symbolism of astrology would lead us to expect that the planet Jupiter would play a significant role in the attainment of success because Jupiter is the planet of good fortune and success. For this reason, the following Jupiter enhancements are Super Aspects and should be of great help to anyone who is lucky enough to be born with any of them; we also include the astrological rationale for why they are Super Aspects:

- *Jupiter enhancement of the Sun,* for the obvious reason that this enhancement symbolizes a person (the Sun) of good fortune and success (Jupiter);
- *Jupiter enhancement of Venus,* because this aspect symbolizes extraordinary good luck since both planets are benefics, and each helps the other. Also, this enhancement represents abundance (Jupiter) of money (Venus) and good fortune (Jupiter) in partnerships (Venus);
- *Jupiter enhancement of Uranus,* because the NATIVE (actual person represented by the birth chart) with this aspect would expect great success (Jupiter) in achieving fame (Uranus). This aspect is particularly helpful in achieving success in professions ruled by Uranus, which includes broadcasting, movies, and entertainment in general, as well as politics, because politics involves the masses, and Uranus rules the masses; and
- *Jupiter enhancement of Neptune,* since Neptune is the planet of whatever is "long-term"; this aspect symbolizes long-term good fortune and success, inheritances, landed wealth, and success in businesses through patents, copyrights, and mineral rights.

Each of the above four aspects involve Jupiter, the greater benefic. Venus, the lesser benefic, is also very important to success because it rules money. In this world, money is a common yardstick for measuring success. So any aspect that improves the native's ability to make money will improve his or her ability to become successful. Of the nine Super Aspects we have already listed, two already involve Venus. They are the Pluto-Venus and Jupiter-Venus enhancements. Here are the other two Venus enhancements that are Super Aspects:

- *Uranus enhancement of Venus,* which symbolizes money (Venus) from Uranus-related sources, such as broadcasting, the public, and mass merchandising; and
- *Neptune enhancement of Venus,* because this aspect represents money (Venus) from long-term sources (Neptune), such as land and real estate, oil, patents and copyrights, and inheritances.

Finally, there are two more enhancements of the Sun that are Super Aspects:

- *Uranus enhancement of the Sun,* because this would represent a person (the Sun) of fame. The difference between fame and power is very real, but sometimes fame and power do overlap. For this reason, individuals with Uranus or Pluto enhancements of the Sun can be powerful politicians, famous film stars, or successful athletes. But super-successful businessmen are nearly always Pluto-enhanced, since Pluto rules big business.
- *Neptune enhancement of the Sun,* because Neptune is the planet that rules artistry and talent of all kinds.

So, according to the symbolism of astrology, it is these 12 Super Aspects that we would expect to see the most of in the charts of the super-rich and famous, the super-powerful and famous. And fortunately, this is exactly what we find.

The orbs of aspects are also important. We will continue to have a narrower and tighter orb than most astrologers. The orb for longitudes will remain three degrees, and the orb for the declinations will also remain 2:20 degrees. The only exception is for the Uranus-Pluto declinational aspects. We have found that the orb for the Uranus-Pluto declinational enhancement must be closer than for other aspects. This is probably because these two planets move so slowly. The orb for the declinational aspects for these two planets will be just one degree.

On the basis of the above expectations, we investigated the birth charts of essentially every super-rich and super-famous American whose birthdays we could find. Here are the highlights of our research.

Billionaires

Forbes magazine publishes an annual listing of the 400 richest people in America. According to *Forbes,* the three richest men in America at the time of this writing are:

- **Bill Gates**, worth about $9 billion. He is the founder and principal stockholder of Microsoft Corporation, the company whose software runs 70 percent of the personal computers in the world.
- **Warren Buffett**, also worth about $9 billion. He is the president of Berkshire Hathaway, a public holding company. He made his money by making very profitable long-term investments.
- **John Kluge**, worth almost $6 billion. His fortune was amassed in the business world through his dealings in radio and television stations, cellular licenses, long-distance telecommunications, and other enterprises.

We used *America's Who's Who* for their birth dates. We do not know their time of birth. But remember, we do not need the time of birth; we only need birth dates. We are not using midheavens, ascendants, or houses. Astrology will live or die by aspects alone, and without the Moon. For the purposes of this book, every chart is cast for 1:00 P.M. Eastern Standard Time. That would be the equivalent of 10:00 A.M. Pacific Standard Time. We chose this time because it most closely averages out to noon time through all four American time zones. The birth charts of these three billionaires, with the declinations in the form of Magi Astrocharts, can be found at the end of this chapter.

From the symbolism of astrology, the Jupiter-Pluto enhancement is the single most powerful aspect for success and amassing a fortune in big business. All three of these billionaires were born with precisely this astrological aspect, the Jupiter enhancement of Pluto. These men have one parallel, one contra-parallel, and one conjunction of Jupiter and Pluto. These three types of aspects, as we learned earlier, all act the same. They are enhancements. And in the case of these three billionaires, they were very strong enhancements, because the aspects were very close to being exact. The astrological rule is that the more exact any aspect is, the stronger the aspect is.

The Jupiter-Pluto enhancement is the strongest possible enhancement of Pluto. Although Pluto is not associated directly with money, per se, it is the planet of power, and money is power. It is also the planet of big business, and these men all made their money through big business.

All three billionaires also have at least one of the other 12 Super Aspects. Bill Gates has the Jupiter enhancement of the Sun, which makes him a very lucky man. And both Buffett and Kluge have the Neptune enhancement of Venus, which gives them long-term moneymaking capabilities. In addition, Kluge was born with an additional five Super Aspects. They are: Jupiter contra-parallel Neptune, Jupiter parallel Uranus, Jupiter parallel Venus, Uranus parallel Pluto, and Pluto contra-parallel Venus. This means that the three richest men in America have a total of eleven Super Aspects in their birth charts. Notice that ten of these Super Aspects are in the declinations. Now you know why nobody could prove astrology before—no one used the declinations!

What about some other billionaires? Would we find more Jupiter-Pluto enhancements? Yes! From *Forbes'* listing of the richest men and women in America, every single one of the billionaires who made their money themselves (those who did not inherit the billions), have at least 2 of the 12 Super Aspects we expected, and 7 of 8 have the Jupiter-Pluto enhancement. The charts of each of these billionaires are at the end of this chapter. Here are the other richest people in America, according to *Forbes* magazine:

- **Edward C, Johnson III**, the man behind Fidelity Investments, has Jupiter parallel Pluto (that makes it 4 for 4), and also has a Sun-Pluto parallel and a Sun-Jupiter parallel. Johnson has a fourth

Super Aspect, the Uranus trine Venus. He and his family are worth $5.1 billion.

- **John van Andel**, co-founder of Amway Corporation, is worth $4.5 billion. He also has Jupiter contra-parallel Pluto, so he is the fifth billionaire in a row that has Jupiter enhancement of Pluto. He also has Pluto parallel Sun and Jupiter trine Neptune.

- **Richard Marvin Devos** is the other co-founder of Amway Corp. He has two Super Aspects. He was born with Pluto trine Sun and Jupiter conjunct Venus. Of the eight richest self-made men in America, he is the only one without a Jupiter enhancement of Pluto. But he has one of the four strongest Pluto enhancements we deemed most helpful in making money. And his son, Richard, Jr., was born with a Jupiter-Pluto enhancement; he was born just one week apart from Bill Gates. Father and son are both involved with Amway, the source of their wealth.

- **Ronald Perelman's** birthday is not available in the publications we researched. He was a king of leveraged buyouts but has now settled into a very successful business in entertainment and broadcasting.

- The **Waltons** and the **Newhouses** inherited their money. They are the family of Sam Walton, the deceased multi-billionaire founder of Wal-Mart Stores, and the sons of Samuel Newhouse, the deceased publishing tycoon.

- **Rupert Murdoch**, the publishing and broadcasting tycoon, was born with Jupiter parallel Pluto. He also has Pluto trine Sun. He is worth $4 billion.

- **Sumner Redstone** of Viacom, Inc., is worth about $4 billion, also. He was born with Jupiter trine Pluto, and Pluto parallel the Sun.

Seven out of eight of the richest self-made men in America have Jupiter enhancement of Pluto in their birth charts. We will refer to this Jupiter-Pluto aspect from time to time as the SUPER SUCCESS ASPECT. But all eight billionaires also have some of the other Super Aspects we anticipated that they would have. Four of them have the Sun-Pluto enhancements. And all of these eight billionaires have at least 2 of the 12 Super Aspects that we decided were the best ones for amassing a fortune.

Seven out of the eight richest self-made men in America have the Jupiter-Pluto enhancement. How rare is a Jupiter enhancement of Pluto? The last enhancement was a conjunction, and it occurred from November 15 through December 18 of 1994. The next enhancement will be a parallel and will occur during part of February and March of 1998. As you can see, it does not occur seven out of eight days. Or even one out of eight days. In a normal decade, it occurs about one out of twenty days. Some decades it is even more rare. Other decades, if Pluto is very high or very low in declinations, it occurs more often because of declinational bias. But although our sampling is small, the presence of so many Jupiter-Pluto enhancements in the birth charts of these richest men in America is strong proof that astrology works. And the fact that all of these billionaires have at least 2 of the 12 Super Aspects is added proof.

Initial Conclusion

Obviously, not everyone with the Jupiter-Pluto enhancement is a billionaire or even a millionaire. In this book, we are not ever implying that any astrological aspect will *always* or even *usually* create any particular set of conditions in anyone's life. What we are saying is that certain astrological aspects will improve a person's chances of achieving super-extraordinary success. This success can be in the form of money, fame, personal athletic accomplishments, team success, political clout, and a host of other achievements, including living a longer, healthier life and appearing more youthful than one's years would suggest.

Also, we are not saying that a person born without certain astrological aspects cannot achieve any of the above-mentioned goals in life. What we do say in this book is that if you have two or more of the 12 Super Aspects, your chances of achieving the highest levels of success are many times better than someone who does not possess any of the 12 Super Aspects. And this proves that astrology works.

Let us now leave the billionaires behind for a while and examine the birth charts of some Americans whose financial wealth is measured only in the tens of millions or hundreds of millions at most. But, nevertheless, they are super-successful, and their faces are much more familiar to most of us than those of any of the billionaires.

The Most Successful Professional Athletes

Not too long ago, America was treated to the basketball-playing prowess of the first Dream Team USA. This was during the 1992 Summer Olympics. Since it is the intention of the Magi Society to cast the birth charts of the super-successful in this book, we think that everyone would have to agree that the five original starters on that basketball team were super-successful in their profession. These five super-athletes were:

- Michael Jordan
- Charles Barkley
- David Robinson
- Karl Malone
- Clyde Drexler

You can find their birth charts at the end of this chapter.

All of these five superstar basketball players were born with a Venus-Pluto enhancement, which is one of the four strongest Pluto enhancements. (We know that skeptics might say that this is just a coincidence—again! But when are they going to realize that too many coincidences create a law?)

Venus, as we discussed earlier in chapter 2, is the lesser benefic, while Jupiter is the greater benefic. This means that the Venus-Pluto enhancement is similar to the Jupiter-Pluto enhancement, but it is not as powerful. We will refer to the Venus-Pluto enhancement as a SUPER SPORTS CHAMPION ASPECT. We will find out later on in the book that there are a number of aspects that are Sports Champion Aspects. All such aspects greatly increase a person's chances of becoming a great athlete.

The Venus-Pluto enhancement is very well suited for athletes. Venus represents possessions, resources, and money. The Venus-Pluto enhancement would symbolize money from Pluto-related endeavors. We learned that Pluto relates to power, big business, politicians, competition, the professional athlete, and professional sports. So in the case of our Olympic basketball stars, the Venus-Pluto enhancement represents money made from competition in sports, as well as money made from the business of sports, including endorsements.

Even among the illustrious company of his fellow superstars, Michael Jordan stands out from the crowd. Could this fact have been predicted from the astrological charts of these five athletes? Yes! Of course. This is because Jordan has *two*—count them, *two*—Super Sports Champion Aspects. He has Venus trine Pluto, and Venus contra-parallel Pluto. So Michael Jordan, the man with the best aspects among these five basketball players, was the one who made the most money and won the most championships.

A planetary eclipse of Venus and Pluto would automatically create two Venus-Pluto enhancements; there would be a Venus-Pluto conjunction as well as a parallel. But Michael Jordan's Venus-Pluto double enhancement was not created by a planetary eclipse. One enhancement was a trine. The Magi Society has found that two-dimensional enhancements of Super Aspects such as Jordan's have awesome power. We call them Magi BI-LEVEL ASPECTS. Any time two planets are not in eclipse alignment, but still form a longitudinal enhancement and a declinational enhancement, it is a Magi BI-LEVEL ENHANCEMENT. It is a very, very special blessing. Just look at Michael Jordan if you have any doubts.

Now, we are not trying to say that the presence of just one Super Aspect is enough for super-success. All of the eight billionaires had at least two Super Aspects. And the same is true for all of these five basketball superstars.

Both Michael Jordan and Charles Barkley have the Sun-Uranus Super Aspect for fame. David Robinson has the Uranus-Venus Super Aspect. Clyde Drexler has Jupiter trine Neptune, and Karl Malone has Sun parallel Pluto. All five superstars have at least two Super Aspects.

Let's look at a different sport now.

Football seems to capture more of America's attention than any other sport. And the players that have won the most Super Bowls would have to be considered the most successful. The Super Bowl ring is what every football player strives to achieve. The quarterback is the most important player on a football team, and there are only two quarterbacks who own four Super Bowl rings: Terry Bradshaw and Joe Montana. When you reflect upon this for a moment, you will come to realize how great an achievement that really is these days with so many teams competing. So much can go wrong. You can lose the title on a bad bounce of the ball.

When you look at the birth charts of Bradshaw and Montana (charts 30 and 31) at the end of this chapter, you will see that they both have the Jupiter-Pluto enhancement, the Super Success Aspect. They are both super-successful even though neither of these two superstars of sports are billionaires. We will learn throughout this book that this one aspect is the single most powerful aspect in providing super-success to anyone who was fortunate enough to be born with it.

We found Montana's chart particularly interesting because he also has a Pluto-Venus enhancement, which is a Super Sports Champion Aspect. In addition, Montana was born with a Sun-Pluto parallel as well. This means that Joe Montana has three of the four strongest Pluto enhancements that we listed early in this chapter as tags of success. That is more than anyone else so far. And it shows, because Montana has been revered as a demigod by the fans—and for good reason.

Please look at Montana's triple parallel involving the Sun, Venus, and Pluto. Don't they look extremely powerful all grouped like that? They are all within one degree of each other, and they are all up at the extremes of the declinations where the planets move the slowest. Bradshaw has a very similar alignment of three planets at birth. He has Pluto-Uranus parallel within a half of a degree and Jupiter contra-parallel to both. All three of these planets are also within one degree of declination. Anytime three or more planets are in such tight alignment, they are very, very powerful. We will see this over and over again in the charts of the great athletes.

Besides the Pluto enhancements, great athletes need Mars enhancements to endure the physical rigors of their profession because Mars symbolizes energy and muscles. We know this idea is contrary to the theory of evolution, but it just does not make sense that genes and chromosomes are the only difference between the average man and the professional athlete. A football player will be hit full force by men weighing over 250 pounds more than a thousand times a year. We are talking full force because our calculations include only real games; we are not including hits during practice. We are sure that if any of us were hit 1,000 times by someone of our own weight, we would not be able to play football ever again. When we watch these games on television and look at the viciousness of some of the tackles, it is hard to believe that there are not more injuries. The receivers sometimes land on their heads. These are not ordinary people. No ordinary person could take this kind of physical punishment beyond high school. It is not just genes and chromosomes, but it is their ASTROLOGICAL ENERGY that allows professional football players to take the kind of physical punishment that they do. Normal people cannot possibly withstand that kind of brutality to their bodies.

One of the astrological reasons that professional athletes can withstand such physical abuse is their enhancements to Mars, the planet that symbolizes energy and muscles. In the case of the seven superathletes whose birth charts we have just done, they all have enhancements of Mars—every single one of them. It is hard to play professional sports without Mars enhancements. Just look at the athletes that have them:

- Michael Jordan and Charles Barkley have Mars-Pluto parallel. This provides enormous energy. Lawrence Taylor, the New York Giants superstar who held the all-time record for sacks when he retired in 1993, also has this aspect. He was also the only football player ever to be named to the Pro Bowl for ten consecutive years. Mars-Pluto enhancements are Super Sports Champion Aspects.
- Clyde Drexler has Mars parallel Mercury; This improves Mars and also Mercury, which rules respiration and the reflexes.

- David Robinson has Jupiter trine Mars, which does exactly what you would expect: this aspect expands (Jupiter) energy (Mars).
- Karl Malone has Mars sextile the Sun, which gives energy to the Sun, the ruler of the heart and circulation.
- Joe Montana has Venus enhancement of Mars, which we will learn later is the single most powerful Mars enhancement. Jordan and Barkley both also have this enhancement of Mars, in addition to their Pluto-Mars enhancements.
- And Terry Bradshaw has Uranus trine Mars. Uranus symbolizes the masses and also massiveness. Uranus-Mars enhancements signify massive amounts of energy.

Any enhancement of Mars is very, very powerful in boosting energy levels. We will learn much more about this later in this book. The sports fans among you will find the games much more interesting when you know which players have the astrological birth charts needed to become superstars and winners.

Let us now do the birth charts of people whose faces are just as familiar as superstar athletes. It is time to go to Hollywood.

Hollywood Megastars

Did the Jupiter-Pluto enhancement and the other three strongest Pluto enhancements work on Hollywood's long-term superstars? Do the 12 Super Aspects work on Hollywood superstars? Will astrology work for the likes of Robert Redford, Harrison Ford, Barbra Streisand, Clint Eastwood, Kevin Costner, and Glenn Close? Of course it does. It works on anything or anybody that has a birth date.

But we do need a correct birth date. So in this regard we do confront a problem when we test astrology on Hollywood superstars. The Hollywood set has an affinity for astrology. Some of them who may have been born in one sign simply decided they did not want to be that sign and changed it, along with a year or two, or more. For this reason, we are suggesting that we do not use these charts for statistical purposes. However, the vast majority, if not all, of the birth dates of the Hollywood megastars we have included in this book are correct.

There is a second problem when we use Hollywood stars to try to validate astrology. In chapter 3, we decided to prove astrology really works by analyzing the birth charts of the most successful persons. But there are no definitive standards available to determine who has achieved the greatest success in the film world. In this book, we have decided to research the birth charts of the most (long-term) successful individuals in various professions. The success of billionaires can be measured in dollars. The success of athletes is measurable in their career records. However, it is much more difficult to find a yardstick for success in Hollywood. The Oscar is a great achievement, and virtually all actresses and actors would like to win as many as possible. But there are an incredible number of one-time winners, and both Hollywood and the public seem to be very fickle. At the end of chapter 3, we decided on our methodology of proving astrology—that is, doing the birth charts of essentially all of the long-term super-successes. Being a one-time Oscar winner does not qualify anyone as a long-term super-success in Hollywood. In this book, we are only interested in the superstars who have had lasting careers.

In our opinion, the following men and women have proven themselves to be the longest term superstars and are included in our research: Sean Connery, Clint Eastwood, Robert Redford, Barbra Streisand, Harrison Ford, Sylvester Stallone, Glenn Close, Arnold Schwarzenegger, Meryl Streep, Richard Gere, Kim Basinger, Kathleen Turner, Denzel Washington, Kevin Costner, Bruce Willis, and Mel Gibson.

All of these superstars have at least one of the four strongest enhancements to Pluto. We have already seen that this type of enhancement gives the individual a jump start to fame and fortune. Most have two or more of them. And, as was the case with all the other super-successful persons in this chapter, all of these Hollywood superstars have at least 2 of the 12 Super Aspects.

Of the 11 charts of Hollywood's most successful leading men, 9 have the Jupiter-Pluto enhancement, the Super Success Aspect. Only the two muscular men, Schwarzenegger and Stallone do not. But both of these leading men have Uranus-Pluto parallel; in Arnold's case, that aspect was just about exact, which makes the beneficial influences of the aspect as strong as possible. Besides a Uranus-Pluto parallel, Stallone also has the Sun-Pluto parallel. In fact, 10 of the 16 actors and actresses have the Sun-Pluto parallel or contra-parallel. The Sun-Pluto enhancement is the most common enhancement to the Sun of the super-famous.

Of the five women we are looking at, three have the Jupiter-Pluto enhancement, and the other two each have the Uranus-Pluto enhancement.

Astrology worked again.

Which star has the strongest chart for lasting fame and fortune? If we use the yardstick of who has the most Super Aspects, we would have to say that Harrison Ford has the strongest chart. He has three of the four strongest Pluto enhancements. He also has Jupiter parallel the Sun, Jupiter parallel Venus, and Uranus parallel Venus. This means that he has a total of 6 of the 12 Super Aspects for long-lasting success. Is it any wonder that he has starred in 7 of the 25 all-time highest-grossing films? No one else is even close. So just as Michael Jordan and Joe Montana have the greatest number of Pluto enhancements in their respective categories, and just as they are at the top of their professions, Harrison Ford has the most Pluto enhancements among Hollywood megastars, and he is also the most successful in his profession. (See Harrison Ford's birth chart at the end of this chapter.)

We have also provided you with the birth charts of Clint Eastwood, Robert Redford, Sean Connery, Kim Basinger, Kathleen Turner, Meryl Streep, and Denzel Washington.

Like the other groups, more than half of these men and women also have a cluster of at least three planets in the same degrees of declination. This type of alignment, as we will see continually in this book, is very powerful and useful. This cluster is so powerful that it deserves a special term so that we can refer to this type of alignment easily. The term we will use is MAGI PYRAMIDS, which is any declinational alignment of three planets, where each of the three planets is in equal degree aspect to each other. The aligning planets, however, must be comprised of only the Sun, Venus, Jupiter, Uranus, Neptune, and Pluto. Of the 16 Hollywood superstars we have mentioned, 15 have at least one Magi Pyramid.

Six of these sixteen superstars share the same particular Magi Pyramid. Clint Eastwood, Harrison Ford, Kathleen Turner, Kim Basinger, Kevin Costner, and Denzel Washington all have the Jupiter-Pluto-Sun Magi Pyramid. This means that in each of their six birth charts, Jupiter, Pluto, and the Sun make mutual equal-degree enhancements to each other. In the cases of Eastwood, Ford, and Turner; Jupiter, Pluto, and the Sun are all in triple parallel. With the other three superstars, Jupiter and Pluto are in parallel, and the Sun is contra-parallel to both Jupiter and Pluto. Since a contra-parallel has the same astrological effect as the parallel, there is no need to distinguish between them. Therefore, all six superstars have the Magi Pyramid of Jupiter, Pluto, and the Sun.

Just as Mars was enhanced in the charts of the athletes, so is Uranus enhanced in the charts of actors and actresses. Uranus is the planet that symbolizes broadcasting and communication to the masses. Uranus is the planet of fame. Of the 16 Hollywood superstars whose charts we have examined, 9 of them have the Jupiter-Uranus enhancement. A Jupiter-Uranus enhancement means success and good fortune in broadcasting and communication to the masses; Jupiter-Uranus enhancement represents fame. As such, it makes sense to call it the SUPER FAME ASPECT.

A Closer Look at Pluto

Most of you have probably observed that the vast majority of these birth charts have Pluto very high in declination. You may be wondering if this is always the case with Pluto. The answer is "no." As with all the other planets, Pluto moves from one extreme of the declinations to the other. But it does so slower than any other planet because it is the planet that is farthest from the Sun. From the years 1922 until 1963, the declination of Pluto was between 20 and 24 degrees north. From 1922 to 1947, Pluto was rising to higher declinations as it moved from 20 to 24 degrees. From 1948 to 1963, Pluto was falling in declination as it was moving from 24 to 20 degrees. This is a lot of years in a few degrees. We had touched upon the reason for this in our last chapter, which explained the declinations. The fact is, the planets move through the various degrees of the declinations at a different pace. All planets slow down their pace as they approach the extremes on either side of the Celestial Equator. The slower the planet revolves around the Sun, the slower the planet will move through each degree of declination. But they will always move slowest through the extremely high or low declinations. This means that Pluto, the slowest planet to revolve around the Sun, will also move slowest through the declinations. And Pluto will move the slowest through the extremes of the declinations.

At this moment in early 1995 as the Magi Society's founders are completing this book, Pluto is in 7 degrees south declination. This is obviously a long way from its declinations of over 20 degrees north in virtually all of the birth charts we have examined so far. And Pluto will not reach 20 degrees south declination until 2014.

None of the above in any way reduces the validity of our discovery that the Jupiter-Pluto enhancement provides the NATIVE (the actual person represented by the birth chart) with inordinate amounts of good fortune. This is because even during the years when the Jupiter-Pluto enhancement occurs the most, over the span of any generation, it is still a rare aspect.

In fact, what we have just discussed even helps to validate astrology. During the years 1925 to 1963, Pluto was high in declination, so our knowledge of declinational bias tells us that there were more Pluto enhancements than normal. This means that people born during this period of time were more likely to have Pluto enhancements than normal. These same people born between 1925 and 1963 are the people who now control the destiny of essentially all the nations and all the economies. This control began to take shape in the 1980s when persons born later than 1925 began to achieve positions of power. Since the population of people born during the 1925 to 1963 period have more Pluto enhancements, we would expect the world to become more and more oriented to matters associated with Pluto and its symbolisms. And this is exactly what has happened. Pluto is the planet that rules big business; during the last fifteen years, countries have become much more oriented towards the free enterprise system. Communism has failed and fallen; so has socialism. Free trade is a watchword. Countries that had previously socialized or nationalized whole industries have reversed this process. We believe all this is in large measure a direct result of the phenomenon that the people who are now in control have more Pluto enhancements than the historical norm, and they believe in what Pluto represents, which is big business and free enterprise.

But the planets will continue to move on, and this ensures change in the future. Neptune and Uranus have been in extreme declination during the last 15 years. Neptune rules religion and spirituality; Uranus rules technology and astrology. People born in the last 15 years will begin to rise to positions of power in 30 years. We will have a very significant change in world orientation starting about that time.

Let us now look at the natal charts of some men and women who have the most power in this country.

The Astrology of Politicians

Since Pluto is the planet that represents power, then it should again be greatly enhanced in the birth charts of America's most successful long-term politicians. In addition, just as in the acting profession, many politicians should have Uranus enhancements because they have to be able to communicate to the masses, and Uranus is the planet of the masses.

In November of 1994, a political event of monumental significance occurred. The Republicans gained control of the House of Representatives for the first time in 40 years, and Newt Gingrich became the first Republican to become Speaker of the House in 40 years.

Referring now to Gingrich's birth chart, which is at the end of this chapter, Gingrich was born with an exact Jupiter parallel Uranus, the Super Fame Aspect. This gives Gingrich enormous power as a politician and good luck in dealing with the voting public. This ability is further enhanced by the fact that Venus is also parallel to Jupiter and Uranus, thus creating a Magi Pyramid of Jupiter, Uranus, and Venus. He also has a Sun-Pluto parallel, which means that this is the chart of a man able to obtain and handle power. The combination makes him a very strong political force, which you would expect from the first Republican Speaker of the House in 40 years!

Robert Dole, the Republican Majority Leader in the U.S. Senate, has a similarly powerful chart. (Dole's birth chart is also at the end of this chapter.) He has the Sun-Pluto parallel as well. His success in gaining power is further helped by his Jupiter trine to Pluto. Here we are again and again and again. The Super Success Aspect, Jupiter enhancement of Pluto, is an incredibly powerful aspect that helps the native attain extraordinary success in any profession. In this case, the symbolism is success and good fortune (Jupiter) in Pluto-related endeavors, which includes politics. The Jupiter-Pluto enhancement also symbolizes good fortune in achieving power. Different people attain it in different ways, though. The eight billionaires listed early in this chapter reached their high levels of power by amassing billions of dollars; in their cases, money gives them power. Senator Dole gained power by winning elections and becoming Majority Leader in the Senate.

President Clinton's birth chart also confirms that astrology works. Like Newt Gingrich, he has the aspect that allows him to succeed with the voting public. He has the Jupiter-Uranus enhancement in the form of a trine of these two planets, so he has the Super Fame Aspect. And he has one of the four strongest enhancements of Pluto, Uranus parallel Pluto, which is interpreted astrologically as power (Pluto) from the masses and voting pubic (Uranus). President Clinton's wife, Hillary, was born with the Super Success Aspect as well as four other Super Aspects! These two birth charts make a very powerful team. The birth charts of both Clintons are at the end of chapter 9.

The most important aspect for success, the Jupiter-Pluto enhancement, is dominant in the charts of our recent First Ladies and Presidents. Besides Hillary, three other recent First Ladies have this aspect. They are Barbara Bush, Nancy Reagan, and Jackie Onassis. Among the recent presidents, George Bush, Ronald Reagan, Jimmy Carter, and Jack Kennedy were born with it.

Ronald Reagan, the "Great Communicator," has probably been one of the most fortunate men in politics during this century. He never lost an election, including when he ran for Governor of California, and president of the Screen Actors' Guild. His birth chart is very instructive (please see his chart at the end of this chapter).

For all the years that Reagan was in U.S. politics, most Democrats and many reporters wondered what in the world the voting public saw in him. Part of the answer is that Ronald Reagan has the best of all Magi Pyramids. He has the Jupiter-Pluto-Sun Magi Pyramid, the astrological tag of someone most likely to be super-successful. Reagan also has exceptional aspects when it comes to communicating with the voting public. He has Uranus parallel Mercury. This aspect symbolizes speech and oratory (Mercury) to broadcast to the masses (Uranus). No wonder they call him the "great communicator." Reagan's good luck comes from this Jupiter-Sun parallel; his ability to obtain power comes from his Jupiter-Pluto contra-parallel and his Sun-Pluto contra-parallel. This means he has three of the four strongest Pluto enhancements. And he has Uranus-Neptune contra-parallel, which means that he obtains long-term security (Neptune) from the general public (Uranus) and from Uranus-related endeavors such as broadcasting.

As you can see, the more you know about astrology, the better you can make intelligent observations about what is happening in this world. And the more you observe the world through the eyes of astrology, the more you realize that knowledge of astrology and its symbolisms is indispensable.

America's Top CEOs

There is one last group of super-successful people we would like to discuss in order to prove that astrology works. They are the people who run America's most successful corporations, the 30 companies that make up the Dow Jones Industrial Average. The Dow Jones Publishing Company, which publishes the *Wall Street Journal*, has been maintaining a stock index called the Dow Jones Industrial Average for longer than anyone can remember. This index is famous around the world. When you ask someone what happened in the stock market, the reply will be given to you in terms of the Dow Jones Industrial Average. The 30 companies that the Dow Jones Publishing Company choose to include in the index are widely regarded as 30 of the most successful companies in the United States. These 30 companies are:

- Alcoa
- Allied Signal
- American Express
- American Telephone and Telegraph
- Boeing
- Caterpillar Tractor
- Chevron
- Coca-Cola
- Disney
- Dupont
- Eastman Kodak
- Exxon
- General Electric
- General Motors
- General Tire
- International Business Machines
- International Paper
- J.P. Morgan
- McDonald's
- Minnesota Mining and Manufacturing
- Merck
- Philip Morris
- Procter & Gamble
- Sears
- Texaco
- Union Carbide
- United Technologies
- Westinghouse
- Woolworth's

If astrology works, then it should work on the birth charts of the 30 executives who run these companies. Because Pluto symbolizes big business, we would again expect it to be the most heavily aspected planet in the charts of these 30 businessmen. The Magi Society researched the birth charts of the Chief Executive Officers (CEOs) of all 30 companies and found that, indeed, Pluto is the key planet in the birth charts of almost all of these 30 powerful and wealthy business executives.

The Jupiter enhancement of Pluto was found to be present in 10 of these 30 charts. This percentage is not as high as that of the billionaires or the Hollywood superstars, but it was still high enough to be statistically significant. The Jupiter-Pluto enhancement certainly helped all of the executives that were fortunate enough to possess it.

The Pluto-Sun enhancement occurred in 14 of these 30 birth charts. This is a phenomenal statistic, since the normal occurrence of this aspect in a random group of 30 individuals would have been about 2 or 3. Fourteen is very statistically significant, and this is another validation of astrology.

In addition, there were eight Sun-Jupiter enhancements. The normal occurrence is only about two. And 19 of the 30 have at least one Magi Pyramid.

Again, the 12 Super Aspects continue to appear so much more often in the charts of the super-successful that the conclusion must be that astrology really works, and it works very well.

🪐   🪐   🪐

Chart 22: October 28, 1955
Birth date of William Gates III

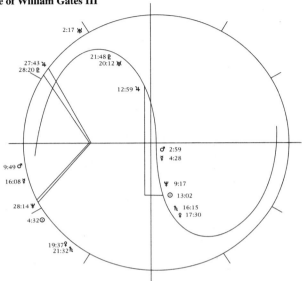

Chart 23: August 30, 1930
Birth date of Warren Buffett

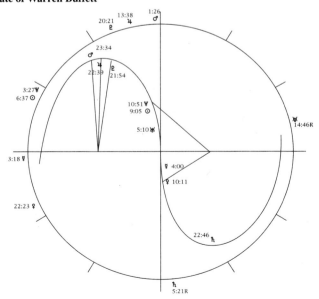

Chart 24: September 21, 1914
Birth date of John W. Kluge

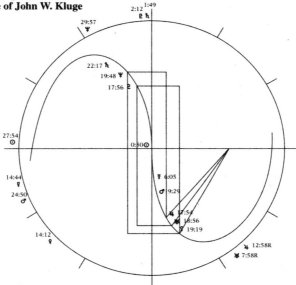

Chart 25: June 29, 1930
Birth date of Edward C. Johnson III

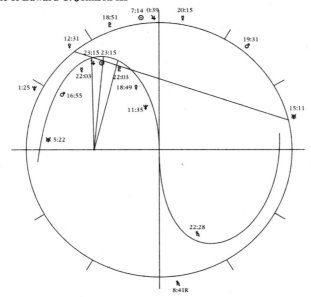

Chart 26: June 3, 1924
Birth date of John Van Andel

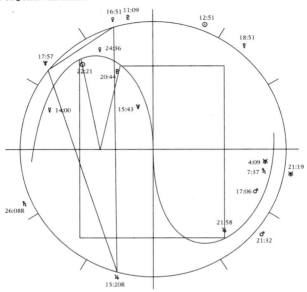

Chart 27: March 4, 1926
Birth date of Richard M. Devos (Sr.)

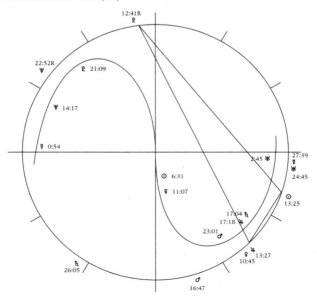

Chart 28: March 11, 1931
Birth date of Keith Rupert Murdoch

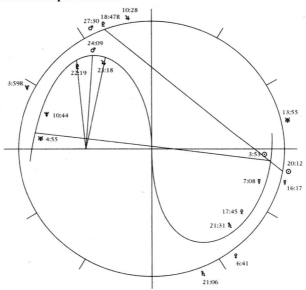

Chart 29: May 27, 1923
Birth date of Sumner Redstone

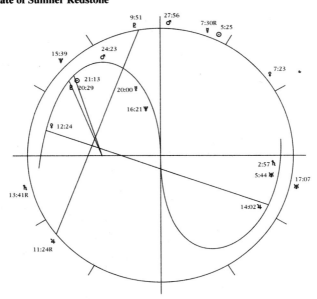

Chart 30: September 2, 1948
Birth date of Terry Bradshaw

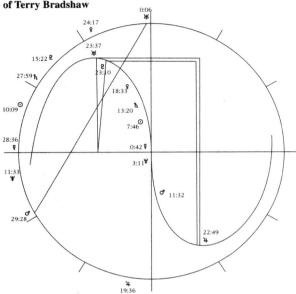

Chart 31: June 11, 1956
Birth date of Joe Montana

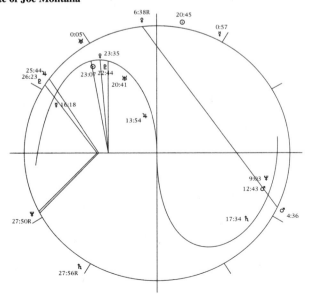

Chart 32: February 17, 1963
Birth date of Michael Jordan

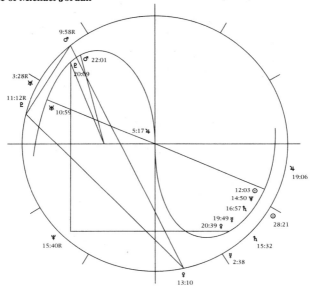

Chart 33: February 20, 1963
Birth date of Charles Barkley

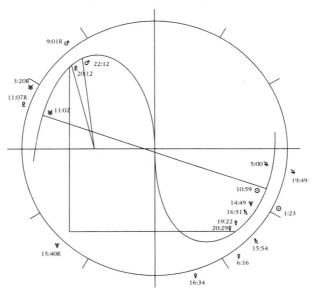

Chart 34: August 6, 1965
Birth date of David Robinson

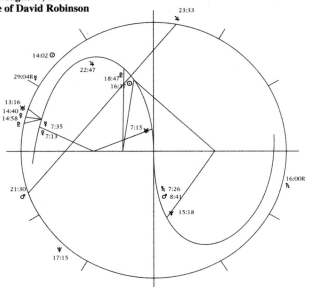

Chart 35: July 24, 1963
Birth date of Karl Malone

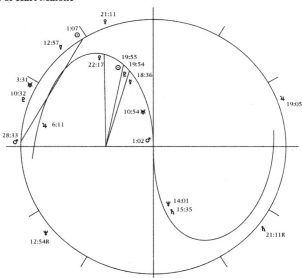

Chart 36: June 22, 1962
Birth date of Clyde Drexler

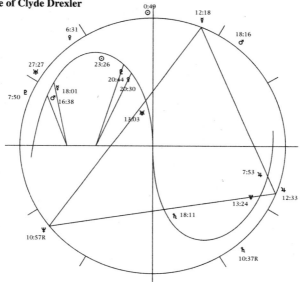

Chart 37: July 13, 1942
Birth date of Harrison Ford

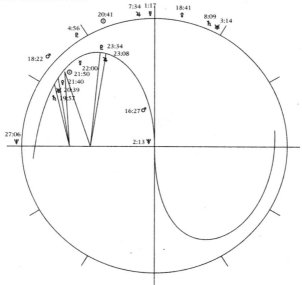

Chart 38: May 31, 1930
Birth date of Clint Eastwood

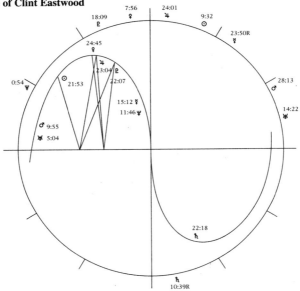

Chart 39: June 22, 1949
Birth date of Meryl Streep

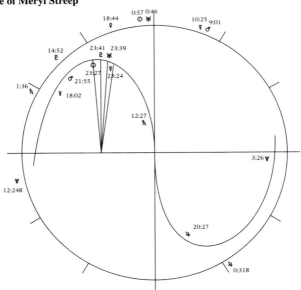

Chart 40: August 18, 1937
Birth date of Robert Redford

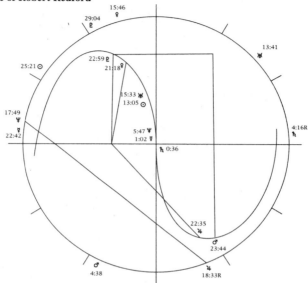

Chart 41: December 8, 1953
Birth date of Kim Basinger

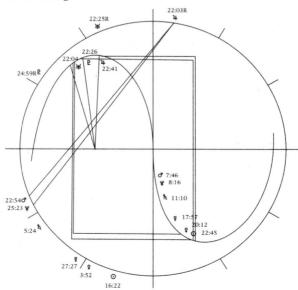

Chart 42: August 25, 1930
Birth date of Sean Connery

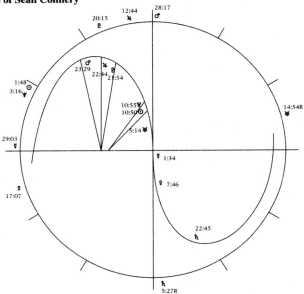

Chart 43: June 19, 1954
Birth date of Kathleen Turner

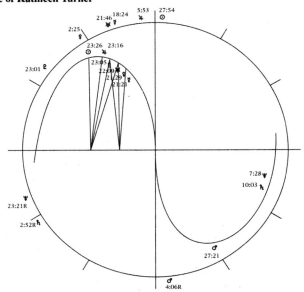

Chart 44: December 28, 1954
Birth date of Denzel Washington

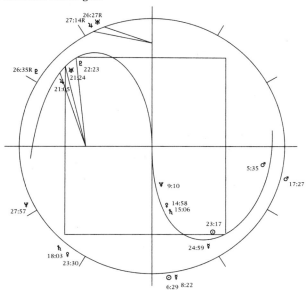

Chart 45: June 17, 1943
Birth date of Newt Gingrich

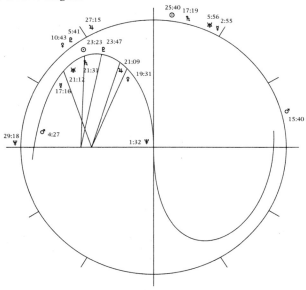

Chart 46: July 22, 1923
Birth date of Bob Dole

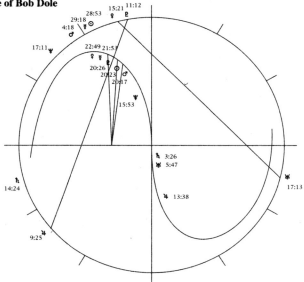

Chart 47: February 6, 1911
Birth date of Ronald Reagan

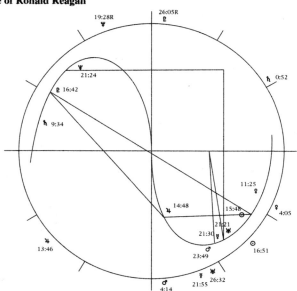

ASTROLOGY WORKS
ON STOCKS AND BONDS

I n the last chapter, we examined the birth charts of dozens of men and women, all of whom were either the most successful in their professions, or they were very close to being so. Every single one of them had at least 2 or more of the 12 super astrological aspects that we, at the Magi Society, have learned were most likely to help the native become very successful over the long term. They were all aspects of enhancement. Some were trines, and some were conjunctions, which are longitudinal aspects. Most of the Super Aspects were declinational aspects because most were parallels or contra-parallels.

Applying Aspects Are Better than Separating Aspects

There is another very important concept we must now discuss. If you look back at the birth charts of the eight billionaires, you might have noticed something amazing about the seven who had the Super Success Aspect, the Jupiter-Pluto enhancement. Jupiter was always moving towards the natal Pluto at the time of birth. All seven men who had the Super Success Aspect had the planets aligned such that Jupiter was moving towards the natal Pluto immediately after birth. Astrologers refer to this by saying that Jupiter was APPLYING to natal Pluto. If Jupiter were moving away from the natal Pluto, astrologers would say that Jupiter was SEPARATING from Pluto.

In fact, of all the birth charts that had the Super Success Aspect, Jupiter was applying to Pluto more than 90 percent of the time. This is statistically significant because it means that when Jupiter is applying to an aspect, it is stronger than when it is separating—which is to say that the day is better when Jupiter is still applying toward an exact aspect. This fact helped direct us to our next proof of astrology, which is mind-boggling.

A Dream Comes True

Having learned in the last chapter that it's helpful to be born on a day with Super Aspects, and having also discovered that days when Super Aspects are applying are better than days when the Super Aspects are separating, we can make the assumption that it is probable that other good things happen during days that have at least 2 of the 12 Super Aspects applying to a peak. We can also assume that the more Super Aspects that are applying on any given day, the better that day is, and the better the things that happen on such a day will be. Wouldn't it be nice if the stock and bond markets reacted to the Super Aspects day by day as the aspects were occurring? If they did, we would have a quantifiable measure of the power of the aspects, and this would be another proof that astrology works. We would actually see prices of stocks going up and down as the aspects came together and then dissipated.

Skeptics might say to us, "Dream on." But it is better than a dream; it actually happens.

Subsequent to an extensive study conducted by the Magi Society, there can be no doubt that the movement of planets influence the stock and bond markets. When the planets are applying towards forming certain exact Super Aspects, stock prices rarely go down. After these certain aspects are exact, and the planets are separating, a change in the momentum of stock and bond prices occurs. The Super Aspects that are most effective in this manner are the Super Success Aspect (Jupiter enhancement of Pluto) and the Jupiter enhancement of the Sun. Jupiter is the strongest component to this astrological effect. As Jupiter is applying toward multiple Super Aspects, stock prices rarely go down. If Pluto is also involved, then bond prices are also influenced in the same way. In other words, when Jupiter is applying towards a Super Aspect with Pluto, bond prices rarely go down.

The Magi Society is happy to report that astrology is further proven by the fact that Saturn has the opposite effect of Jupiter. It works most dramatically in the declinational aspects. When Saturn is applying toward multiple declinational aspects, the stock market rarely goes up.

Let us now look at some examples of the influence of planetary motion on stock and bond prices. The examples will also help clarify what we have discovered.

The Effect of the Jupiter-Pluto Enhancement on Bond Prices

What follows is a list of every Jupiter enhancement of Pluto in the last decade and what happened to bond prices before and after the exact enhancements occurred. There are only six of them, since it is a rare aspect.

Case 1: On March 21, 1986, Jupiter made an exact trine to Pluto. This is a remarkably powerful alignment. We expected that the bond market would not fall as this date approached, and we were correct. In fact, during the previous four months, the U.S. bond market had its greatest rally in history, having risen about 35 percent. After the exact trine occurred, during the following two months, the bond market fell 15 percent. This is a picture-perfect confirmation of the beneficial power of the Jupiter-Pluto enhancement. Bond prices went up as Jupiter was moving into trine to Pluto, and bond prices fell as Jupiter was moving away from the trine to Pluto because the Jupiter-Pluto enhancement was no longer applying.

Case 2: On March 24, 1987, Jupiter was parallel to Pluto. Again astrology worked. Bond prices did not fall as the Jupiter-Pluto enhancement was applying. Although the bond market did not rise as the aspect was applying, the bond market fell 20 percent after the alignment dispersed, and as the aspect was separating. In our opinion, this means that the bond market was so weak internally that the only thing holding it up was the Jupiter-Pluto enhancement while it was still applying; once this aspect dispersed and was separating, the bond market crashed because the Jupiter-Pluto enhancement was no longer holding bond prices up.

Case 3: On June 12, 1990, Jupiter made another trine to Pluto. The bond market rallied for the seven weeks just before the trine. After the trine occurred, bond prices went sideways for six weeks. Here again, it is possible to see the beneficial effects of Jupiter trine Pluto; bond prices rose as Jupiter was applying, but stopped rising after the aspect was separating.

Case 4: On September 4, 1992, Jupiter was contra-parallel to Pluto. For the three months prior to this date while the Jupiter-Pluto enhancement was applying, the bond market had a strong rally. Then after the aspect was dispersing, bond prices eased off at first and then fell.

Case 5: On August 30, 1993, Jupiter was parallel Pluto. As was the case in all the other examples of Jupiter-Pluto enhancements, for the months before the Jupiter-Pluto aspect became exact and was applying, bond prices rose. As the aspect was dispersing, bond prices lost upside momentum and went sideways.

Case 6: Finally, on December 1, 1994, Jupiter was conjunct Pluto. This was during the longest bear market in bonds during this last 10 years. In spite of that, bond prices had risen for five weeks as the aspect of enhancement was applying. After the exact aspect was made on December 1, bond prices quickly lost upside momentum for a brief period.

As we expected, bond prices never went down overall during the period that the Jupiter-Pluto enhancement was applying. By overall, we naturally mean the general trend, because obviously, bonds can have some down days even if the overall trend is steady, or up in price. In all six cases of Jupiter-Pluto enhancement during the last ten years, bond prices overall rose or held steady during the weeks or months as the aspect was applying. Bond prices never fell overall as the Jupiter-Pluto aspect was applying. Shortly after the aspect was exact, the momentum of bond prices changed. Bond prices either fell or they stopped going up for a while. This is what we would expect from the principles of astrology. And this is another proof that astrology works.

The Effect of the Sun-Jupiter Planetary Eclipse

As we learned earlier in the book, the Sun-Jupiter planetary eclipse is the single most beneficial aspect to the Sun. Since the Sun represents the day itself, the day of the Sun-Jupiter planetary eclipse must be the most fortunate of days. So although the Jupiter-Pluto enhancement is fabulous, by itself the aspect does not involve the Sun. Virtually every day has more than one aspect. From aspect integration, we know that it is the total effect of all the aspects of a day that determines the type of day it is. And the aspects to the Sun have the strongest influence on the type of day it is. For this reason, the Jupiter-Sun planetary eclipse is the single most beneficial aspect because there are two Sun-Jupiter enhancements on such a day. The Sun is conjuncted by Jupiter, and the Sun is parallel to Jupiter.

Sometimes the aspects on any given day may be contradictory. For example, it is possible to have a Jupiter-Pluto enhancement at the same time as a Saturn conjunction Sun. We know from our second chapter on symbolism that a Saturn conjunction Sun is not good. So a day with the Saturn-Sun conjunction and the Jupiter-Pluto enhancement is a mixed day. A mixed day will result in mixed influences on the financial markets. This means that the impact on stock and bond prices would not be significant because there are both positive and negative influences at the same time, and they approximately cancel each other out. However, a day with a Sun-Jupiter planetary eclipse and a Jupiter-Pluto enhancement is a remarkably fortunate day because these two aspects are the two strongest Super Aspect influences on the stock or bond markets. Such a day could be a major peak for the financial markets. And we have found this to be the case.

Because there is always more than one aspect in a day, the planetary effect on the stock market of any given day will have a number of influences. The net influence depends on the net directional power of the sum of all of the aspects. But the Jupiter-Sun planetary eclipse is so powerful that it would require a number of strong negative aspects to neutralize its beneficial influences. Therefore, during the vast majority of time periods that precede an exact Jupiter-Sun planetary eclipse, the stock market should not fall.

To test this theory, let us look at the effect of each of the last 10 Sun-Jupiter planetary eclipses. A Sun-Jupiter planetary eclipse occurs about every 13 months, or 400 days. If astrology works, we would expect that during the period preceding the Sun-Jupiter planetary eclipse, stock prices would rarely fall; the stock market would not decline during the days that precede the eclipse. After the eclipse, the momentum of stock prices would change; often they would decline precipitously because the cushion of the beneficial effects of the impending Sun-Jupiter eclipse had passed.

After examining the movement of stock prices around the Sun-Jupiter planetary eclipses, we found that stock prices reacted the way we would expect astrology to work. We list below the financial market reactions to each of the last 10 Sun-Jupiter planetary eclipses. **Once again, astrology worked every single time!**

- February 18, 1986 was the date of the first of these 10 most recent Sun-Jupiter planetary eclipses. The stock market went up approaching that date.
- On March 26, 1987, there was a Sun-Jupiter planetary eclipse. It was a high in stocks and bonds. But it was a much more significant high in bonds because three days earlier, there was a Jupiter-Pluto parallel. Bond prices fell from 104 to 77 during the following seven months.
- On May 2, 1988, there was another Sun-Jupiter planetary eclipse. There was a high that day for stock prices.
- The next Sun-Jupiter planetary eclipse was June 9, 1989. It was a modest high in the stock market.
- Then there was a Sun-Jupiter planetary eclipse on July 15, 1990, which was on a Sunday, when the financial markets are closed. But the next day was the high in stock prices for the whole year.
- The next Sun-Jupiter planetary eclipse was on Saturday, August 17, 1991. Again the financial markets were closed. But during the weekend, after the planetary eclipse began separating, hard-line communists in Russia tried to remove Mikhail Gorbachev from power in an attempted coup. After the eclipse, when the stock market opened on Monday, it was down about a hundred points.

- September 18, 1992 was the date of the next Sun-Jupiter planetary eclipse. A high in stocks was reached earlier in the week, but again stock prices took a big fall afterwards. The Dow Jones Industrial Average fell over 200 points during the next couple of weeks. This is just another example of the power of the stars.
- On October 17, 1993, we had the most interesting of these Sun-Jupiter planetary eclipses, and Pluto was involved. On that day, Jupiter was conjunct to the Sun, in trine to Saturn, and semi-sextile to Pluto. Because Pluto is aspected by Jupiter and Saturn that day, it should be a significant day for the bond market. It was. That day was the all-time high in bond prices. Once again, this is a very dramatic example of the power of astrology. As for stock prices, they rose going into that day.
- The most recent Sun-Jupiter eclipse was on November 18, 1994. It was a Friday. On the following Monday and Tuesday, stock prices fell 135 points.

Our analysis shows that in all 10 cases of the Sun-Jupiter planetary eclipses, the eclipse was either pushing stock prices up, or holding stock prices up until the actual occurrence of the eclipse. There were 10 planetary eclipses in 10 years. In six of these eclipses, stock or bond prices fell significantly after the eclipse dispersed. And these six falls in prices were the most significant drops of those years. But in all 10 cases, the financial markets confirmed that astrology works. When we add these ten cases to the six instances of the Jupiter-Pluto enhancements, the result is that in 16 out of 16 cases, astrology worked. There can be no doubt that the financial markets confirm that astrology really works.

THE MORE JUPITER ENHANCEMENTS, THE MORE POWERFUL THE RESULTS

We have learned that on any given day, a lot of aspects may be occurring, but on the whole, if Jupiter is conjunct the Sun, it is a good day. It would appear logical to extend this principle and expect that if Jupiter enhances more than just one of the planets, it is better than if Jupiter enhances only one planet. Therefore, the financial markets should react more strongly to multiple enhancements by Jupiter than to single enhancements.

This turns out to be the case.

During the last 10 years, the dates when Jupiter enhanced the most planets are August 24 and 25, 1987. During this two-day period, Jupiter was in trine to the Sun, Moon, Venus, and Mars. At the same time, Jupiter was parallel to the Sun, Mercury, Moon, Venus, and Mars. On those two days, Jupiter made more total positive aspects to the other planets, and in tighter degrees, than any time in centuries. For this reason, New Age advocates called it the HARMONIC CONVERGENCE. Other planets were close to being enhanced by Jupiter as well. If astrology influences the stock market, it should have done something monumental then. And it did. During that week, on Tuesday, August 25, the Dow Jones Industrial Average (DJIA) made its all-time high before dropping 1,000 points during the following 60 days. From October of 1985 to August 25, 1987, the stock market gained about 1,200 points and peaked at the harmonic convergence of August 25, 1987, to the very day. To the very day!

Here is the astrological explanation:

The harmonic convergence of August 25, 1987 was the most significant positive multiple alignment of planets in this century. There were more Jupiter enhancements on that day than on any other day for centuries. For this reason, it's natural that positive events, including expansion of stock prices, would peak on approximately that day. Once the alignment broke up after August 25, 1987, stock prices no longer had the positive influence of the Jupiter enhancements applying and creating positive influences. The dispersal of the alignments is like letting air out of a balloon. To more easily deal with these concepts, let us call the beneficial effects that precede an enhancement ASTRO-EXPANSION.

Our second example of when Jupiter was in aspect to the most planets was between July 12 and July 16, 1990. During that time, Jupiter was conjunct to the Sun, and Jupiter was in parallel to the Sun, Venus, and Moon; and contra-parallel Saturn, Uranus, and Neptune. Again, astrology really worked. This time the stock market also had an all-time high and then crashed. And again, the drop was severe, although not as bad as the 1987 crash; it fell "only" 650 points in the next 100 days.

So the two days that had the most Jupiter enhancements were both all-time highs in the stock market, and they were both followed by crashes. The two most significant price reversals this last decade were astrologically timed. We figure the odds against this happening by mere coincidence is about a billion to one. A chart of stock prices covering these two dramatic examples is at the end of this chapter, along with astrological charts of the alignments on the days when the stock market was at the highs.

Saturn Has the Opposite Effect of Jupiter

Astro-expansion is caused by enhancements by Jupiter. Stock or bond prices, or both, have gone up as Jupiter was applying to exact enhancement aspects. Since the symbolism of Saturn is the opposite of Jupiter, we can expect that the opposite will be true of alignments involving Saturn rather than Jupiter. And this has been the case. We will see that multiple-applying aspects by Saturn causes stock prices to go down. The term ASTRO-CONTRACTION will refer to the contraction of wealth caused by a convergence of Saturn to the Sun and at least one other planet. We did not discuss Saturn aspects in the last chapter because we were focusing on the most successful individuals, not the worst failures, which are generally associated with Saturn aspects. Let us look at some examples of astro-contraction.

After the crash of October 19, 1987, the stock market actually recovered nearly 300 points, then drifted sideways in a volatile manner. On December 4, seven weeks after the crash, stock prices dropped to a low that has not been tested since that date. The DJIA (Dow Jones Industrial Average) fell 200 points in seven days going into that day and then rallied 200 points in the next two weeks. On that December 4, Saturn was exactly parallel Neptune and the Sun, which is the opposite type of aspect as Jupiter being parallel to these planets. The aspects dispersed after that date.

This same negative alignment occurred again about a month later on January 8, 1988. The stock market fell 160 points that day. This is another example of astro-contraction.

A third significant event occurred on October 18, 1990. On that day, there was an exact parallel of Saturn to Neptune, and Saturn was exactly contra-parallel to Mars. The actual precise low in stock prices for the year was just one week earlier when Saturn was square the Sun, and at the same time Saturn was moving towards a closer and closer parallel to Neptune. Stock prices could not rally, though, until after the Saturn contra-parallel to Mars broke up. Again, astrology really worked.

As you can see from the graph of the stock prices at the end of this chapter, those three days were very important lows in the stock markets. During the last decade, those three days had the tightest alignments of Saturn to two other planets, not including the Moon, and all three days were the most significant lows in stock prices during this last decade. These are three more examples of astrology working on stock and bond prices. This makes it 21 times in a row that astrology worked in the financial markets.

Twenty-one successful applications of astrology out of 21 tries is not coincidence. It is not only statistically significant, it is irrefutable validation.

Jupiter Overpowers Saturn

In the first chapter, we asserted that astrology seems to have been designed such that the good overcomes the bad; in other words Jupiter overpowers Saturn. In fact, Jupiter overpowers Saturn so much so that we believe the negativity of Saturn is totally neutralized by the conjoining of Saturn by Jupiter. We know that this is a new concept, even to those of you who are long-time astrologers. But we have a great deal of evidence to back up this assertion.

Take, for example, the movement of stock prices during mid-October, 1989. On October 10, stock prices were at an all-time high after rising 150 points in less than two weeks. There was an exact Jupiter contra-parallel Saturn on that day. After the aspect dispersed, the stock market dropped 250 points in just 4 days. Because Saturn was the only planet enhanced by Jupiter on that day, we do not have to take into account other Jupiter enhancement aspects to explain the stock price movements.

There were four other dates when Jupiter was either parallel or contra-parallel to Saturn in the last decade. In all four cases, stock prices increased as the aspect was moving towards exactness. This is further evidence that Jupiter overpowers Saturn.

Then most recently, on August 31, 1994, there was a GRAND TRINE of Jupiter, Saturn, and Mars. The stock market roared upwards about 200 points going into that date.

There is also the example of July 12 to 16, 1990, dates when Jupiter enhanced the Sun, Venus, Moon, Neptune, Uranus, and Saturn. At the same time, Saturn was parallel Neptune and Uranus, and contra-parallel Venus and the Moon. But the presence of Jupiter overpowered Saturn's influences, and those days were highs in stock prices. In fact, those days were the highs in stocks for the whole year.

Summary

During this decade, the two most significant highs before crashes in stock prices were on days when there were the most exact multiple aspects of Jupiter enhancement. And the three most significant lows occurred on days when there were multiple exact aspects by Saturn to Sun and another planet. Five for five. The odds of this happening by chance is a trillion to one or so.

To the Magi Society, what has been discussed in this chapter proves the following:

1. Planetary alignments affect the stock and bond markets.
2. Aspects of Jupiter enhancement to other planets are beneficial for stock prices while Jupiter is applying.
3. Aspects of Saturn to other planets are negative while Saturn is applying, except that if Jupiter is involved, Jupiter overpowers Saturn.
4. The more applying aspects of Jupiter enhancement there are, the more beneficial the effects.

The beauty of associating astrology to the stock and bond markets is the ease with which astrological effects can be checked. If you want to check out the effect of the planets on stocks or bonds, all you need is an EPHEMERIS and charts of stock and bond prices. But make certain you buy the ephemeris that Hay House publishes, because it includes the declinations, as well as other information on the planets that are not available from any other ephemeris.

WARNING: Please do not go out and try to make money using astrology. We do not know of anyone who has been able to use astrology to make money without first losing money, sometimes a great deal of money for a long time. Although there is no question that the planets are the primary cause of all stock and bond prices, you are almost certain to lose money trying to invest based on the planets because the planets influence *you* as well.

When the planets are aligned favorably to your own birth chart, it means you are having good TRANSITS and you will make money with or without knowledge of astrology. When the planets are not aligned favorably to your birth chart, and you are having bad transits, then you will lose money with or without knowledge of astrology. That is, something is bound to go wrong with your investments even if you were correct in your analysis of stock market direction. For example, you tell your broker to buy but he sells. We will publish a book in the near future that will teach you to read the transits to your birth chart and plan your life so that you will not invest money when the planets are unfavorably aligned to your natal planets. No one has ever been able to beat the stars by making money when he or she was having bad transits. Since the planets are powerful enough to influence the entire stock and bond markets, they are certainly also strong enough to influence all of us and all of you.

But none of this diminishes the value of astrology. As we write this book in the spring of 1995, a financial astrologer is rated the number-one stock market timer for the last two years.

Stock Chart 1: August 25, 1987
Significant high in stocks

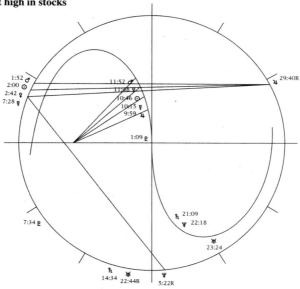

Stock Chart 2: December 4, 1987
Significant low in stocks

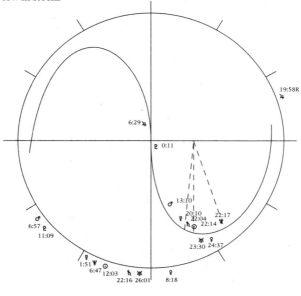

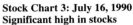

Stock Chart 3: July 16, 1990
Significant high in stocks

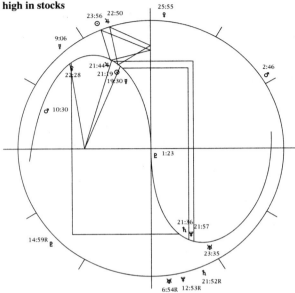

Stock Chart 4: October 18, 1990
Significant low in stocks

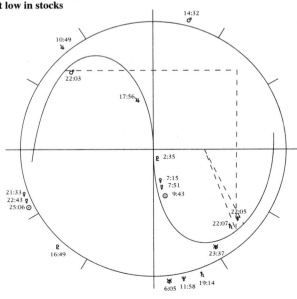

Stock Chart 5: October 18, 1993
All-time high in bond prices

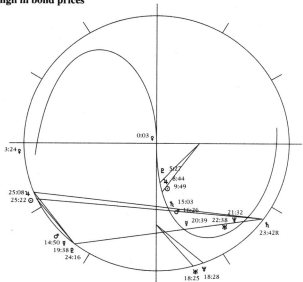

**Stock Chart 6: Graph of U.S. Treasury Bond Prices
from March 23, 1990 through March 10, 1995.
The all-time high was October 15 to 18, 1993.**

Oct. 15-18, 1993

Stock Chart 7: Graph of prices of Dow Jones Industrial Average (DJIA) from January 2, 1987 through December 20, 1991.

DJIA at 2722.40
on August 25, 1987

DJIA at 2999.75
on July 16, 1990

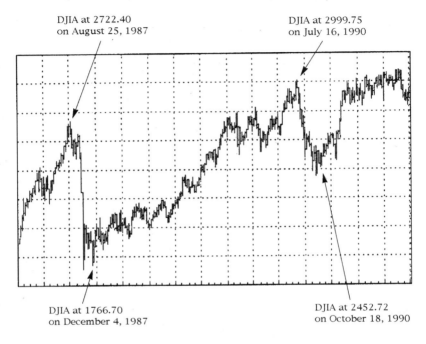

DJIA at 1766.70
on December 4, 1987

DJIA at 2452.72
on October 18, 1990

TRANSITS AND PROGRESSIONS:
THE TOOLS OF PREDICTION

In the opinion of the Magi Society, we have already provided strong evidence supporting the validity of some of the most important symbolisms of astrology. We have also shown that astrological aspects really work because they accurately apply to the most successful people in America. We accomplished this by analyzing the key aspects of the birth charts of the richest people in America, as well as some of the most successful superstars of American professional sports and Hollywood. We also analyzed the birth charts of the most successful CEOs of U.S. corporations and some of the most powerful politicians in this country.

As we progress through the rest of this book, we will compound the proof that astrology works. But we will also provide information about certain areas of astrology that we will not prove at this time. Remember that this book is written for the 47 percent of Americans who believe that astrology contains some scientific truths. It is our intention to teach Magi Astrology to all those who wish to learn it. So a large part of the balance of this book is devoted to just presenting a great deal of new astrological knowledge so that you can learn how to use astrology to help live better lives. As we teach you Magi Astrology, we will also be correcting some common misconceptions about astrology.

So far, the only areas of astrology we have dealt with are symbolisms and aspects. In our opinion, the most powerful and interesting part of astrology is prognostication. As you all know, astrologers believe they can predict the future conditions experienced by an individual.

The emphasis here is on the word *conditions.* Astrologers no longer believe that anything is fated or predetermined. There is free will. But we do believe that the planets influence our lives in such a way that the background conditions of our lives change, and these changes are caused by the movement of the planets. What kind of changes will occur? And when? Questions such as these can often be answered by studying the areas of astrology called TRANSITS and PROGRESSIONS. They are the most powerful parts of astrology once you know how to use them.

Transits

To understand transits, we need to understand the following: astrologers believe that the regular daily movement of the planets influences our lives. The greatest influence in our lives is felt when one or more of the moving planets are making a TRANSIT to any NATAL POSITION in our birth charts. A natal position is the position of a planet at the time of birth. If, for example, a person is born with his or her Sun in 2 degrees Pisces, the natal position of that Sun is 2 degrees Pisces. Since there are 10 planets, there are 10 natal positions for the longitudes, and 10 natal positions for the declinations. Obviously, the natal positions of planets never change because it is the position of the planets at the time of birth. Since the actual planets in the sky are always in motion, all of the planets will move to a new position every hour, every minute, and every second.

From time to time, on a regular basis, each planet in the sky will make an angle to a natal position such that the angle made will be considered meaningful by astrologers. Such an occurrence is called a TRANSIT. The angles that are considered meaningful angles by astrologers are the same angles as those that are interpreted to be meaningful as aspects in a birth chart, and we are already familiar with these. For the longitudes, they are multiples of 30 degrees. These angles are 30 degrees, 60 degrees, 90 degrees, 120 degrees, 150 degrees, 180 degrees. and zero degrees. Astrologers call these angles TRANSITING ASPECTS as opposed to natal aspects. For example, if Venus is in 2 degrees Capricorn on a birth chart, then we say that the natal position of Venus is 2 degrees Capricorn. Then as Mars revolves around the Sun, every time Mars is in 2 degrees of any of the 12 signs, it is making a transit to the natal position of Venus in the birth chart. Since any of the 10 moving planets can create a transit to any of the 10 natal positions of a birth chart, there can be a large number of transits at the same time.

That is how the transits work for the longitudes. But we also have transits for the declinations. And the principle is the same. A transit is made by a planet in motion whenever the transiting planet is in the same degree as a natal planet's position. If Pluto is in 8 degrees North declination at birth, then any time one of the ten moving planets passes 8 degrees on either the North or South side of the celestial equator, a transit has occurred.

You are probably aware that astrologers believe that certain transiting aspects are good, and certain transiting aspects are not so good. Whether or not a particular transit by a particular planet is positive or negative is not the subject of this book, but it will be one of the subjects of a subsequent book written by the Magi Society. At this time, we only need to know that any transit by a planet to a natal planet that makes an enhancement aspect is beneficial but Saturn is the exception. If Saturn makes an enhancement aspect to a natal planet, it is not beneficial unless the natal planet is Mercury or Uranus. All other transiting aspects made by Saturn are stressful. When a planet other than Saturn makes a transiting aspect to a natal planet that is not an enhancement aspect, there are no general rules. For example, a Jupiter quincunx to a natal planet is good, but a Uranus quincunx to a natal planet is not. But as we just said, we will deal with all possible transits in another book, but this is all that we need to know for the purposes of this book.

Astrologers generally use an orb for transits, just as they use an orb for aspects. The orb they generally use is plus or minus five degrees or so. In other words, astrologers tend to believe that if a planet is applying towards one of your natal planets, there is a transiting influence from the time the transiting planet is five degrees from your natal planet until the transiting planet has passed your natal planet by an angle of five degrees.

The Magi Society strongly disagrees with the plus and minus orb in transits. It has been our experience that a transit is active and effective only as the transiting planet is applying towards the natal planet up until the transit is actually exact and begins to separate; the transit is not in effect very shortly after the passing of the transiting planet. Sometimes, if it is a negative transit, there will be what we will refer to as FALLOUT from the bad transit for a brief period. But we believe that the actual influence of the transit is complete and peaks at the time of the exact transit. Once the transiting planet is moving away from exact aspect to the natal position, the transit itself is no longer an influence. In the last chapter, we discovered that the planets work in this way when they affect the financial markets. So we are sure that this is also how the planets work as transits.

But please remember that the Magi Society does believe that everyone has free will. To the Magi Society, the following analogy is an apt one to explain how the moving planets and our birth chart interacts with our free will. We are given a house as our home; it is our birth chart. How we paint and decorate the home is up to us. We can also remodel it and even build additions to it to suit our fancy. It is up to us to landscape the grounds, and we can do it in any way we wish. The one thing we cannot do is sell the house, or live elsewhere. The exception is if we get married; there is a new house for us to live in, but the old house always exists. (We will deal with weddings and marriages in chapter 14.)

What we mean by all of this is that your birth chart is like your house; you will live in that house, so the house represents the conditions you will live under. The study of transits is designed to predict the timing of the changes in the conditions, and whether the changes will be inclined to lean toward improvement or deterioration. If we know our transits, we will have more free will. This is because we can adjust our activities to take our transits into account.

For example, if we know that we will have transits that will hinder us from making money on investments during the next month, we can avoid losing money by not investing during that period. This is what we meant in chapter 6 when we wrote that it is impossible to make money on investments during the times that your transits are such that you are *not supposed to* make money on investments. We have found that it is virtually impossible to make successful investment decisions when transiting Saturn is making an aspect to natal Pluto or Neptune. Even though the members of the Magi Society are extraordinarily knowledgeable in astrology and investments, none of our members has ever made money when Saturn was transiting natal Pluto or Neptune. It is not possible to overcome the influences of the transits. But it is possible to minimize their power by avoiding certain activities during Saturn transits. This increases our free will, because we are better able to navigate through the transits, and we can avoid getting into trouble.

***

SECOND CHALLENGE TO SKEPTICS

As an astrological skeptic, you certainly do not believe in transits. But the Magi Society knows that transits are very powerful, and we challenge skeptics to make profits investing money during times when they have bad transits. To be able to truly verify whether money was really made or lost, the investments will be limited to publicly traded stocks or commodities—no real estate. Of course we have to be provided with accurate birth dates so we can determine the times when there will be bad transits. If you are a skeptic of astrology, and you are also a professional investor, you are likely to be making investments most of the time. The Magi Society will tell you when you cannot make money. Contact us and we will prove it.

***

Two Examples of the Power of Transits

We present in this chapter two very high-profile examples of how transits work. Our examples focus on O.J. Simpson and George Bush. O.J. was born on July 9, 1947, and his Pluto is 12:11 Leo. On July 8, 1994, a judge ruled that there was enough evidence to hold Simpson over for trial. This meant that he would be in jail at best until his trial was over and at worst for the rest of his life. On that day of July 8, Saturn was exactly quincunx Simpson's Pluto. Pluto's symbolisms include dramatic change and beginnings and endings. Saturn symbolizes crystallization of problems beyond the control of the native, as well as possible tragedy and losses. As we said earlier, we believe that any transit by Saturn (except some of the conjoining transits) is bad. Obviously, the interpretation of a Saturn transit to a natal Pluto would be that of disastrous and tragic change in Simpson's life as he begins a new segment of his life, and he will lose (Saturn) power (Pluto). His problems were such he was no longer in control of his destiny, meaning he was powerless.

We have found that a Saturn aspect to Pluto is the most disruptive transit that there is.

What is a good transit? Uranus to the Sun is one of the best ones you can have. It provides fame, public acclaim, and popularity (all Uranus) to the native (the Sun). Remember how popular President George Bush was when we won the Kuwait War? (See the end of this chapter for his birth chart.) All the polls showed him having an approval rating of over 80 percent. Almost nobody thought he would lose the 1992 election. So why did he? It was the fault of his transits. Bush's transits were fabulous during the Kuwait War, but these positive transits had vanished before the elections. The most important good transit he had before the elections was transiting Uranus contra-parallel natal Sun.

George Bush's Sun is 23:07 north declination. During the Kuwait War, Uranus, a very powerful benefic, was making an exact contra-parallel to his Sun. Uranus made three positive contra-parallel aspects to Bush's Sun between the war and the 1992 election. The interpretation is that Uranus, provider of universal fame and mass appeal, helped Bush (represented by his natal Sun) until Uranus made its last contra-parallel transit in October of 1992, one month before the election. George Bush lost the very helpful and powerful Uranus transit just before the November election in 1992. Without the help of the positive transit, Bush lost the election by just 3 percent of the vote.

The Progressions Are More Important than the Transits

Transits are a very powerful influence. But there is a second influence on our daily lives, and these are called the PROGRESSIONS. They are similar to transits except that the time parameters are different. This is the most difficult concept in normal astrology to understand and accept.

Astrologers use several types of progressions, but in this book we are only interested in the so-called SECONDARY PROGRESSIONS. The concept of secondary progressions is that in addition to being influenced by the transits of the planets as they revolve around the Sun, our daily lives are also influenced by the transits that occurred immediately after we were born. To be more precise, the transits of each day after we are born are programmed into our future such that these transits "overlay" our normal daily transits for an entire year of our lives. Each day represents a whole year, so that the transits we experience during the third day of our lives are carried forward to the third year of our lives and are overlaid on top of the daily transits that we have during the third year. The transits we experience during the 35th day after we are born will be overlaid on top of our daily transits during our 35th year of life.

We realize that this is a difficult concept to understand and an even more difficult concept to swallow. But we promise you that it is not only valid, it is the most powerful tool in astrology. So, please stay with this idea until you get used to working with it.

Progressions are one of the tools that help us prove astrology works. Good progressions are extraordinarily beneficial and powerful. Progressions are much more powerful than daily transits because progressions usually last years. As is the case with the transits, in our opinion, a progression by any planet is working only when a planet is moving towards a natal planet. In other words, if Jupiter is moving towards natal Pluto, it is working until the progressing Jupiter reaches the natal position of Pluto. Once it is past, the progression is no longer working. A person who is born with Jupiter having already passed Pluto, and where Jupiter continues to move away from Pluto, is not experiencing a positive progression of Pluto by Jupiter. The

Jupiter-Pluto enhancement aspect is still there. But the help from that particular progression is not.

Going back to the birth charts in chapter 5, remember that the natal charts with the Jupiter-Pluto enhancement almost always had Jupiter applying to Pluto. In such a circumstance, we will refer to the aspect as an APPLYING ENHANCEMENT by Jupiter. This is a very, very important concept to understand. When people are born with a Jupiter applying enhancement to Pluto, not only do they have the advantages of the Jupiter-Pluto enhancement aspect, they also have the beneficial influences of the progression with Jupiter applying to Pluto, until the progression separates. Keeping in mind that each day a progression lasts is the equivalent of a whole year of life, such a progression is so powerful that its influence cannot be overstated. Evidence of this is that, as we already said, almost all of the persons whose birth charts we did in chapter 5 have applying enhancements of Jupiter to Pluto; so these persons had the help of the positive progression as well as the natal Super Success Aspect.

Below, we will provide three very high-profile examples of the validity and power of the progressions. We will look at the lives of Clint Eastwood, Cher, and Ronald Goldman, the man who was killed along with Nicole Brown Simpson. The birth chart of the latter two appear at the end of this chapter; Clint's (chart 38) can be found in chapter 5.

In the case of Ronald Goldman, he was born with no Super Aspects. But of course there are other aspects. The most interesting aspect in his chart was Saturn quincunx to Uranus. Uranus is the planet of the masses, public acclaim, and fame. Uranus is also the planet of change. Goldman was born with Saturn in applying quincunx towards Uranus. Again, if progressions work, we can expect that the negative Saturn applying Uranus progression could be used to time major events in his life. There is no greater event in Goldman's life than his death. He was 25 years old. After Goldman was born, Saturn was applying to Uranus for 25 days and then reached peak. This means that 25 years after Goldman was born, this Saturn progression was peaking and created a condition such that Goldman was most susceptible to the disruptive loss (Saturn) of life, which was the greatest change (Uranus).

Also, the Saturn negative progression to Uranus gave Goldman an un-desired (Saturn) fame (Uranus) aspect.

Please do not have nightmares if you find that you or a loved one has the same progression. It is a very tough progression, but there is no progression so bad that it cannot be overcome, especially if you are forewarned of it. We are certain that in Goldman's case, he had very strong negatives to his calculated points, such as the midheaven and ascendant, as well as other negative progressions to his natal planets. One of the advantages of knowing astrology is to be aware of any problematic progressions and transits. It is true when they say "to be forewarned is to be forearmed." By being extra, extra careful during negative progressions, you can readily survive them. Remember also that Saturn crystallizes problems that have not been handled correctly or that have been overlooked. Great care can ensure that there are only minor problems to be crystallized.

Now let us analyze Cher's birth chart.

Cher had a major RULING PROGRESSION in her life that ended sometime in 1988 or 1989. She was born with Jupiter trine Uranus, which is one of the 12 Super Aspects; it is the best aspect a person can have for success in the entertainment field because this is the aspect of super-fame. In the last chapter, we noted that 9 of the 16 Hollywood superstars had this same Super Aspect in their birth charts, which the Magi Society calls the Super Fame Aspect. For Cher, the aspect was also a progression; Uranus applied towards Jupiter. This progression symbolizes obtaining good fortune (Jupiter) from the public (Uranus) and from the entertainment industry (also Uranus). Uranus was applying towards Jupiter for 32 to 33 days after Cher was born, depending on her exact time of birth. On the basis of a day for a year with this pro-gression, this would time the progression to last until 1988 to 1989. She won an Oscar for her role in the movie *Moonstruck* in 1988. But since then, fans have been wondering where she has been. We all love Cher, and we're sure Cher will be back. She has a fabulous natal chart.

To most fans of Clint Eastwood, it seems as if he has always been successful. But actually there was a time when Clint had to settle for being in low-budget cowboy movies filmed abroad. Clint was born with a Jupiter-Pluto parallel. But Jupiter was separating from Pluto at birth for 31 days, which equates to 31 years. Then Jupiter reversed direction and began to apply to Pluto. Not long after Clint turned 31, he starred in his now-famous role in *A Fistful of Dollars.* His career took off, and the rest is history.

Through our massive research, we have found a number of progressions that have an enormously beneficial impact on the native. They are progressions by Jupiter to the Sun, Venus, Saturn, Uranus, Neptune, and Pluto; and also the progressions of Uranus to the Sun, Venus, Jupiter, Saturn, Neptune, and Pluto. These are the 12 SUPER PROGRESSIONS. The very best one is Jupiter to Saturn.

The exact same 12 Super Progressions are also Super Transits. For example, if Jupiter is trine natal Sun, or Venus, or Saturn, or Uranus, or Neptune or Pluto, the native is having a Super Transit.

Any transit or progression by Saturn is negative, except if Saturn makes an enhancement aspect to Mercury or Uranus, in which case it is good.

We have also found in our research that the progressions of Uranus seem to provide more fame and fortune than those of Jupiter. There are two reasons for this: first, it is because Uranus moves slower than Jupiter; therefore, the progressions of Uranus last longer. For this reason, Uranian progressions can be a more lasting influence and, therefore, a stronger one. Sometimes a Uranian progression can last decades. Obviously, the longer a progression lasts, the stronger the influence. The second reason Uranian progressions appear to be stronger influences is that while Jupiter provides good fortune, Uranus provides fame and acclaim, which brings the native to the attention of the public. It is possible for Jupiter to provide enormous success without fame. But Uranus will bring the fame.

We know that skeptics are jumping up and down in total disbelief as they read this chapter. They are probably thinking that just the few examples of transits and progressions given are not anywhere near enough to validate their influence. But as we said earlier, parts of this book are meant only to teach astrology to those who already know it works. And now, we do have another challenge for the skeptics.

***

THIRD CHALLENGE TO SKEPTICS

The Magi Society is completely confident that we can apply Magi Astrology to predict the future better than any skeptic or group of skeptics. We challenge all skeptics to a contest of predicting the future. Let us do it in a way that can be followed and enjoyed by the public. Let the skeptics choose any well-known group of American athletes and predict how well they will do over the course of the next several years. The Magi Society will also make predictions on the future performance of these same people. The reason we choose athletes is because their performances are quantifiable and will allow for easy undisputed determination of whose predictions are the best. Wouldn't it be interesting to know if astrology can predict when Michael Jordan can score 50 points or when Greg Maddux will pitch a shutout? There are thousands of professional athletes in the United States, so there are more than enough to choose from. The skeptics are allowed to recruit all the experts they can to help them make their predictions. But they are not allowed to use astrology. To be certain of this, the rule will be that they are not allowed to predict performances that would match the rules of transits and progressions explained in this chapter. For example, if baseball player "A" has transiting Uranus parallel the Sun, skeptics cannot use him as a choice for good performances. This is because skeptics are supposed to be trying to disprove astrology as opposed to secretly using it. The Magi Society would be choosing player "A" to perform well when transiting Uranus parallels the Sun because everyone performs better under the influence of this transit.

We are very anxious to compete with skeptics on this challenge. Please do not disappoint us.

(Skeptics and friends are welcome to contact us. Our telephone number is 212-867-2905.)

☄   ☄   ☄

Chart 48: May 20, 1946
Birth date of Cher

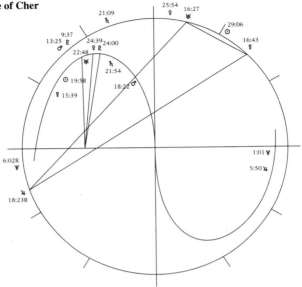

Chart 49: July 2, 1968
Birth date of Ron Goldman

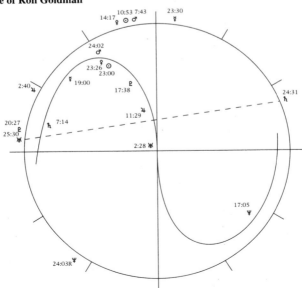

CORRECTING OLD ASTROLOGY AND LEARNING MAGI ASTROLOGY

Astrology is much more complex than most people realize. There are two groups of people holding astrology back—the public and the astrologers. We are not trying to be funny. Both the public and the astrologers have misconceptions about astrology. It is important to correct some of these misconceptions before we go deeper into astrology. That is the purpose of this chapter.

The 12 Constellations of the Zodiac

It is generally assumed by the public that the 12 constellations of the zodiac are directly related to the 12 signs of the natal chart. Almost everyone believes that when an astrologer says that a planet is in the sign of Gemini, the astrologer is saying that the planet is also actually visible in the constellation of Gemini when we look at the sky. This is not the case.

Thousands of years ago, when the Babylonian astrologers first formulated astrology with the 12 signs, it was true that at that time, when an astrologer referred to a planet being in Gemini, that planet really was visible in the constellation of Gemini. But it is not the case now. The reason for this is the PRECESSION OF THE EQUINOXES, which refers to the phenomenon of the backwards movement of the constellations in the sky, a phenomenon that requires about 2,145 years to move 30 degrees. An explanation for all this is provided in the following paragraphs.

Astrologers do not use a fixed point in the sky in or near the constellation of Aries to define the astrological position of zero degrees Aries. If we look up at the sky precisely at the time spring begins every year around March 21, and if we could see the Sun, the position of the Sun at that precise time is regarded by astrologers to be zero degrees Aries. That is the astrological definition of zero degrees Aries. Astrologers then use that position as the reference point to divide the sky into the 12 signs drawn in a natal chart.

Now, when we talk about the position of the Sun at the beginning of spring, we are referring to the part of the 12 constellations where the Sun is at that time. For the last 2.000 years, that position has been in the constellation of Pisces, but it has been moving one degree every 71.5 years. For approximately 2,000 years prior to the birth of Christ, the Sun's position on the first day of spring was in Aries. For the last 2,000 years, the position of the Sun on the first day of spring has been in the constellation of Pisces. That is why astrologers call the last 2,000 years the Age of Pisces. Sometime not all that long from now, on the first day of spring of a future year, the position of the Sun will be such that it will definitively be located in the constellation of Aquarius, and this will verify that we will be in the Age of Aquarius. We use the term *definitively located* because the boundaries of the actual constellations in the sky are debatable.

The *precession of the equinoxes* is the term used to refer to the fact that the backdrop of the constellations in the sky moves one degree every 71.5 years This very small change each year adds up to 30 degrees in about 2,145 years. And what it means is that now in 1995 when astrologers say that a planet is in 15 degrees Pisces, that planet is actually visibly in the middle of the constellation of Aquarius. When an astrologer says that a planet is in 15 degrees Scorpio, it means that the planet is visibly in the constellation of Libra.

For the purposes of this book, it is not necessary to understand the actual reasons of the cause of the precession of the equinoxes. It is important, however, to realize that this does not reduce the validity of astrology in any way whatsoever. In fact, it enhances the validity of astrology. Claudius Ptolemy was one of the greatest astrologers of all time. He understood the precession of the equinoxes 1,850 years ago. It is Ptolemy who devised the astrological system of using the position of the Sun on the first day of spring as being the zero degree point of Aries. This system is called the system of the TROPICAL ZODIAC. What it all means is that the reference point of an astrological chart is the zero degree point of the natal chart. This point is the position of the Sun at the first day of spring, which in turn is defined as the day when the length of the day equals the length of the night, and when, on the next day, the length of the day is greater than the length of the night. This is opposed to the autumnal equinox, wherein the day following the first day of autumn has a longer night than day.

Astrologers have been using this Tropical Zodiac successfully for nearly 2,000 years. All of this underscores the validity of equal-degree aspects because there have never been defined borders between the 12 constellations that the 12 signs were named after.

Aristotle's Influence on Astrology

So far in this book, you have been presented with ample evidence that astrology works. It should be obvious by now that the planets have a strong influence on our lives. Astrology had not been proven or disproved for 4,000 years. But once we employed the astrology of the Magi Society, where we added and used the declinations (our second dimension of astrology), it was relatively easy to prove the validity of astrology. The power of additional knowledge can do so much. For this reason, our goal should be to increase our knowledge of astrology even more. Also, we should not allow old astrological rules and principles to prejudice us in our search for new knowledge, and the truth. We say this because the principles and rules of today's astrology are riddled with a number of incorrect ideas. Just as it was difficult to prove astrology when we did not have enough knowledge, it is even more difficult to prove astrology when parts of it are simply wrong.

After extensive research into the birth charts of over 2,000 of the super-successful, it has become obvious to the Magi Society that some of the old rules of astrological interpretation have to be amended or discarded altogether. Although astrology certainly works, some of its rules of interpretation were fashioned by Greek astrologers who did not believe in the empirical system. They did not employ observations of events to test their rules. Aristotle, one of the Greek astrologers who greatly shaped astrology as it stands today, was not an empiricist; he was a theoretician. Some of the incorrect rules that prevail in astrology were devised by Aristotle and his followers. Unfortunately, these inaccuracies have contributed greatly to the failure of astrology to gain greater support.

One example of Aristotle's lack of empiricism is his analysis of falling objects. Although this has nothing to do with astrology, it is illustrative of how Aristotle's mind worked and why he was wrong in much of his astrological work. He believed that an object that was ten times as heavy as another object would fall to the ground ten times faster than the lighter object would fall. In other words, Aristotle believed that objects fell to the earth at a speed that was directly proportional to its weight. We know that this is not the case. Newton's laws of gravity tell us the truth. Objects of all weights begin falling at the same speed and they accelerate according to Newton's laws of gravity. The acceleration in the falling speed is the same no matter what the weight of the object is. In other words, objects of different weights fall at the same speed to the ground, except where the object is so light that air resistance is a factor; examples of such objects are feathers and sheets of paper. This was first demonstrated by Galileo when he dropped two objects over the Leaning Tower of Pisa. One object was much heavier than the other; both were dropped at the same time, and both fell to the ground at the same time.

It was not necessary to drop objects from a high building to test Aristotle's law about falling objects and find out that it was wrong. If someone was on a roof of a house during Aristotle's time 2,300 years ago, and he dropped a heavy stone at the same time as he dropped a very small coin, it would be obvious to any observer that the two objects hit the ground at the same time. This illustrates that no one in Aristotle's day designed and conducted experiments to test their theories.

To a certain extent, most astrologers are guilty of making the same mistakes as Aristotle. Astrologers have heretofore not subjected some of their beliefs to appropriate tests. It is an absolute imperative that all of the rules of astrology be subjected to scientific and statistical testing. There will be rules that will not withstand such tests. Such rules have to be revised until they are statistically valid. Any rule or principle that cannot be improved enough to meet stringent statistical testing will have to be discarded altogether. Unless this is done, astrology is being ill served by anyone who practices it yet is using unproven rules of interpretation. We should not assume that every principle of astrology is valid. Most are, but over the years, some bad ones have crept in and somehow have not been discarded.

In our opinion, there are presently at least two significant rules (and many less significant ones) in astrology that are wrong. The first incorrect principle of astrology is the rule that days when planets are in RETROGRADE MOTION are less favorable than when there are no planets in RETROGRADE (defined and explained below). The second incorrect important rule of astrology relates to whether an aspect is good or bad.

Retrograde vs. Direct Motion

Retrograde motion is a very important concept in astrology. It is not necessary to understand exactly why it occurs; it is only necessary to know that it occurs regularly. In order to have some understanding of retrograde motion, it is important to realize that astrology is based on the apparent movement of the planets, not the actual movement. The emphasis is on the word *apparent*, as opposed to the actual movement of the planet because astrologers are only interested in what the visual movements of the planets are. If you happen to look up at the sky and mark the night-to-night position of the planets relative to the backdrop of the constellations, you would find that some of the planets appear to be moving backwards. Astrologers refer to a planet that appears to be moving backwards as a planet that is in retrograde. All the real planets (Mercury through Pluto) all revolve around the Sun in the same direction. They never actually move backwards even though there are times when they appear as if they are. But when you are on a highway in a car and you pass another car, it appears that the other car is moving backwards even though that other car is moving forwards. The apparent backwards movement is caused by the fact that the other car is moving slower than the car you are in. In the same manner, the Earth and all the planets revolve around the Sun at different orbits and speeds. The actual motions of the planets are such that on a regular basis, the rate of change of the angle between the Earth and one or more of the planets creates a situation such that it "appears" that one or more planets are moving backwards and therefore is in retrograde motion.

For whatever reason, virtually all astrologers and astrology books regard days that have planets in retrograde motion as less positive than days when there are no planets in retrograde. In particular, astrologers generally regard days when Mercury is in retrograde as particularly problematic. Contrary to other astrologers' beliefs, the Magi Society knows that when planets are in retrograde, it is better than when they are in DIRECT MOTION. One reason is below.

Very few astrologers seem to know this, but whenever Jupiter is trine to the Sun, Jupiter is in retrograde motion. The motions of the planets and the positions of the Earth and Jupiter are such that Jupiter is always in retrograde on a day when it trines the Sun.

Always.

Since astrologers believe that Jupiter trine Sun is one of the very best aspects, and one of the most beneficial, how can Jupiter in retrograde be bad? The answer is that Jupiter in retrograde is not bad. It is at least as good as Jupiter in Direct Motion.

This is a perfect example of one of the problems with astrology today and is one of the main reasons astrology is not respected by the scientific community. In general, astrologers have not been scientific enough, and they blindly follow the dictates of old ideas, right or wrong. We have probably all heard astrologers say "Mercury is in retrograde! Watch out! Be extra careful!" Mercury is in retrograde about three weeks every eight months, or roughly 10 percent of the time. But 8 out of 30 of the corporations that comprise the Dow Jones Industrial Average were incorporated on days with Mercury in retrograde. These companies are:

- Boeing
- Caterpillar
- Disney
- Eastman Kodak
- Goodyear Tire
- General Motors
- International Paper
- United Technologies

This means that more than 25 percent of these companies were founded when Mercury was in retrograde, and Mercury is in retrograde only about 10 percent of the time. How can Mercury in retrograde be bad? If anything, we should consider the possibility that Mercury in retrograde is a good period to form corporations.

In our research, we have found that it is better to have some retrograde planets in your natal chart than to have no retrograde planets at all. And by the way, the United States was founded with Mercury in retrograde.

Good and Bad Aspects

In chapter 2, we listed all of the equal-degree aspects along with astrologers' normal evaluations of whether or not these aspects were positive or negative. You may have thought at the time that astrologers were a pessimistic group of individuals since there were more bad aspects than good ones. In traditional astrology, the trine and sextile are regarded by astrologers as good, and the conjunction is regarded as sometimes good and sometimes bad. But all the other equal-degree aspects are regarded as being stressful. That would mean that 7 out of 12 aspects are bad, which in turn would mean that in the average birth chart, 7/12ths (or, almost 60 percent) of the aspects were bad. This would obviously create a strong negative tilt to the average birth chart. The world would be full of people with bad birth charts. We, of the Magi Society, do not believe the world is like that.

To add insult to injury, astrologers generally believe that there are other aspects that are not equal-degree aspects, and all of them are negative. For example, the semi-square aspect is 45 degrees, and this is regarded as always bad. Also bad is the quintile aspect of 72 degrees. Et cetera.

What a horrible state of affairs this would be. If you accepted this generally advocated interpretation of the aspects in astrology today, there would be several times more bad aspects as good ones. We might as well all give up.

But we are about to come to the rescue of humanity. Remember, we will not accept anything in astrology that is not provable.

A New Way of Looking at Aspects

Based on the extensive research conducted by the Magi Society, we have found no aspect to be *provably negative*. There *are* aspects between two particular planets that have a negative tilt; and all of them involve Saturn, meaning that Saturn is one of the two planets that forms such an aspect. But unlike the Jupiter enhancement of Pluto, which we know gives a person a jump start on success, we have not found any aspect that makes a person the likely prisoner of failure, or even just more likely to fail. In fact, quite the opposite is true. All equal-degree aspects, except those involving Saturn, are helpful. The more exact the aspect is, the more positive the influence of the aspect. This means that we believe that the Jupiter opposition Sun aspect is helpful, not harmful. And the Jupiter square Sun aspect is also helpful and not harmful.

Saturn aspects are the only equal-degree aspects that have any negative influences. But the influences can be overcome because the aspects act on the personality and character of the native such that they will have flaws, and these flaws can be overcome. For example, a Saturn aspect to Pluto makes the native susceptible to being reckless; he sees only the possible rewards of an action; he does not pay attention to the possible risks of the action. But this is a trait that can be overcome through controlling the ego and with the help of a loving partner in life.

You might ask: If all equal-degree aspects not involving Saturn are good, then what is bad in a birth chart? What appears more important in any determination of what is negative in a birth chart is this: the lack of equal-degree aspects is a probable hindrance to achievement of super-fame and fortune. But the lack of equal-degree aspects does not hinder achievement on a less grandiose level, and does not reduce the native's chances of finding happiness in life.

The planets and astrology seem to have been designed to help rather than hinder a person. This is true for both the aspects, as well as the transits and progressions. There are more good transits and good progressions than there are bad ones because Jupiter overpowers Saturn, and because Saturn is the only planet with a negative tilt.

With regard to the aspects, the more equal-degree aspects a person has in his or her birth chart, with the exception of ones that are formed by Saturn, the more likely the person is to achieve unusual success and fame. Persons with essentially no equal-degree aspects in their natal charts are less likely to achieve great success, but they can still be successful.

We believe that the confusion astrologers have about aspects is caused in large measure by the progressions. Astrologers have noticed that when a person is born with certain aspects, the natives with those aspects often have significant problems during their lives. But in our opinion, most of the time, the real cause is that the natives are having multi-year bad progressions, which is often the case when there is a so-called bad aspect.

In the last chapter, we saw that Ronald Goldman was born with a Saturn quincunx Uranus. This is universally regarded by astrologers as a very bad aspect. But we think it was really just the progression that was Goldman's problem, not the aspect itself. If Goldman had the same aspect, but Saturn was separating from Uranus so that he did not have the negative progression to contend with, his life would have been greatly improved. When you think about it, if an aspect were bad, and the progression was also bad, a person with an applying aspect that is traditionally regarded as negative would have to go through horrible times. It would mean disaster would befall a high percentage of the population. We are certain that this is not the case. There are no aspects that are very bad.

The Magi Society has found that all equal-degree aspects by Jupiter, Uranus, and Venus are very helpful. But the enhancement aspects are the most powerful. Therefore, a trine, conjunction, parallel, or contra-parallel by Jupiter, Uranus, or Venus to any other planet is very helpful, whereas the opposition, quincunx, square, sextile, and semisextile are merely helpful. In all cases, if Jupiter, Uranus, or Venus is applying, or the aspect is very close to exact, then the positive influences of such aspects are increased dramatically. We will refer to the extra strength of very close aspects as PROXIMITY ENHANCEMENT. Such enhancements are very powerful. Any time an aspect is less than 0:3 degrees apart, there is proximity enhancement. Proximity enhancement is especially beneficial for athletic performance because it provides enormous amounts of energy.

Aspects involving Saturn are the only ones that we have found to have a negative tilt. But we repeat that they are not so negative that the native is a prisoner of failure. Let us give you an example. (Please refer to the birth chart of Billy Martin at the end of this chapter.)

Billy Martin was a Yankee baseball player and manager. He was born with Saturn parallel Pluto. As we already said, this aspect has a negative tilt to the extent that the aspect makes the native lean towards the reckless side. For instance, persons with this aspect see the rewards but not the risks of an action. In Billy Martin's case, when he managed the Yankees, he took risks that most managers would not have taken. He might instruct a player to bunt even though he had two strikes. This is considered risky by most other baseball managers. But the beauty of astrology is, when Billy Martin had good transits, his disregard of risk would pay off more than the conservative play of another manager. Those of you who follow baseball know that Billy had the stormiest career of any baseball manager. He won world championships. He was hired and fired five times by Yankee owner George Steinbrenner, who has a Jupiter enhancement of Pluto in his birth chart. Steinbrenner's Jupiter-Pluto enhancement clashed with Martin's Saturn-Pluto aspect. George, Billy's boss, was less of a risk taker. And Billy was also having other problems. But together, they won championships and provided a lot of excitement to the game of baseball.

Problematic Aspects Are Counterbalanced

The Magi Society has found that aspects that are traditionally judged to be bad all have another side to them. All such aspects provide the native with a counterbalance. For example, we have found that just about everyone with the Saturn-Pluto aspect is a risk taker, and often they overlook the risks. But such tendencies inherent to those born with the aspect are counterbalanced so that people who have this aspect also always have another characteristic: they have indomitable confidence. You can never fully suppress the fighting spirit of such persons. They can fail today, but you can be certain that they will be back tomorrow. They almost always keep trying. Sooner or later, they will hit upon good progressions or transits and will have successes.

Another interesting example of our counterbalance principle is the Saturn-Neptune aspect. In chapter 5 of this book, we examined the birth charts of five great basketball players. They are Michael Jordan, Charles Barkley, David Robinson, Clyde Drexler, and Karl Malone. They were the five men picked to have the honor of starting for the U.S.A. Olympic basketball team. Besides the fact that all five were born with the Venus-Pluto enhancement Super Aspect, and they all had an enhancement of Mars, they also all had a Saturn-Neptune aspect. Michael Jordan, Charles Barkley, and Clyde Drexler were all born with Saturn square Neptune. David Robinson has Saturn trine Neptune, and Karl Malone has Saturn parallel Neptune.

The Saturn-Neptune aspect is an aspect that traditional astrology would interpret as being negative. According to the symbolism we presented in chapter 2, this aspect would include the interpretation of having limited (Saturn) inheritances (Neptune). We assume that this is true of these five men. The Jupiter-Neptune enhancement can bless the native with inheritances. The best example of this symbolism is Queen Elizabeth of England, who is the world's richest woman. She inherited her wealth. She was born with an exact Jupiter-Neptune contra-parallel.

But there is a counterbalance to the Saturn-Neptune aspect. These people do not give you an inch; they are so competitive that they do not even give you a micron. But this is a characteristic that is necessary if you want to achieve the highest level of success in competitive team sports. And this is another example of our counterbalance theory.

The Bidirectional Aspect—A New Concept

Our research into the birth charts of over 2,000 extremely successful individuals unequivocally tells us that the quincunx is a very positive aspect if it is a BIDIRECTIONAL quincunx. A bidirectional aspect is one created by two planets where one of the two planets is in retrograde motion and the other is not. In the past, astrologers have generally not made a distinction between aspects that have both planets moving in the same direction versus bidirectional ones. **Our research shows that all bidirectional aspects have a more positive influence than MONODIRECTIONAL aspects.**

In fact, a bidirectional quincunx where Uranus or Jupiter is applying towards another planet is the equivalent of a Super Aspect. So are all bidirectional quincunxes involving the Sun and Jupiter, or the Sun and Uranus, or the Sun and Neptune, or the Sun and Pluto.

You may recall that of the eight richest self-made men in America, seven of them had Jupiter enhancement of Pluto. The only billionaire who was not born with such an aspect was Richard Devos. But guess what? Devos has a bidirectional quincunx of Jupiter and Pluto. He also has a bidirectional quincunx of Pluto and Venus. Now the billionaires all fit perfectly under a nice, neat little umbrella. They all have Super Aspects involving Jupiter and Pluto.

Other bidirectional aspects involving any pair of the Sun, Venus, Mars, Jupiter, Uranus, Neptune, and Pluto are powerful and beneficial, although these are not quite Super Aspects.

But we do need to tighten the orb for these aspects. A bidirectional quincunx is a Super Aspect if it is within 2:30 degrees. And the bidirectional squares and oppositions are beneficial aspects within the same orb of 2:30 degrees.

Because of the nature of the cause of retrograde motion, it is impossible to have bidirectional aspects that have angles smaller than the square aspect. In other words, it is not possible to have a bidirectional sextile, semi-sextile or conjunction. The possible bidirectional aspects are square, trine, quincunx, and opposition.

As is the case with all aspects, even in a bidirectional aspect, it is not helpful to have Saturn applying to any planet that it is in aspect with because this would create a stressful progression (except to Mercury or Uranus). But it is very helpful to have Jupiter or Uranus applying to any planet that Jupiter or Uranus is in bidirectional aspect with.

Now we need to introduce another new concept that we call PLANETARY SYNCHRONIZATION.

Planetary Synchronization—Another New Concept

Planetary synchronization is the term the Magi Society has chosen to refer to an alignment of planets that involve more than two planets, and where all planets are in equal-degree aspect to each other. The same term applies to both the longitudes and the declinations. After our examination of the birth charts of over 2,000 of the most successful or influential people in America, it is obvious that any time there is planetary synchronization in a birth chart, the native derives strong benefit from it (except when Saturn is positioned in a way that creates negative progressions).

A simple example of planetary synch (our shortened term for synchronization) is the chart of Bill Gates, America's richest man. Bill Gates was born with Jupiter, Pluto, and Neptune all within 0:41 degrees of the signs. Looking back at his chart in chapter 5, we see that:

- Jupiter was 27:43 degrees Leo,
- Pluto was 28:20 degrees Leo, and
- Neptune was 28:14 degrees Libra.

This fits the requirements of planetary synch. There are at least three planets that are all in equal-degree aspect to each other.

In a certain sense, planetary synchronization is very similar to a grouping of interrelated equal-degree aspects. But we will learn that it is usually much more than that.

There are two types of planetary synchronizations. LONGITUDINAL SYNCHRONIZATION occurs whenever at least three planets are located such that they are all within a few degrees of one or more signs, regardless of the signs they are in, as was the case above with Bill Gates.

DECLINATIONAL SYNCHRONIZATION is when at least three planets are within a few equal degrees, regardless of whether the planets are in the north or south declination.

In both cases, however, the Moon is always excluded in this book because we do not know where the Moon is in the charts we will use. As we have discussed before, we are not sure of the exact time of birth for the charts we are using, and the exact times are not necessary.

During our research, we found that longitudinal synchronization of planets has an effect similar to the beneficial power of sextiles. A sextile is a positive aspect, but not as strongly beneficial as an enhancement aspect. In the case of longitudinal planetary synchronization, all planets that are in synch appear to be helped by each other to the same extent as if each planet is in sextile to each other. If the longitudinal planetary synchronization already has planets in trine, conjunction, or sextile, then the power of these planets' aspects are increased by the synchronization to other planets and are therefore much more powerful than sextiles.

In the past, astrologers have given names to certain specific alignments of three or four planets. The GRAND TRINE and the GRAND CROSS are examples. And collectively, such alignments are called CONFIGURATIONS. But astrologers have not previously formulated the concept of planetary synchronization, wherein all the planets in synch are thought of as enhancing all the other planets in synch. A grand cross has four planets in synch. This means that in the case of the grand cross, all four planets are working together such that it is the equivalent of each being in sextile to each other. To more fully understand this, let us look at some real examples.

Please look again at the birth chart of Terry Bradshaw (chapter 5), the football player who led his team to four Super Bowl victories. In Terry's birth chart, Uranus, Mars, Saturn, and Mercury were in longitudinal synchronization of just 2:07 degrees. And at the same time, Jupiter, Pluto, and Uranus were in declinational synchronization of just

0:49 degrees. Terry only had 2 of the 12 Super Aspects. But his planetary synchronization gave him the equivalent of a few more.

Another interesting example of planetary synchronization among the birth charts from chapter 5 is that of John Kluge, America's third richest man, where we see that:

- Neptune is in 19:48 degrees north declination,
- Pluto is in 17:56 degrees north declination,
- Jupiter is in 17:54 degrees south declination,
- Uranus is in 18:56 degrees south declination, and
- Venus is in 19:19 degree south declination.

As you can see, planetary synchronization depends upon the degrees of declination, and not whether the planet is north or south. In Kluge's case, he was born with five planets synchronized to within 1:54 degrees.

After having examined the birth charts of absolutely all of the most successful American professional athletes, we have come to the inescapable conclusion that planetary synchronization is an extremely powerful astrological influence that greatly improves a person's athletic performance. Planetary synchronization increases energy, respiratory capacity, and stamina, improves coordination and reflexes, and extends the number of years an athlete can perform at peak levels.

But in the case of an athlete, a very tight aspect of even just two planets is able to provide enormous energy to the native. But the more planets in synch, the better. The rules are:

1) the tighter the synchronization of planets, the better the athlete; and
2) the more planets that are in synch, the better the athlete.

Take, for example, the birth charts of the following five athletes who have been generally regarded as among the very best in their respective sports: Larry Bird, Bill Russell, and Julius Erving, three of the best basketball players in the history of the sport; and Ivan Lendl and Arthur Ashe, the tennis greats. (As always in this book, all birth charts can be found at the end of the chapter.)

After examining the last five birth charts, you can better understand the power of planetary synchronization. We chose to show five charts with longitudinal synchronization rather than declinational synchronization because the visual effect is stronger. But declination synchronization is just as powerful, and we will have many examples of it later in this book.

As far as athletes are concerned, planetary synchronization is as powerful as the aspects. An aspect involves only two planets; synchronization involves at least three planets. Certain synchronization configurations involving three planets are more powerful and more beneficial than other configurations with the same three planets. The same is true with configurations of four or more planets; some are more powerful than others with the same planets. The reason for this involves what astrologers call MIDPOINTS. In the past, astrologers have not used midpoints in the way we will learn to use them. So it is now important that we understand this concept.

Midpoints—An Old Concept Applied in New Ways

These days, especially in England, astrologers are making very good use of MIDPOINTS in their astrological interpretations. What are midpoints? Midpoints are exactly what it sounds like they should be. Astrologers use the term *midpoint* to define the position on a birth chart that is the middle point between two planets. In other words, the Jupiter-Saturn midpoint is the point on a chart where the angle between Jupiter and Saturn is divided in half, with the resulting midpoint being equidistant to Jupiter and Saturn. This means that there are always two midpoints, and the two are always opposite each other. But just as astrologers always choose the lesser angle to define an aspect, they also always choose the midpoint that is nearer to the planets creating the midpoint. (Please refer to the midpoint charts under "Midpoints" in the Glossary.)

Astrologers believe that the midpoint of two planets is sometimes as important as the actual position of the planets and that a transit by a planet to the midpoint affects both of the planets that create the midpoint.

Since there are 10 planets, there are 10 times 9 midpoints. Ninety represents a lot of midpoints, but that is only for the longitudes. The declinations have midpoints, also, which means that there are 2 times 90 midpoints, and 180 midpoints is a very large number of midpoints.

The Magi Society does not attest to, or deny, the validity of midpoints used in the way that astrologers now use them. That is a subject for a subsequent book. In *Astrology Really Works!,* we will use midpoints in a different way. We will learn about midpoint aspects in birth charts, which are very, very important, and how they improve planetary synchronization.

One of our primary interests in midpoints is how they are related to planetary synchronization. Midpoints increase the power of planetary synchronization. Generally, when there is synchronization, there are also interesting relationships between the midpoints of the planets in synch, and the actual synchronized planets. Take, for example, the chart of Larry Bird. In Bird's chart, the midpoint of Pluto-Neptune makes three equal-degree aspects. It is conjunct to Jupiter, in opposition to Mars, and square to Mercury. But there is much more. The midpoint of Jupiter-Mars is in trine to Pluto, conjunct to Mercury, and sextile to Neptune. In fact, the configuration pattern formed by Larry Bird's five-planet synchronization of Jupiter, Pluto, Neptune, Mars, and Mercury creates a total of 12 midpoint aspects to the planets that form the configuration. In addition, they form midpoint aspects to planets that are not any of the synchronized planets, the most important of which are:

- the midpoint of Jupiter-Neptune sextile to the Sun, and
- the midpoint of Jupiter-Pluto sextile to Venus.

How does one interpret these midpoint aspects? In the same way we interpret everything else—we use the SYMBOLISM of the planets. In Larry Bird's case, the Jupiter-Neptune midpoint sextile to the Sun is interpreted as: success and good fortune (Jupiter), especially in long-term security (Neptune), which will be provided to him (the Sun). The Jupiter-Pluto midpoint sextile Venus means that he will make money (Venus) from success (Jupiter) in professional sports (Pluto).

Larry's birth chart dramatically illustrates one of the reasons that planetary synchronization is so powerful. Besides the fact that all planets in synch are in aspect to each other, the midpoints of the planets in synch form additional aspects.

Earlier, we explained that the midpoint of Jupiter-Neptune is in sextile to Larry Bird's Sun. In other words, the midpoint of two planets acts like a planet. Midpoints actually make aspects to other planets. This concept is essentially new and has not been used by astrologers. But the Magi Society has great confidence in its belief that midpoints do act as planets as far as making aspects to planets is concerned. Also, midpoints work as transits to other planets. In other words, the midpoint of Jupiter-Pluto can make a transit to any natal planet. Our Society has found that such transits are as powerful as the transits of the actual planets.

We mentioned earlier that there are two possible midpoints between two longitudinal planets. Each of these two midpoints is 180 degrees from the other. Astrologers who use midpoints prefer to use the closer or "near" midpoint as opposed to the "far" midpoint (see example in Glossary under "Midpoint"). The Magi Society believes that both midpoints are always active. Referring to chart 54, one Jupiter-Neptune midpoint is in trine to Mars, and the other is in sextile to Mars. Both midpoints are actually working; therefore, both aspects exist. But in Magi Astrology, we will always use the trine aspect when we discuss aspects by midpoints because midpoint aspects are very powerful, and the sextile aspect is not so powerful.

Two very interesting examples of the power of midpoints are the birth charts of Elton John and Glenn Close. Both are superstars in their professions. As you can see in their charts at the end of the chapter, Glenn Close has four Super Aspects. She has Jupiter and the Sun in trine, Neptune-Sun parallel, a Uranus-Venus enhancement, and a Uranus-Pluto enhancement. It means that she is a very fortunate person, will have an extended career, will make money from movies, and has power and appeal with the masses.

Elton John has two Super Aspects, the Neptune-Sun enhancement, and Uranus parallel Pluto. He was born six days apart from Glenn Close. In the declinations, both the midpoint of Jupiter-Pluto and the midpoint of Jupiter-Uranus are parallel to Elton John's Sun. And these same two midpoints are contra-parallel to Glenn Close's Sun. In other words, the natal Suns of both Glenn Close and Elton John are enhanced by the same two natal midpoints, the Jupiter-Pluto and the Jupiter-Uranus midpoints. This is not a coincidence. In the case of Larry Bird, his Sun had a midpoint enhancement by Jupiter-Neptune. All of these midpoints involve Jupiter. The fact is that the midpoints of Jupiter-Saturn, Jupiter-Uranus, Jupiter-Neptune, and Jupiter-Pluto are very powerful. An enhancement by any of them is almost as powerful as a Super Aspect.

For a greater understanding of midpoints, let us now look back at the billionaires in chapter 5. From the symbolism of astrology, we would expect that the Venus-Pluto and Jupiter-Pluto midpoints would be very important to the making of billionaires. Here are the aspects made by these two midpoints to the eight billionaires in chapter 5.

Bill Gates:

- Jupiter-Pluto enhances Venus by contra-parallel. We interpret this as money (Venus) from success (Jupiter) at big business (Pluto).
- Jupiter-Pluto trine Neptune. This means long-term security (Neptune) from success (Jupiter) at big business (Pluto).
- Venus-Pluto conjunction Mars, which means Gates has energy (Mars) to make money (Venus) from big business (Pluto).
- Venus-Pluto contra-parallel Mars. Same as above.

Warren Buffett:

- Venus-Pluto conjunct to the Sun. This means that Buffett is a man (the Sun) who has the capacity to make money (Venus) from big business (Pluto).

John Kluge:

- Venus-Pluto parallel the Sun. Buffett has this aspect.
- Venus-Pluto enhancement of Uranus. This gives Buffett fame (Uranus) from making money (Venus) in big business (Pluto).
- Jupiter-Pluto parallel the Sun. Kluge is a man (the Sun) who is able to succeed (Jupiter) in big business (Pluto).

Edward Johnson III:

- Jupiter-Pluto parallel the Sun. Kluge has this aspect.

John Van Andel:

- Venus-Pluto parallel the Sun. Same as Buffett and Kluge.

Richard Devos:

- Venus-Pluto enhancement of the Sun. Same as Buffett, Kluge, and John Van Andel.
- Jupiter-Pluto enhancement of Uranus. Means he can achieve fame (Uranus) from success (Jupiter) in big business (Pluto).

Rupert Murdoch:

- Venus-Pluto enhancement of the Sun. Same as Warren Buffett, John Kluge, John Van Andel, and Richard Devos.

Sumner Redstone:

- Venus-Pluto enhancement of Neptune. This aspect helped Redstone obtain long-term security (Neptune) from an ability to make money (Venus) from big business (Pluto).
- Jupiter-Pluto enhances Saturn. This is a very special aspect. Remember that Jupiter overpowers Saturn. Any aspect by Jupiter to Saturn is very good, including midpoint aspects.

All eight billionaires had at least one important enhancement by either the Jupiter-Pluto midpoint or Venus-Pluto midpoint. Five of eight had an enhancement of the Sun by the Venus-Pluto midpoint. Normally, only one of eight would have this aspect. If you add these statistics to the fact that seven of them had the Super Success Aspect of Jupiter-Pluto enhancement, and five also had Pluto-Sun enhancement, the weight of evidence that astrology really works is overwhelming.

It also means that the midpoint aspects work, and are also very powerful.

We know that calculating all of these midpoints can be tedious and time-consuming. But you can see that they are a very important part of astrology. If you are going to learn to use astrology, it will be necessary for you to obtain some astrological aids. An ephemeris is a must, and as we already mentioned, the publisher of this book also publishes an ephemeris that comes complete with declinations, important midpoints for the longitudes and declinations, and a listing of planetary eclipses. If you have a personal computer, you may also want to consider obtaining a software program that provides this information and more. If you contact the Magi Society, we will recommend a software package for your needs. (Our telephone number is near the end of this book, just before the Glossary.)

Chart 50: May 16, 1928
Birth date of Billy Martin

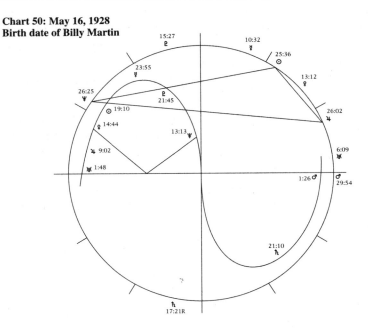

Chart 51: December 7, 1956
Birth date of Larry Bird

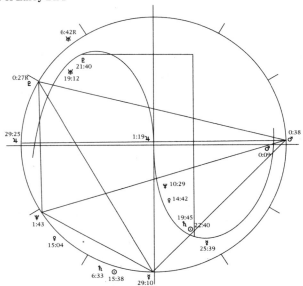

Chart 52: March 7, 1960
Birth date of Ivan Lendl

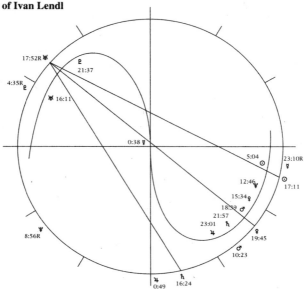

Chart 53: February 12, 1934
Birth date of Bill Russell

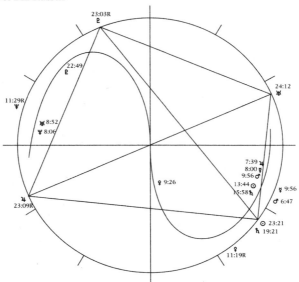

Chart 54: July 10, 1943
Birth date of Arthur Ashe

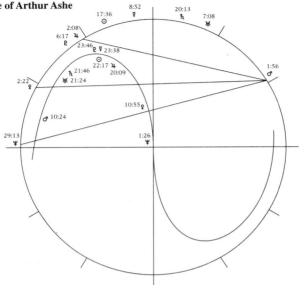

Chart 55: February 22, 1950
Birth date of Julius Erving

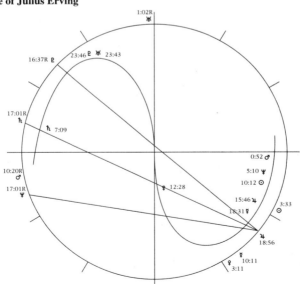

Chart 56: March 19, 1947
Birth date of Glenn Close

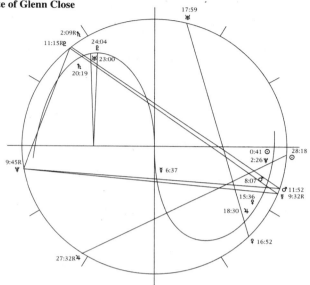

Chart 57: March 25, 1947
Birth date of Elton John

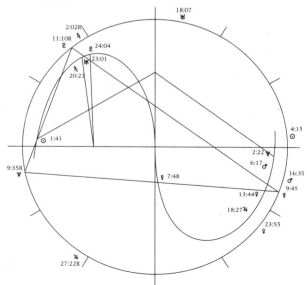

SUPER CHARTS

In previous chapters, we introduced you to some new concepts in astrology and corrected some old ideas that were not useful. With this increased knowledge of Magi Astrology that we have gained in this book, let us now examine the birth charts of some of the most successful people in the Western world. Every single person we have chosen has been at the very top of his or her profession for an extended time period. Each birth chart confirms that the symbolism of astrology, as well as astrological aspects, work. Whenever there is planetary synchronization, it also works.

For each chart, we will give you the particular person's qualification to be included in this chapter of super-successful natal charts. We will also list the Super Aspects of each birth chart along with any important planetary synchronizations and eclipses.

SUPER CHART 1: Prime Minister John Major

Qualification: Prime Minister of the United Kingdom

Super Aspects: Jupiter parallel Pluto; Jupiter parallel Uranus; Pluto trine the Sun; Neptune parallel the Sun

Planetary eclipse: Saturn and Uranus

Planetary synchronization: Uranus, Neptune, and Mercury in the longitudes; the Sun, Venus, Saturn, and Pluto in the longitudes

John Major never seems to do well in the opinion polls, but he has done well at the voting polls. His political prowess stems from his

Jupiter enhancement of Uranus, which President Clinton and Newt Gingrich also have. The Prime Minister also has the Super Success Aspect, which never hurts. And his ability to achieve power is foretold by his Pluto trine Sun.

SUPER CHART 2: Chancellor Helmut Kohl

Qualification: Chancellor of Germany for what seems like forever

Super Aspects: Jupiter parallel Pluto; Uranus parallel the Sun; Uranus conjunct the Sun

Planetary eclipse: Uranus and the Sun

Planetary synchronization: Jupiter, Uranus, the Sun, Mercury, and Mars in the longitudes; Jupiter, Pluto, and Saturn in the declinations

Helmut Kohl will go down in history as the man who presided over the unification of Germany. This was no small feat. Kohl also has the Super Success Aspect. But the astrological key to his chart is the Uranus-Sun planetary eclipse. Uranus rules fame, the masses, and revolutions. He was able to orchestrate the unification in part because his Uranus-Sun planetary eclipse means that he is a man (the Sun) who can govern the masses (Uranus) and produce revolutions (Uranus). Uranus also rules change. East Germany certainly changed.

SUPER CHART 3: Bill Clinton

Qualification: President of the United States

Super Aspects: Jupiter trine Uranus; Uranus parallel Pluto

Planetary eclipses: Mars and Neptune; Mars and Venus

Planetary synchronization: Mars, Neptune, and Mercury in the longitudes

As of this writing, President Clinton has been having negative transits. For most of 1994, Uranus has been quincunx his Sun. Although a natal quincunx is positive if it is bi-directional, the quincunx is stressful if in transit. In addition, Pluto squared his Sun in 1993 and 1994.

And Neptune will quincunx his Sun in 1995 and 1996. During 1995, Saturn will square Uranus, and quincunx his Sun and Jupiter three times. These are not good transits to have, especially when the eyes of the nation are watching you. But Clinton has always been amazingly resourceful and has shown an unbelievable ability to overcome roadblocks that would be fatal to most politicians—which is an admirable quality for a President. Jupiter makes very strong positive transits in 1996 as it parallels Uranus and Pluto during the election year. It will definitely be a very interesting election year.

Where does President Clinton get his power? He has an alignment similar to a Magi Pyramid. Jupiter is trine Uranus, and the Sun is almost in sextile to both. Any longitudinal alignment of three synchronized planets is very powerful so long as the Sun, Venus, Jupiter, Uranus, Neptune, or Pluto are the three component planets. We call this type of longitudinal alignment a Magi TRIANGLE, and we will see it regularly in the charts of the super-successful. Magi Triangles have the same effect as Magi Pyramids; the pyramids are always in the declinations, and the triangles are always in the longitudes.

SUPER CHART 4: Hillary Clinton

Qualification: First Lady of the United States

Super Aspects: Jupiter contra-parallel Pluto; Jupiter contra-parallel Uranus; Uranus parallel Pluto (a Magi Pyramid); Neptune contra-parallel Venus; Uranus trine the Sun

Planetary synchronization: Jupiter, Pluto, Uranus, and Mars in declination

Hillary Clinton has five Super Aspects. As much as conservatives would love to see her disappear from the political scene, individuals with so many Super Aspects rarely get pushed aside for long; and Hillary certainly will not voluntarily step aside for long, either. We notice that she has been having a super-negative progression that will be leaving in the not-all-too-distant future. Also, she has the super progression of Jupiter contra-parallel natal Pluto when she turns 66 (in the year 2014). This is the progression that helped Jack Kennedy become

President. American politics will be fascinating to watch in the upcoming decades.

SUPER CHART 5: Pope John Paul II

Qualification: The leader of the Catholic Church

Super Aspects: Jupiter parallel the Sun; Pluto parallel the Sun; Neptune parallel the Sun; Jupiter parallel Pluto; Jupiter parallel Neptune; Jupiter conjunction Neptune (a Magi Pyramid)

Planetary eclipse: Jupiter and Neptune; Venus and Mercury

Planetary synchronization: The Sun, Jupiter, Pluto, and Neptune in declination

This is the chart of a wonderful man, one who does a lot of good for the Catholic Church. His birth chart has the extremely rare Jupiter-Neptune planetary eclipse, which leads us to the interpretation that he brings success, good fortune, and expansion (Jupiter) to the Catholic Church (Neptune). He is also blessed with another planetary eclipse, that of Mercury and Venus, which gives him a sharp mind and the ability to communicate (Venus acts as the lesser benefic and enhances Mercury, which rules the mind and communication). Imbedded in his quadruple parallel is the Magi Pyramid of Jupiter, Pluto, and the Sun. This brings power (Pluto-Sun parallel) and good fortune (Jupiter enhancement of the Sun and Pluto).

SUPER CHART 6: Princess Grace (Grace Kelly)

Qualification: American commoner who married a reigning European monarch, Prince Rainier of Monaco. She was also a very successful movie star in Hollywood for a number of years.

Super Aspects: Jupiter parallel Pluto; Neptune contra-parallel Venus; Pluto trine Sun

Planetary eclipse: The Sun and Mars

Planetary synchronization: Jupiter, Pluto, and Saturn

Grace Kelly was born with an extraordinarily tight aspect of Jupiter-Pluto enhancement (the Super Success Aspect). It is the dominant aspect of her natal chart and helped her in all her endeavors throughout her life. Her Pluto trine Sun gave her the desire for, and the ability to obtain, power (Pluto). In addition, her Neptune contra-parallel to Venus helped her to achieve long-term (Neptune) security and possessions (Venus). This same aspect can also provide for long-term (Neptune) beauty (Venus), which she certainly possessed.

SUPER CHART 7: Queen Elizabeth II

Qualification: She is the Queen of England and the richest woman in the world.

Super Aspects: Pluto trine Venus; Jupiter contra-parallel Neptune

Planetary eclipse: Jupiter and Mars

Planetary synchronization: Jupiter, Neptune, Mars, and Saturn

Queen Elizabeth has two Super Aspects, which both involve money. Her Jupiter enhancement of Neptune gave her the gigantic inheritances needed to be the richest woman in the world. Is $10 billion good enough? Her Pluto trine Venus gives her even more money, but it also means partnerships (Venus) in power (Pluto).

SUPER CHART 8: Princess Diana of Wales

Qualification: She is, arguably, the most famous (and most photographed) woman in the world.

Super Aspects: Neptune trine Sun; Uranus parallel Venus; Jupiter parallel Pluto

Planetary synchronization: Jupiter, Neptune, Pluto, and the Sun in the longitudes

Princess Di has had a very rough marriage to Prince Charles. Nonetheless, she remains the Princess of Wales, and her son, Prince William, is likely to one day become King of England. Princess Di's most powerful astrological feature is the Magi Triangle of Jupiter, the Sun, and Pluto.

SUPER CHART 9: Bill Cosby

Qualification: The comedian is generally reputed to be the wealthiest African-American in Hollywood.

Super Aspects: Jupiter contra-parallel Pluto; Jupiter contra-parallel the Sun; Pluto parallel the Sun (a Magi Pyramid)

Planetary synchronization: Jupiter, the Sun, and Mars in the declinations

The Cosby Show was the top-rated television show for years. Bill Cosby has been equally successful and talented in comedy and drama. His versatility is legend. He won Emmys, a Golden Globe, and several Grammys.

SUPER CHART 10: Oprah Winfrey

Qualification: This ultra-famous talk show hostess is probably the richest woman on television.

Super Aspects: Jupiter parallel Pluto; Jupiter parallel Uranus; Uranus parallel Pluto

Planetary eclipse: The Sun and Venus

Planetary synchronization: The Sun, Venus, and Saturn

Oprah, like so many other broadcasting and film stars, has Jupiter enhancement of Uranus. This is the best aspect for success in any area of the mass media. The Uranus enhancement of Pluto also helps because it gives her power and appeal (Pluto) in dealing with the general public (Uranus). Of course she also has the Super Success Aspect. Note how closely the planets are aligned in her Magi Pyramid of Jupiter, Pluto and Uranus.

SUPER CHART 11: Mick Jagger

Qualification: Along with Rod Stewart and Elton John, Mick Jagger of The Rolling Stones is one of the longest-lasting rock and pop superstars. He is still going strong in his late forties.

Super Aspects: Jupiter conjunct Pluto; Pluto conjunct the Sun; Jupiter conjunct the Sun (Magi Triangle); Jupiter parallel the Sun; Jupiter parallel Uranus; Uranus parallel the Sun (Magi Pyramid)

Planetary eclipse: The Sun and Jupiter

Planetary synchronization: Jupiter, the Sun, and Uranus

Mick Jagger is another one of those super-lucky souls who has the Sun-Jupiter planetary eclipse in their birth charts. Besides the good fortune that this aspect gives the native, the aspect also makes them very benevolent and fair. Mick is no exception to this characteristic of Sun-Jupiter-enhanced persons. As most people know, Mick Jagger has been more than equitable with the members of The Rolling Stones. All of the band members earn just as much as Mick Jagger because they all share equally. That is extraordinary. People with Sun-Jupiter enhancements are very fair and loyal. That is one reason why astrologers have always regarded Jupiter as the planet of peace. Mick has six Super Aspects.

Mick also has the Jupiter-Pluto enhancement. Jagger also has Venus trine Mars, an aspect of great energy (Venus, the lesser benefic, enhances Mars, which symbolizes energy); no wonder he can jump up and down on stage so energetically. His intensity and attention-getting abilities stem from his Sun-Pluto conjunction, although it is a wide aspect. Here we have to divert from the general trend of this book and bring in one of the 12 astrological signs to explain Mick more completely. Mick's Sun-Pluto conjunction is in Leo. We all know what that means. He commands and demands attention.

He is also a very intelligent man; you have to be in order to be so successful for so long. The Sun-Jupiter enhancement gives him sound judgment. But his high level of intelligence comes from the Mercury-Jupiter parallel (Jupiter, the greater benefic, enhances the mind, Mercury.)

SUPER CHART 12: Elvis Presley

Qualification: He was the "king" of pop music for two decades when he was alive.

Super Aspects: Pluto contra-parallel the Sun; Pluto contra-parallel Venus; Neptune trine the Sun; Magi Triangle of Neptune, Jupiter, and the Sun

Planetary synchronization: Pluto, Uranus, and Saturn in the longitudes; the Sun, Venus, and Pluto in the declinations

Elvis was the most idolized American-born singer of all time. His Sun, Venus, and Pluto Magi Pyramid was the most obvious of the enhancements that helped him achieve what nobody else has actually replicated. We have seen the Sun-Jupiter-Pluto Magi Pyramid a lot. But here Venus replaces Jupiter in the alignment. Jupiter is more helpful to the attainment of good fortune; and Venus is more useful when it comes to money, love, and beauty. This is why Elvis had so much sex appeal.

He also had a trine of Neptune to the Sun. The Neptune trine Sun will sometimes make a person uninhibited, and Elvis had few inhibitions, as evinced by his "Elvis, the Pelvis" moniker.

SUPER CHART 13: Rod Stewart

Qualification: Along with Mick Jagger and Elton John, Rod is one of the longest-lasting and most successful music superstars.

Super Aspects: Jupiter contra-parallel Neptune; Pluto contra-parallel the Sun; Uranus contra-parallel the Sun

Planetary synchronization: Neptune, Venus, and Saturn in the longitudes

Mick Jagger has the Sun-Pluto-Jupiter Magi Pyramid; Elvis Presley had the Sun-Pluto-Venus Magi Pyramid; and Rod Stewart has the Sun-Pluto-Uranus Magi Pyramid. Of the three benefics, Venus provides for the most beauty, so it makes sense that Elvis is considered to have been the sexiest and best-looking of the three music men. Jupiter provides the most good luck, and Mick, does indeed seem to be the most fortunate. And Uranus is also great. Rod's Jupiter enhancement of Neptune gives him the longest-lasting security of the three, which may be the reason that he has had two hit albums in his late forties.

SUPER CHART 14: Steven Spielberg

Qualification: The most successful motion picture producer/director of the last two decades.

Super Aspects: Jupiter trine Pluto and Jupiter contra-parallel Pluto (Magi Double Aspect); Pluto contra-parallel the Sun; Jupiter parallel the Sun; Uranus contra-parallel the Sun; Venus is enhanced by Jupiter, Uranus, and Pluto; Pluto parallel Uranus; Jupiter contra-parallel Uranus. Ten super aspects! And a Magi Triangle of Jupiter, Pluto, and Neptune, as well as a Magi Triangle of Uranus, the Sun, and Venus.

Planetary eclipse: Jupiter and Mercury

Planetary synchronization: The Sun, Uranus, Venus, and Saturn in the longitudes; Jupiter, the Sun, Pluto, Uranus, and Venus in the declinations

This super-genius of Hollywood directed *Jaws* while he was in his twenties. He was able to achieve such a remarkable accomplishment at such a young age because he was born with not just one, but two Jupiter-Pluto enhancements. Jupiter trined Pluto at birth, and also Jupiter was contra-parallel Pluto. This means he has two Super Success Aspects and this gives him a Bi-level Enhancement of Jupiter and Pluto. He also has eight other Super Aspects, including Jupiter enhancement of his Sun, making him a very lucky man. His three enhancements to Venus give him superlative ability to make money. The Sun-Pluto contra-parallel provides him with the desire for, and ability to attain, power. And the Uranus-Pluto parallel allows him to succeed in big business (Pluto) involving the public (Uranus) through filmmaking (Uranus).

In addition to all of these aspects of success, Spielberg has a brilliant mind. He was born with a planetary eclipse of Mercury and Jupiter, which is the best single enhancement of the mind and intelligence (Mercury).

Now here is a great example of how accurate astrology is. Spielberg has experienced nothing but success in his life because the Uranus progression to Pluto began at birth, and continues until age 72.

How fortunate can you get? We all love your movies, Steven Spielberg. Please keep them coming.

SUPER CHART 15: Walt Disney

Qualification: The genius of animated film, his Walt Disney Company was number one worldwide in children's entertainment for decades.

Super Aspects: Jupiter parallel the Sun; Uranus parallel the Sun, and Uranus conjunct to the Sun; Jupiter parallel Uranus; Jupiter, Uranus, and Neptune all enhancing Venus in the declinations; Jupiter contraparallel Neptune. Neptune contra-parallel the Sun. Nine super aspects!

Planetary eclipses: Uranus and the Sun, Jupiter and Saturn; Jupiter and Mars

Planetary synchronization: Jupiter, the Sun, Neptune, Saturn, Uranus, and Venus in the declinations; the Sun, Jupiter, Pluto, Uranus, and Saturn in the longitudes.

Walt Disney was the Steven Spielberg of the 1930s through the 1950s, although he concentrated his efforts on entertaining children. Parents knew that they could always depend on Disney's movies for their wholesomeness, moral values, and lack of violence. We all miss him.

SUPER CHART 16: Martina Navratilova

Qualification: Martina has won more tennis tournaments (166) than anyone else, male or female.

Super Aspects: Neptune parallel the Sun

Planetary eclipse: Jupiter and Venus

Planetary synchronization: Neptune, Saturn, and Pluto in the longitudes; the Sun, Neptune, and Mars in the declinations

Skeptics might be shouting "Ah-ha! Only one super aspect! Astrology does not work." That is a skeptic for you. Astrology has been working for nearly a hundred charts, and when one seems to be off center, the skeptic rants and raves. But in reality, Martina confirms the astrology of athletes. And when you see the natal charts of the other great tennis players, you will be amazed by the similarities.

Although Martina has only one Super Aspect, the other aspects she does have are picture perfect for what she is. And she does have the Jupiter-Venus planetary eclipse, which is one of the most beneficial of the planetary eclipses and certainly can be graded as equivalent to a Super Aspect.

Her career lasted 19 years. We already saw her chart earlier and noted that she owes her longevity to the Sun-Neptune parallel. Although the Sun-Neptune enhancement is the most effective aspect for longevity and also provides enormous reserves of energy, enhancements to Mars are also very helpful because they increase energy and stamina, and promote healing of the muscles. We learned in chapter 5 that Mars rules energy and the muscles. Notice that Martina has three strong enhancements to Mars. The Sun-Mars parallel gives her energy (this is the same aspect that baseball pitching greats Tom Seaver and Steve Carlton have). The Mars-Neptune parallel gives her still more energy. And remember that planetary synchronization provides enormous reservoirs of energy; she has extremely close synchronization in both the longitudes and the declinations.

Martina is a perfect example of the power of proximity enhancement. In the last chapter, we explained that if two planets are in very tight aspect, the aspect is particularly strong and is especially important when dealing with athletes because the tighter the aspect, the more energy it provides. Well, Martina's Neptune sextile Pluto is 0:01 degrees apart. This provides enormous energy, and you need extraordinary amounts of energy in order to last 19 years on the pro tennis circuit. It is not the genes. Children of people with these Super Aspects will not be nearly as successful as their parents unless the children have similar Super Aspects. Therefore, we can see that if we use the consistent interpretation of astrological symbolism, Martina's athletic skills are confirmed by astrology. Her midpoint enhancements also confirm astrology. Part of her ability to be a champion of champions lies in her midpoint enhancements which, remarkably, are very similar to those of Jimmy Connors, the male tennis player who has won the most tournaments. We will go into more detail on him when we get to his chart later on.

Midpoint enhancements: Neptune-Uranus midpoint parallel to Jupiter and Venus; Neptune-Pluto midpoint parallel to Jupiter and Venus; Jupiter-Uranus midpoint conjunct to Pluto; Jupiter-Uranus midpoint trine to Neptune; Neptune-Pluto midpoint trine to Saturn; Jupiter-Saturn midpoint conjunct to the Sun.

The midpoint enhancements to Venus, Neptune, and Pluto provide the money. And the enhancements of Jupiter provide the good fortune. Also, all the midpoint enhancements increase Martina's athletic skills.

There are more midpoint enhancements, but these are the major ones.

You were fabulous, Martina. All tennis fans will miss you.

SUPER CHART 17: Chris Evert

Qualification: Before Martina Navratilova, Chris was the best female tennis player in the world. She won the U.S. Open title six times and the French Open seven times. Chris is second only to Navratilova in tournaments won (157).

Super Aspects: Jupiter parallel Pluto; Pluto contra-parallel the Sun; Uranus contra-parallel the Sun; Jupiter conjunct Uranus; Pluto trine the Sun. Multiple Magi Triangles formed by Jupiter, Uranus, Pluto, Neptune, and the Sun. Also a Magi Pyramid of the Sun, Pluto, and Uranus.

Planetary eclipse: Jupiter and Uranus; Venus and Saturn

Planetary synchronization: Jupiter, Uranus, Pluto, Neptune, Mercury, and the Sun in the longitudes; Jupiter, Uranus, Pluto, Mercury, and the Sun in the declinations.

Martina Navratilova and Chris Evert are the two female tennis professionals who won the most tournaments. And they are also the two with the greatest degree of planetary synchronization.

Chris's chart is an excellent example of the enormous power of planetary synchronization. She has six planets in longitudinal synchronization of less than 3 degrees. That is two-thirds of the planets (remember we do not use the Moon) in ten percent of the degrees. She also has a five-planet declinational synchronization. As we have said before, synchronization is most effective for the athletes. The more planets in synch, and the tighter the synchronization, the better the athlete. Chris is just about at maximum in both number of planets in synch and the closeness of the synch. Besides strength and endurance, synchronization provides steadiness and balance, great coordination and reflexes, and great ability to play under pressure.

But we should not overlook the Super Aspects. She has five Super Aspects.

Some people thought Chris was boring to watch because she was a baseline player and rarely rushed the net. But we always enjoyed her play and wish she were still in the game.

SUPER CHART 18: Jimmy Connors

Qualifications: Won more tennis tournaments (109) than any other male tennis player.

Super Aspects: Uranus parallel Pluto; Neptune contra-parallel the Sun. Magi Triangle of Jupiter, Pluto, and Neptune.

Planetary synchronization: Jupiter, Uranus, Pluto, Mercury, and Neptune in the longitudes; Pluto, Uranus, and Mars in the declinations.

Is it a coincidence that all these tennis greats have such fabulous planetary synchronizations? We do not think so.

Here are interesting similarities between Connors and Navratilova. Both have:

- Neptune in declinational enhancement of the Sun;
- two nearly exact declinational enhancements of Mars; and
- the Jupiter-Uranus midpoint enhancing both Neptune and Pluto.

Also, both have won more tennis tournaments than any other player of their sex. Astrology really works—especially because these similar aspects symbolize superhuman-caliber energy and stamina, extreme longevity, and the highest level of athletic skills.

SUPER CHART 19: Ivan Lendl

Qualification: Won more tennis tournaments (94) than any other male tennis player except for Jimmy Connors.

Super Aspects: Jupiter contra-parallel Pluto; Uranus contra-parallel Venus

Planetary synchronization: Uranus, the Sun, Venus, Mercury, and Saturn in the longitudes

With Navratilova, Evert, Connors, and Lendl, we have the four tennis players who have won the most tournaments ever. And all four players' natal charts prove that astrology really works.

Even more interesting is that all four players confirm each other astrologically. For example, Connors and Navratilova each have the best aspects to Mars, which determine how much power a person can muster. Enhancements to Mars provide more power in the tennis game. So these two should have the most power in their game. And they do. Remember how Connors attacked every ball? His was a power game. Martina is well known for having had the greatest power game of any female player. Evert and Lendl do not have the great power in their tennis games; they were baseline players who won championships because they rarely made mistakes and had great stamina and coordination. And they rarely charged the net the way Connors and Navratilova did. Neither Lendl nor Evert have the double declinational enhancements to Mars that Connors and Navratilova have. So they did not have the power. But Lendl and Evert have great planetary synchronization, which provides stamina and coordination.

In addition, Lendl has Uranus in bi-directional quincunx to the Sun. We have explained that bi-directional quincunxes are very beneficial and powerful aspects. **Many professional athletes have such aspects.** It is the equivalent of a Super Aspect.

SUPER CHART 20: Rocky Marciano

Qualification: The only heavyweight boxing champion to retire un-defeated. He won 49 fights; 43 of them were knockouts.

Super Aspects: Jupiter trine Pluto; Jupiter trine Uranus; Jupiter con-tra-parallel Neptune; Uranus contra-parallel the Sun. Magi Triangle of Jupiter, Pluto and Uranus

Planetary eclipse: Mars and Venus; Venus and the Sun

You need to have an awesome astrological chart to accomplish what Rocky Marciano did; his natal chart was magnificent. Rocky had a grand trine of Jupiter, Pluto, and Uranus, which is also a Magi Tri-angle. Imbedded in this configuration is the most fortunate of all as-pects for great success, the Jupiter-Pluto trine. It also means he had the Uranus-Pluto trine (wide) and the Jupiter-Uranus trine. If you are going to stand in the boxing ring toe to toe with 200-pound muscle-men who want to knock your block off, it is quite good indeed to have this grand trine. Since Marciano was born, this alignment has never occurred again. It will not occur again for more than 100 years, which means that none of our children will reap the benefits of such a grand trine. Marciano also has Jupiter enhancement of Neptune, which gives him longevity and helps him to physically regenerate and heal; we have already learned it also provides financial security.

SUPER CHART 21: Deion Sanders

Qualification: The only person to ever play in a Super Bowl and the World Series. Sanders is considered by most football coaches to be the best cornerback in the game, and also the fastest player. He helped the San Francisco 49ers win the franchise's fifth Super Bowl in 1995.

Super Aspects: Jupiter parallel Pluto; Jupiter parallel the Sun, Jupiter contra-parallel Neptune; Pluto parallel the Sun; Jupiter con-junction the Sun; Neptune contra-parallel the Sun

Planetary eclipse: The Sun and Jupiter

Planetary synchronization: Saturn, Mars, and Venus in the longitudes; Jupiter, the Sun, Pluto, Neptune, and Mars in the declinations.

Deion Sanders is the only man to ever play two professional sports successfully. Bo Jackson was the first to play two professional sports well, but he was injured in football. Sanders hit .533 in the 1992 World Series for the Atlanta Braves, and was All-Pro as a football player four times as of the 1994 season. He is only 27 years young.

Sanders' natal chart has a very strong similarity to the Pope's, with one major addition. The Pope has mutual declinational enhancements of the Sun, Jupiter, Pluto, and Neptune. With Sanders, you add Mars to the list. That is why he is an athlete. As we keep saying, Mars rules energy and muscles, and represents the athlete. Since both Neptune and Jupiter are involved in this synchronization, we can expect that the odds favor a long and brilliant career. But you never know if he will opt out of sports for singing or some other career. He has a rap song hit, and he likes to be called "Prime Time," so he has ambitions in the entertainment industry, which stem from his Pluto/Neptune aspects.

SUPER CHART 22: Bobby Fischer

Qualification: At the age of 14, he was the youngest person to win the U.S. Chess championship. The only American to ever be world chess champion; he held the title from 1972 to 1975. He never lost the title; it was taken from him when he refused to defend it.

Super Aspects: Jupiter parallel Pluto; Jupiter trine the Sun. Magi Triangle of Jupiter, Venus, and the Sun

Planetary eclipse: Saturn and Uranus

Planetary synchronization: Uranus, Neptune, and Mars in a grand trine

Bobby Fischer is the temperamental genius from Brooklyn who made chess popular in this country during the first five years of the 1970s. His natal chart is a good example of proximity enhancement. It has a remarkably tight grand trine of major planets. His grand trine of Uranus, Neptune, and Mars had a spread of only :06 degrees and was perfectly suited for chess, although if personal computers existed during his youth, he would have been one of the world's best computer programming geniuses. Uranus rules technology, inventions, computer programming, astrology, and chess. The Mars trine Uranus gives Bobby Fischer an energization (Mars) of Uranian pursuits, which includes chess. He has this enhancement twice because he also has the Uranus-Mars contra-parallel, providing him with a Magi Double Aspect. There was no escaping Uranian endeavors for him. His success comes from the Jupiter-Pluto parallel and the Sun-Jupiter trine. Bobby Fischer's Uranus trine Neptune also contributed to his success, since it meant that he could derive long-term security (Neptune) from chess (ruled by Uranus).

SUPER CHART 23: Luciano Pavarotti

Qualification: Pavarotti is widely regarded as the best opera singer of modern times. He commands up to $100,000 for a performance.

Super Aspects: Jupiter trine Pluto; Neptune parallel Venus; Neptune contra-parallel the Sun

Planetary eclipse: Neptune and Venus

Pavarotti is 60 and still going strong. He has the fountain-of-youth aspect; Neptune enhances his Sun. As is usual with those who are super-successful, Pavarotti has the Super Success Aspect: Jupiter enhances Pluto. His natal chart also has a planetary eclipse of Neptune and Venus. Neptune rules artistic talent. In Pavarotti's case, this eclipse means financial success stemming from artistic talent.

SUPER CHART 24: Connie Chung

Qualification: Female anchorperson on the CBS network; winner of two Emmys

Super Aspects: Jupiter trine Uranus; Uranus parallel Pluto

Planetary eclipses: Mars and Neptune; Mars and Venus

Planetary synchronization: Mars, Neptune, and Mercury in the longitudes

Born just one day after President Clinton, Connie Chung's Super Fame Aspect is the key to the strength of her birth chart. This aspect helps her to achieve great success in communicating to the masses, which is exactly what an anchorperson is supposed to do. Her two planetary eclipses provide her with enormous reserves of energy. The three-planet synchronization of Mars, Neptune, and Mercury provide great mental stamina and give her artistry and talent (Neptune) in the way she communicates (Mercury).

SUPER CHART 25: Cindy Crawford

Qualification: According to *Forbes Magazine,* she is the highest-paid model in the world.

Super Aspect: Uranus conjunct Pluto

Once in a while, we encounter a birth chart that does not seem to entirely fit the person. Cindy Crawford has only one Super Aspect. But closer examination of her birth chart helps to fill in some of the missing pieces. Cindy Crawford has a planetary synchronization of Jupiter, Uranus, Neptune, and Pluto. Included in this configuration is a bidirectional quincunx of Jupiter applying to Neptune, which we have said in chapter 8 is very powerful and the equivalent of a Super Aspect. The synchronization itself provides success (Jupiter) in the business (Pluto) of modeling (Uranus) and talent (Neptune).

There you have it. Between the birth charts in chapter 5 and the ones in this chapter, we have examined the birth charts of some of the most famous men and women in the world. They all have at least two Super Aspects. If you think we left any out, feel free to check out their birth charts, also. Chances are extraordinarily high that super-successful and famous people have Super Aspects.

Super chart 1: March 29, 1943
Birth date of Prime Minister John Major

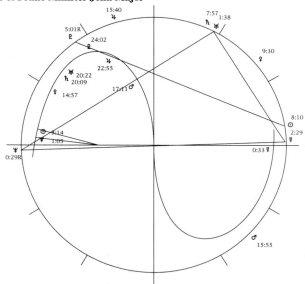

Super chart 2: April 3, 1930
Birth date of Helmut Kohl

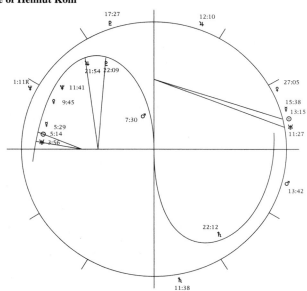

Super chart 3: August 19, 1946
Birth date of President Clinton

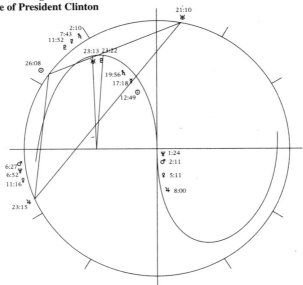

Super chart 4: October 26, 1948
Birth date of Hillary Clinton

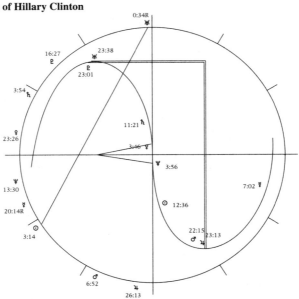

Super chart 5: May 18, 1920
Birth date of Pope John Paul II

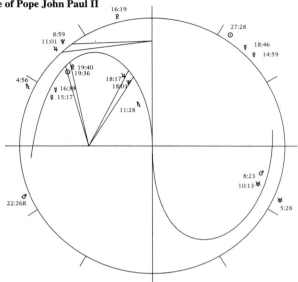

Super chart 6: November 12, 1929
Birth date of Princess Grace Kelly

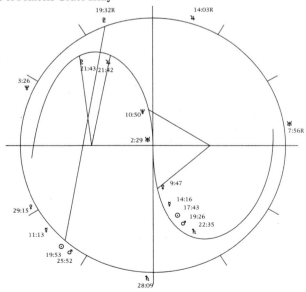

Super chart 7: April 21, 1926
Birth date of Queen Elizabeth II

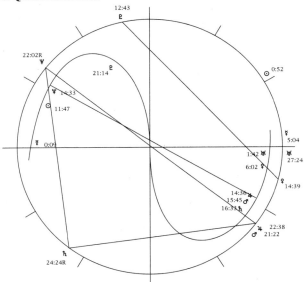

Super chart 8: July 1, 1961
Birth date of Princess Diana of Wales

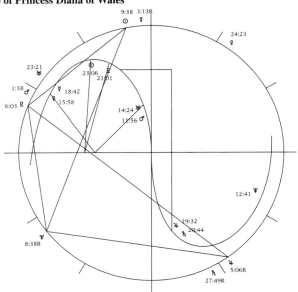

Super chart 9: July 12, 1937
Birth date of Bill Cosby

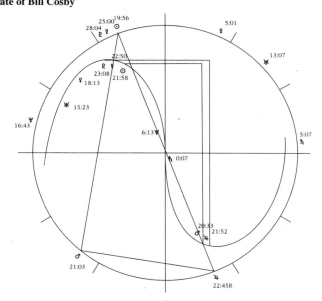

Super chart 10: January 29, 1954
Birth date of Oprah Winfrey

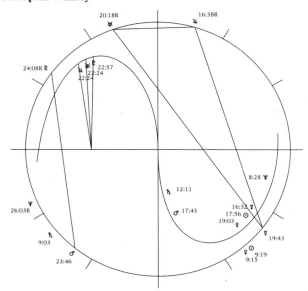

Super chart 11: July 26, 1943
Birth date of Mick Jagger

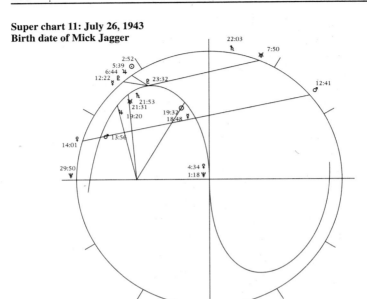

Super chart 12: January 8, 1935
Birth date of Elvis Presley

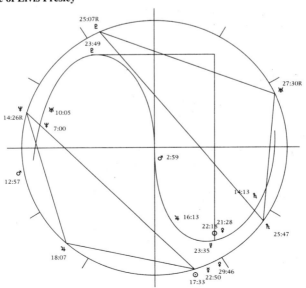

Super chart 13: January 29, 1945
Birth date of Rod Stewart

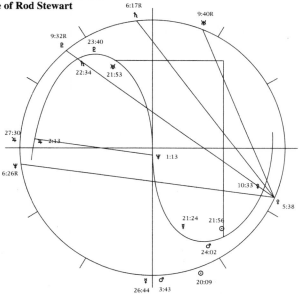

Super chart 14: December 18, 1947
Birth date of Steven Spielberg

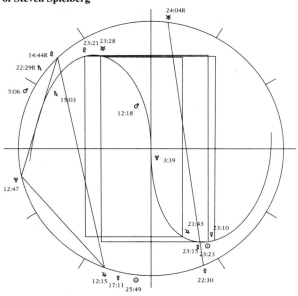

Super chart 15: December 5, 1901
Birth date of Walt Disney

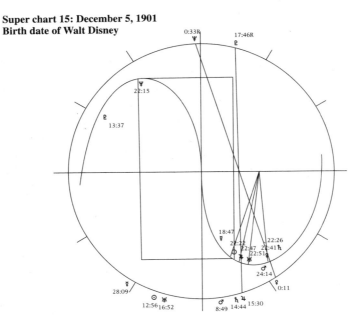

Super chart 16: October 18, 1956
Birth date of Martina Navratilova

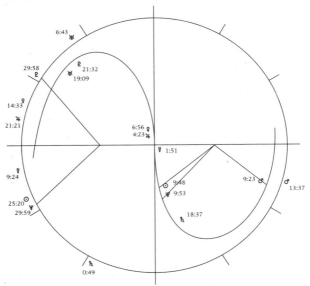

Super chart 17: December 21, 1954
Birth date of Chris Evert

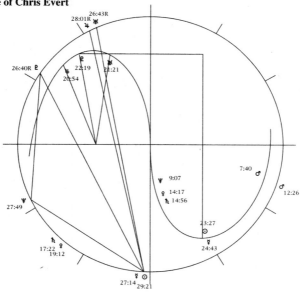

Super chart 18: September 2, 1952
Birth date of Jimmy Connors

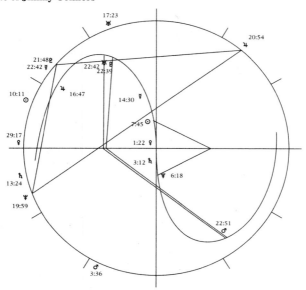

Super chart 19: March 7, 1960
Birth date of Ivan Lendl

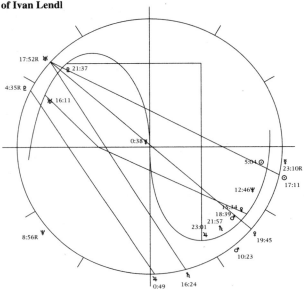

Super chart 20: September 1, 1923
Birth date of Rocky Marciano

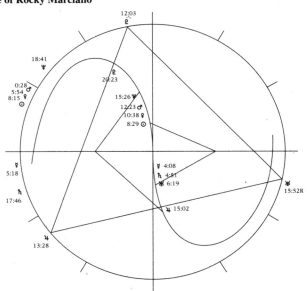

Super chart 21: August 9, 1967
Birth date of Deion Sanders

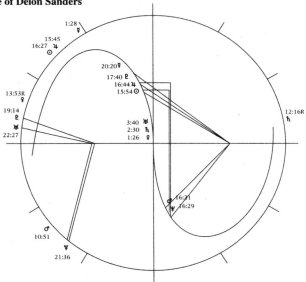

Super chart 22: March 9, 1943
Birth date of Bobby Fischer

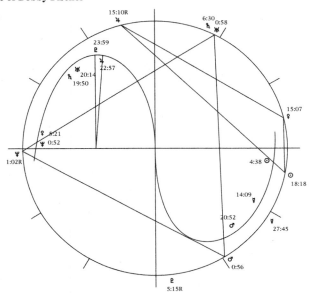

Super chart 23: October 12, 1935
Birth date of
Luciano Pavarotti

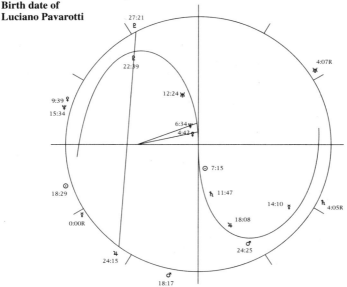

Super chart 24: August 20, 1946
Birth date of Connie Chung

Connie Chung's chart is essentially the same as President Clinton's (Super Chart 3), whose birth date is August 19, 1946.

Super chart 25: February 20, 1966
Birth date of Cindy Crawford

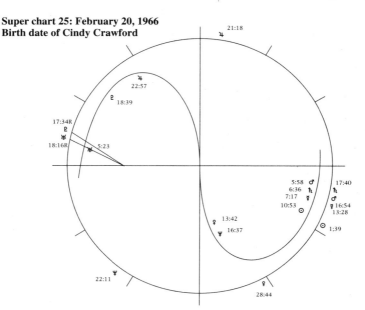

ASTROLOGY WORKS
ON GREAT ATHLETES

We are now ready for another proof of astrology. This could forever change the world of sports and the way you view them.

Great Athletes Have Mars Enhancements

For thousands of years, astrologers have associated Mars with war, aggression, and action. For at least the last several hundred years, astrologers have also associated Mars with the muscles, initiative, and the urge to take action and energy. Due to these associations, astrologers have believed that Mars represents the athlete. The key word for Mars is *energy*.

Astrologers have also believed for a couple of decades that Pluto is somehow associated with energy; Pluto has an influence on energy, but the influence is not as strong as the influence of Mars. In astrological terminology, Pluto is the SUB-RULER of energy, and Mars is the RULER.

The astrologers got this all very right.

The Magi Society conducted a study into the astrological charts of every single professional baseball and basketball player that ever played. We are not exaggerating this assertion. In addition, our society studied the birth charts of every football player and North American hockey player of recent times, as well as every superstar of all times in these sports. Every one of them. Finally, we also studied the birth charts of the best tennis players and the best golfers in history.

As a result of this extraordinarily thorough study, the Magi Society discovered that Mars is indeed the planet that rules energy. Enhancements to Mars are remarkably helpful to anyone who wishes to become a professional athlete. We also confirmed that Pluto is the sub-ruler of energy, and certain enhancements of Pluto are also very beneficial in helping the native succeed as an athlete.

In chapter 5, we had pointed out that the Mars-Pluto enhancement and the Venus-Pluto enhancement were Super Sports Champion Aspects. There is another enhancement that is probably even more powerful than these two. The aspect that provides the most energy is the Mars-Venus enhancement. We have therefore added this enhancement to the list of aspects that are Super Sports Champion Enhancements.

Here are some of the best athletes in the recent history of professional sports in America. They all have at least one Super Sports Champion's Aspect, usually the Venus enhancement of Mars. This aspect is exact about once in 25 days. Midpoint enhancements are more important to the athlete than to most people, so in the charts of these super-athletes, we will include midpoint enhancements.

CHAMPION CHART 1: Nolan Ryan

Qualification: During his career as one of the most gifted baseball pitchers of all time, he pitched seven no-hit games, a greater number than anyone else has pitched. He is the all-time leader in strikeouts and the only person to throw a no-hitter over the age of 40; he did that twice, once when he was 42, and the other time when he was 43. Nolan Ryan probably had the strongest arm of any baseball pitcher in history.

Super Aspects: Jupiter parallel the Sun; Jupiter parallel Venus; Uranus parallel Pluto; Neptune trine Sun

Midpoint enhancements: Jupiter-Pluto trine Mars and Saturn; Jupiter-Pluto contra-parallel Neptune; Jupiter-Uranus contra-parallel Neptune; Venus-Jupiter trine the Sun and Pluto

Magi Triangle of the Sun, Pluto, and Neptune within 1:31 degrees

Magi Pyramid of Jupiter, Venus, and the Sun

Planetary eclipse: Mars and the Sun (great energy)

Enhancement Aspects to Mars: Venus parallel Mars; Jupiter parallel Mars; midpoint of Jupiter-Pluto trine Mars; midpoint of Venus-Jupiter parallel Mars

Mars rules energy. You cannot have the strongest arm in baseball history unless you have enormous reservoirs of power and energy, which means that you need many enhancements to Mars. Nolan Ryan has five, including: the Mars-Sun planetary eclipse (which is what a number of other extraordinary fast-ball pitchers such as Tom Seaver and Greg Maddux have), Jupiter-Pluto midpoint trine Mars, Jupiter parallel Mars, and most important of all, Venus parallel Mars. The Venus enhancement of Mars, as we will see in these first 13 charts, is a provider of enormous amounts of power and energy. But power and energy are not all that is necessary to become the all-time leader in strikeouts. Nolan Ryan has good luck with his Jupiter parallel Sun, and his Uranus trine Mercury gives him massive (Uranus) respiratory capacity (Mercury) and virtually unparalleled endurance and longevity (Neptune trine Sun). Besides his Neptune trine to the Sun, Ryan owes his career longevity to his Jupiter parallel Mars, which signifies good fortune (Jupiter) in energy and muscles (Mars).

CHAMPION CHART 2: Sandy Koufax

Qualification: Considered by most baseball experts to be the best pitcher of the modern era, he was certainly the best during the five-year period of 1962 to 1966 when he won 111 games and only lost 34, the best record ever compiled over a four-year period by any pitcher that ever played baseball. Koufax was the youngest player ever elected to the Baseball Hall of Fame.

Super Aspects: Sun-Jupiter parallel; Sun-Pluto contra-parallel; Jupiter-Pluto contra-parallel; Pluto trine Venus

Midpoint enhancements: Jupiter-Uranus contra-parallel Neptune; Neptune-Uranus conjunct the Sun

Magi Pyramid of Jupiter, Pluto, and the Sun

Enhancement aspects to Mars: Venus parallel Mars; midpoint of Uranus-Pluto contra-parallel Mars; midpoint of Jupiter-Saturn contra-parallel Mars

Nolan Ryan and Sandy Koufax were both born with two very rare and powerful aspects. They both have the Sun-Jupiter parallel and the Venus-Mars parallel. The Venus-Mars parallel provided both men with the abundant energy they needed to become great baseball pitchers. It also provided the power they needed to be dominating and overpowering fast-ball pitchers. However, unlike Ryan, Koufax did not have sufficient enhancements to or by Neptune, the planet of longevity. Perhaps this is the reason that Koufax could not fight off traumatic arthritis in his pitching arm.

CHAMPION CHART 3: Warren Spahn

Qualification: Won more games than any other left-handed baseball pitcher; he also won more games than any pitcher born in this century. Spahn won 20-plus games in 13 seasons and led his league in strikeouts for four consecutive years.

Super Aspects: Jupiter contra-parallel Uranus; Uranus trine Pluto; Neptune parallel Venus

Magi Triangle of Jupiter, Pluto, and Uranus

Midpoint enhancements: Jupiter-Neptune parallel the Sun; Jupiter-Venus parallel the Sun; Uranus-Pluto trine Jupiter; Venus-Jupiter conjunct Pluto

Planetary synchronization: Jupiter, Uranus, Neptune, and Pluto in longitudinal synch

Enhancement Aspects to Mars: Venus parallel Mars; Neptune-Pluto midpoint parallel Mars; Neptune parallel Mars; Pluto parallel Mars; Venus-Pluto midpoint parallel Mars

Like Nolan Ryan and Sandy Koufax, Warren Spahn obtained his boundless energy from Venus parallel Mars plus a number of other enhancements to Mars. Spahn's four other enhancements to Mars helped him to become the second oldest pitcher to pitch a no-hitter. Nolan Ryan was the oldest. Ryan had Neptune trine the Sun. Spahn had Neptune parallel Mars; we interpret this as long-lasting and enduring (Neptune) energy (Mars). Martina Navratilova also has this aspect. Spahn's career span was 23 years, 4 years less than Ryan, but more than 99 percent of all other pitchers. Spahn also has Jupiter-Neptune parallel the Sun, which also greatly increases a person's ability to remain physically strong because Neptune is involved as a partner with Jupiter in creating the midpoint aspect.

CHAMPION CHART 4: Mario Lemieux

Qualification: Lemieux was the only hockey player to break Wayne Gretzky's stranglehold as the most dominant player in hockey. For a few seasons, Lemieux was number one. But his career has been curtailed by Hodgkin's disease, a form of cancer.

Super Aspects: Jupiter contra-parallel Venus; Uranus conjunct Pluto; Uranus contra-parallel the Sun

Magi Triangle of Uranus, Pluto, and Neptune

Midpoint enhancements: Jupiter-Neptune contra-parallel the Sun; Jupiter-Pluto contra-parallel Venus; Jupiter-Uranus contra-parallel Neptune

Planetary eclipse: Venus and Mars (great energy)

Synchronization: Uranus, Pluto, Neptune, and Mercury within 1:29 degrees of longitude

Enhancement aspects to Mars: Venus-Mars parallel

During the 1993-1994 hockey season, only eight players scored more than a hundred points. Mario Lemieux scored over a hundred points in six straight seasons and led the league in most points scored during four of them even though Wayne Gretzky was still close to his prime. Mercury rules the reflexes, coordination, and respiratory capacity, and Lemieux's Mercury is greatly enhanced by his Uranus contra-parallel Mercury, the Uranus-Neptune midpoint conjunction to Mercury, and the Pluto-Neptune midpoint conjunction to Mercury. And once again, Lemieux is another great athlete who has the Venus-Mars parallel for abundant energy. But again, just like Koufax, Lemieux's natal chart did not have enhancements of Mars or the Sun by Neptune, the planet of longevity. Lemieux is another good example of proximity enhancement. Besides his Venus-Mars parallel only being 0:19 apart, he has Uranus-Pluto conjunction only 0:07 apart.

CHAMPION CHART 5: Magic Johnson

Qualification: One of the greatest basketball players ever, when Johnson retired, he held the all-time record for career assists and led his team to five championships.

Super Aspects: Jupiter contra-parallel Uranus; Uranus parallel the Sun

Midpoint enhancements: Jupiter-Neptune contra-parallel the Sun; Jupiter-Uranus parallel Venus; Uranus-Pluto contra-parallel Jupiter

Planetary eclipse: Uranus and the Sun (fame)

Synchronization: Uranus, Venus, and Mars within 1:09 longitudinal degrees

Enhancement aspects to Mars: Venus conjunct Mars

Magic Johnson is so gifted and his coordination so extraordinary that he is the tallest player to successfully play the guard position in basketball. When he began his professional career, the average height of all professionals at his position was about 6' 3". Magic Johnson is six inches taller. Like Mario Lemieux, Magic has Uranus enhancement of Mercury, and also like Lemieux, Magic has declinational synchronization of the Sun, Uranus, and Mercury. And, as is the case with Lemieux, Koufax, Spahn, and Ryan, Magic has Venus enhancement of Mars for abundant energy.

CHAMPION CHART 6: Willie Mays

Qualification: In the eyes of many experts, Mays was the greatest baseball player (non-pitcher) of all time. His 660 career home runs ranks third in the all-time rankings. But he not only had the power to hit home runs, he also had the speed to lead the league in stolen bases over four consecutive seasons. There is little question that he was the best defensive outfielder ever to play the game. He won 11 consecutive gold gloves as best defensive center fielder.

Super Aspects: Jupiter parallel Pluto; Jupiter conjunct Pluto

Magi Triangle of Jupiter, Uranus, and the Sun

Midpoint enhancements: Jupiter-Neptune parallel to the Sun; Neptune-Pluto parallel to the Sun

Planetary eclipses: Jupiter and Pluto; Venus and Uranus

Enhancement aspects to Mars: Venus trine Mars (boundless energy)

Athletes the likes of Willie Mays come along once in a lifetime; the astrological key to his success was the Jupiter-Pluto planetary eclipse, which also occurs once in a lifetime. It means that Willie Mays was born with two Super Success Aspects, like Steven Spielberg. Mays got his energy in the same way that Ryan, Koufax, Lemieux, and Magic Johnson did: the Venus enhancement of Mars. Venus was trine Mars when Mays was born. All five great athletes had very tight enhancements of Venus to Mars; the widest one was only 0:20 degree apart. This occurs less than once in 70 days. All five great athletes also have enhancements to Mercury. Magic, Lemieux, and Ryan have Mercury enhanced by Uranus. Mays and Koufax have Neptune enhancement of Mercury.

CHAMPION CHART 7: Joe DiMaggio

Qualification: Voted best living baseball player, DiMaggio hit over .300 during 11 seasons and drove in over 100 runs in each of nine seasons. Joe probably holds the only baseball record considered untouchable; he had at least one base hit in 56 consecutive games. DiMaggio led the Yankees to 10 championships.

Super Aspects: Jupiter parallel Uranus; Uranus parallel the Sun; Jupiter contra-parallel Pluto; Neptune trine the Sun

Magi Triangle of Pluto, Neptune, and the Sun

Magi Pyramid of Jupiter, Pluto, and Uranus

Midpoint enhancements: Jupiter-Uranus contra-parallel Pluto; Neptune-Pluto contra-parallel Uranus

Planetary eclipses: Venus and Mars (boundless energy); Venus and the Sun (beauty); Jupiter and Uranus (fame)

Planetary synchronization: the Sun, Neptune, Pluto, and Saturn in longitude; Jupiter, Neptune, Uranus, and Pluto in declination

Enhancements aspects to Mars: Venus parallel Mars; the Sun parallel Mars

Willie Mays and Joe DiMaggio are the two greatest living baseball players. They share two of the most important astrological aspects for success in sports: Jupiter enhancement of Pluto and Venus enhancement of Mars.

Astrology really works!

CHAMPION CHART 8: Greg Maddux

Qualification: As of the beginning of 1995, he has won the Cy Young award for best baseball pitcher in his league three years in a row and he is only 28 years old. Is he for real? Of course he is. Look at his chart.

Super Aspects: Uranus conjunct Pluto; Uranus contra-parallel Venus

Magi Triangle of Jupiter, the Sun, and Neptune

Midpoint enhancements: Jupiter-Neptune conjunct Venus; Jupiter-Neptune contra-parallel Saturn; Uranus-Neptune parallel Saturn

Planetary eclipses: Mars and the Sun (great energy); Mercury and Saturn (great mental concentration)

Planetary synchronization: The Sun, Mars, Mercury, Jupiter, and Saturn all within 3:38 longitudinal degrees

Enhancement aspects to Mars: Venus parallel Mars and planetary eclipse of Mars and the Sun.

If Greg Maddux quit baseball today at the age of 28, he would still be elected to the Baseball Hall of Fame. He gets most of his energy from the Mars-Sun planetary eclipse, which is a rare astrological aspect that other great pitchers such as Nolan Ryan and Tom Seaver have. But his energy is increased by his wide Venus contra-parallel to Mars and by his five-planet synchronization, which includes Mars. His success is also aided by the proximity enhancement in his Uranus-Pluto conjunction, which is only 0:07 degrees apart. Remember, the tighter the aspect, the greater the benefit.

CHAMPION CHART 9: Bobby Orr

Qualification: Greatest defensive hockey player ever, he was defensive player of the year 8 times; the only defensive player to lead the league in scoring, which he did twice.

Super Aspects: Jupiter contra-parallel Pluto; Jupiter contra-parallel Uranus; Uranus parallel Pluto

Magi Pyramid of Jupiter, Pluto, and Uranus

Magi Triangle of Neptune, Pluto, and Venus

Midpoint enhancements: Jupiter-Pluto parallel the Sun; Jupiter-Uranus parallel the Sun; Venus-Jupiter parallel Neptune; Jupiter-Pluto trine Uranus

Enhancement aspects to Mars: Venus parallel Mars

Bobby Orr was another super-great athlete whose career was cut short. He was injured and could not return. He did not have any enhancements of Mars other than Venus parallel Mars, which is enough to give you boundless energy, but does not provide longevity. Only Neptune or Jupiter can provide that when they are in enhancement to Mars or the Sun; unless there are a lot of other enhancements. Nonetheless, the energy from Venus parallel Mars, and the good fortune from Jupiter contra-parallel to both Pluto and Uranus gave Orr what he needed long enough to be the best defensive hockey player in the history of the sport.

CHAMPION CHART 10: Bill Russell

Qualification: Most successful basketball player in history; playing center, Russell led his Boston Celtics to 11 championships; also won two NCAA championships. This gives him a total of 13 national championships. He was also the first African-American basketball coach. In spite of all the tremendous talent at the center position in basketball today, there is little chance that any of them will surpass Russell's lifetime average of 22.5 rebounds per game, even though Russell was only about 6 feet 9-1/2 inches tall.

Super Aspects: Jupiter trine the Sun; Jupiter parallel Venus; Jupiter contra-parallel Neptune; Jupiter contra-parallel Uranus

Magi Pyramid of Jupiter, Uranus, and Neptune

Multiple Magi Triangle of Jupiter, Pluto, Uranus, and the Sun

Midpoint enhancements: Jupiter-Uranus conjunct Pluto; Jupiter-Pluto conjunct Mars; Jupiter-Pluto parallel to both Uranus and Neptune

Planetary eclipse: Mars and Mercury (energization of mind and respiration)

Planetary synchronization: The Sun, Jupiter, Uranus, and Pluto in the longitudes; Jupiter, Venus, Uranus, Neptune, Mars, and Mercury in the declinations

Enhancement aspects to Mars: Venus parallel Mars; Uranus contra-parallel Mars; midpoint of Jupiter-Pluto conjunct Mars

How many athletes ever win 13 championships? We cannot think of anyone besides Bill Russell, can you? The great thing is that it all makes perfect astrological sense. Russell has more Super Aspects by Jupiter and Venus than any athlete the Magi Society has studied; and we have studied every successful American athlete. Jupiter is the provider of good fortune and success; in other words, it wins championships. Venus, the lesser benefic, provides Russell with five more enhancements. Venus enhances Jupiter, Mercury, Mars, Uranus, and Neptune, all in the declinations. Russell has a total of ten enhancements by Jupiter or Venus. That is why he won more championships than anyone else. He received his athletic ability from the Venus parallel Mars, Uranus contra-parallel Mars, planetary eclipse of Mars and Mercury, and the incredible planetary synchronization in the longitudes and the declinations. Someone like Bill Russell comes along less than once in a lifetime.

CHAMPION CHART 11: Joe Montana

Qualification: Rated football's best quarterback ever, he is number one in efficiency rating and tied with Terry Bradshaw for Super Bowls won (four each). Led the San Francisco 49ers to four championships and was the Super Bowl Most Valuable Player three times, which is more than any other player. Also led Notre Dame to a national championship.

Super Aspects: Jupiter conjunct Pluto; Pluto parallel the Sun, Pluto parallel Venus

Magi Pyramid of Pluto, the Sun, and Venus

Magi Triangle of Jupiter, Pluto, and Neptune

Midpoint enhancements: Jupiter-Pluto contra-parallel Saturn; Jupiter-Uranus contra-parallel Saturn; Venus-Pluto parallel the Sun; Jupiter-Venus trine Mercury and Uranus; Jupiter-Neptune trine Saturn

Planetary synchronization: Jupiter, Pluto, Neptune, and Saturn within 2:12 degrees of longitude. Pluto, the Sun, and Venus within 0:51 degrees declination

Enhancement aspects to Mars: Venus trine Mars; Jupiter contra-parallel Mars

We saw Montana's chart in chapter 5, but since he has the Venus-Mars enhancement, his natal chart is also included in this chapter. Montana has had to come back from a number of injuries. When you are the superstar quarterback, your opponents are not averse to hitting you as hard as they can, and injuries will occur. Montana's Jupiter enhancement of Mars has both protected him from career-ending injuries and helped him to heal when he has been injured. He has the Super Success Aspect and two of the best aspects of athletic ability: Venus enhancement of Mars, and Pluto enhancement of Venus. Uranus is sextile to Mercury, providing him with massive (Uranus) respiratory capacity (Mercury) and great reflexes (also Mercury). But what gave him the ability to be the number-one quarterback are his planetary synchronizations in both the longitudes and the declinations.

Montana's Venus-Mars enhancement is wider than that of any other athlete in this chapter. But he also has the Venus-Pluto enhancement, which we learned in chapter 5 is another key aspect of athletic ability. All five of the superstar basketball players who started for Dream Team USA have this aspect. So Montana has both of these great aspects of energy.

CHAMPION CHART 12: Franco Harris

Qualification: Football running back for the most Super Bowl winning teams; holds the Super Bowl record for most rushing yards gained

Super Aspects: Uranus parallel Pluto; Jupiter parallel Venus; and Sun-Neptune parallel.

Magi Triangle of Pluto, Neptune, and the Sun

Midpoint enhancements: Neptune-Pluto conjunct the Sun; Venus-Jupiter parallel Mercury; Jupiter-Uranus contra-parallel the Sun and Neptune; Jupiter-Pluto contra-parallel the Sun and Neptune

Planetary synchronization: The Sun, Pluto, Saturn, and Neptune in the longitudes; Jupiter, Venus, and Mercury in the declinations

Enhancement aspects to Mars: Venus trine Mars

Franco Harris obtained his energy from Venus trine Mars. Although it was the only enhancement to Mars that he had, he had a lasting career because Neptune paralleled his Sun, and he had powerful synchronization of the important planets in both the longitudes and the declinations. When Franco's team, the Pittsburgh Steelers, were in trouble, they could count on him if they decided to give him the football, which they did a lot.

CHAMPION CHART 13: Emmitt Smith

Qualification: Most successful running back who is actively playing, he has won two Super Bowls and has only played six seasons

Super Aspects: Jupiter trine the Sun; Pluto trine the Sun; Pluto parallel the Sun; Neptune contra-parallel the Sun

Magi Pyramid of Pluto, Neptune, and the Sun

Multiple Magi Triangles of Jupiter, Pluto, Neptune, and the Sun

Midpoint enhancements: Jupiter-Pluto trine the Sun

Planetary synchronization: The Sun, Jupiter, Pluto, and Neptune in the longitudes; the Sun, Pluto and Neptune in the declinations

Enhancements of Mars: Venus trine Mars; Mars contra-parallel Mercury

Smith has Neptune enhancement of the Sun (from contra-parallel), so he recovers from injuries faster and better than 95 percent of the population. He was badly injured the game before the Super Bowl of 1994 but still played and won the Most Valuable Player award for that Super Bowl. This is astrologically understandable because his Venus trine Mars and Mars parallel Mercury give him great athletic ability; his Jupiter trine Sun provides him good fortune, and the Pluto-Sun enhancement gives him recognition. He has a Magi Bi-level Enhancement of the Sun and Pluto.

Enhancement by Extreme Declination

There are quite a number of other great athletes who have the Venus-Mars enhancement. But we think we have proven our point. The Venus-Mars enhancement is to athletes what the Jupiter-Pluto enhancement is to financial success. It does not guarantee the native that he or she will become a championship-caliber athlete, but it greatly improves the chances for extraordinary success in sports.

To continue our proof that Mars symbolizes and rules energy and power, we introduce another new concept in astrology involving the declinations. We will name it ENHANCEMENT BY EXTREME DECLINATION, or EXDEK. As we examined the charts of the most successful athletes, we noticed that there were significantly more natal charts with Mars at very extreme degrees of declination, on either side of the celestial equator. By this we mean that Mars was in a greater degree of declination than its normal range. Normally, in a declinational cycle, Mars reaches its peak declination at 24 to 25 degrees. During some cycles, the peak is less than 24 degrees. In one cycle this century, Mars reached 28:22 degrees. It was over 28:20 degrees for only 30 days since the start of professional football, or one in 600 days—obviously a very rare astrological event. The last time this occurred was in 1993; before that it was 1954. Within 0:03 degrees of the absolute high that Mars made in 1954, Walter Payton was born.

CHAMPION CHART 14: Walter Payton

Qualification: All-time leader in yards gained rushing. He also holds the all-time record in five other categories for rushing, including most yards gained in one game: 275. In terms of rushing yards, Walter Payton is number one and holds six records.

Super Aspects: Jupiter parallel Pluto; Jupiter parallel Uranus; Uranus parallel Pluto

Magi Pyramid of Jupiter, Pluto, and Uranus

Magi Triangle of Uranus, Pluto, and Neptune

Midpoint enhancements: Jupiter-Neptune parallel Venus

Planetary eclipse: Jupiter and Mercury (abundant respiratory capacity and blessed reflexes)

Planetary synchronization: Uranus, Neptune, Pluto, and Mars in the longitudes; Jupiter, Pluto, and Uranus in the declinations

Enhancements to Mars: Pluto trine Mars; super-enhancement of Mars by EXDEK

Any enhancement to Mars provides energy, and Pluto enhancement of Mars is one of the strongest enhancements to Mars. But one of the astrological keys to Payton's energy and power that helped him to become the all-time record holder in six categories of rushing in football is Mars at declination of 28:20 degrees, because the more extreme the declination of Mars, or any other planet, the stronger the benefits from the planet to the native. There is no need for an enhancement by a different planet. The benefits of the planet are improved just because the declination is so extreme, which is why we call this type of enhancement "enhancement by declinational extreme," or EXDEK.

To be more certain that EXDEK works, we need to find more super-athletes with EXDEK of Mars. After all, it could be argued with Payton that the Pluto trine Mars, along with three Super Aspects and planetary synchronization, are enough to have given him his athletic prowess.

From the year that Payton was born in 1954, until 1986, Mars was never over 27 degrees declination except for 30 days in early 1961. If we find some super-athletes born during those days, it would go a long way to helping us prove EXDEK works. How about Wayne Gretzky?

CHAMPION CHART 15: Wayne Gretzky

Qualification: Gretzky is the most dominant player in the history of professional hockey; he is the all-time scoring leader in all three categories: goals, assists, and points; he is also the all-time single-season scoring leader in all three categories; he was Most Valuable Player nine times. Gretzky scores!

Super Aspects: Jupiter contra-parallel Pluto

Midpoint enhancements: Jupiter-Uranus trine Pluto; Uranus-Pluto contra-parallel the Sun

Planetary eclipse: Jupiter and Saturn, both aspects have Jupiter applying to Saturn and creates two Super Progressions

Planetary synchronization: Jupiter, Saturn, Venus, Mercury, and Uranus in the longitudes

Enhancements to Mars: EXDEK Super Enhancement, Mars at 27:09 degrees declination

It is unlikely that we will see any hockey player who will equal Wayne Gretzky anytime soon. Of the 13 best single-season points-per-game performances among all the players that ever played hockey, Gretzky has 9 of them. Mario Lemieux, whose natal chart we examined earlier, has the other four best, including the second best. Walter Payton and Gretzky share the EXDEK of Mars and the Jupiter enhancement of Pluto, along with strong longitudinal planetary synchronization.

Gretzky has Mars at 27:09 degrees declination. With the exception of the weeks surrounding the time he was born, and the time Walter Payton was born, Mars never reached such an extreme declination from 1940 through 1985. This means that if you were born in 1940 or later, and you were an athlete, you could not have enhancement by extreme declination of Mars to the degree that Payton and Gretzky had unless you were born near their birth dates.

Mark Messier, the great hockey player who (in 1994) captained the New York Rangers to their first Stanley Cup championship since 1940, was born just eight days before Gretzky, and his Mars was 27:13. Messier has the Sun parallel Pluto as well, but he does not have the five-planet synchronization that Gretzky has. Another astrological aspect that Gretzky has is a bi-directional quincunx of Pluto and the Sun, which we have explained is as helpful as the Pluto trine Sun.

So far, we have learned how important Venus enhancement of Mars can be to an athlete. We also know that the Venus-Pluto enhancement is very helpful to sports professionals; all five of the basketball players who represented us as starters in the 1992 Olympics (Dream Team America) have this aspect. So did Joe Montana and Sandy Koufax. The reason for this phenomenon, as we mentioned earlier in this chapter, is that Pluto is the sub-ruler of energy (Mars is the ruler). Therefore, the Venus-Pluto enhancement can provide influences very similar to those of Venus-Mars enhancements.

If Mars is the ruler of energy, and Pluto is the sub-ruler, it would follow that the enhancement of Mars and Pluto would be a very powerful force in providing boundless energy. And this is the case. Tony Dorsett, the football running back who is the third all-time leading rusher, has this aspect of Pluto-Mars enhancement. So does Lawrence Taylor, the football lineman who is considered by many experts to be the best outside linebacker to have ever played the game. Taylor retired after the 1993 season holding the record for being the all-time leader in sacks.

As we said earlier in this chapter, we will refer to each of these three enhancements as Super Sports Champion Aspects.

But does any player have all three of these enhancements? Does any player have Venus enhancement of Mars, plus Pluto enhancement of Mars, plus Venus enhancement of Pluto? Yes!

CHAMPION CHART 16: Michael Jordan

Qualification: The unstoppable offensive scoring machine of basketball, he holds the all-time record for highest career scoring average. Jordan led the league in scoring for seven consecutive seasons and was also a great defensive player who led his team to three straight championships before he retired early.

Super Aspects: Uranus contra-parallel the Sun; Venus parallel Pluto; Venus trine Pluto

Midpoint enhancements: Jupiter-Pluto trine Saturn; Venus-Jupiter conjunct Saturn; Jupiter-Pluto contra-parallel the Sun

Enhancement aspects to Mars: Venus contra-parallel Mars; Pluto parallel Mars

Michael Jordan, like all of the other super-athletes whose natal charts are presented in this book, is a confirmation of the symbolism of astrology and is also a confirmation that astrological aspects work. So strong is his chart that he has been undisputed demigod of basketball. In the final quarter of all his playoff games, whenever it was necessary, he would carry his team on his back. He was at his best in the final moments of a game, when it counted most; he was virtually indefatigable and truly a cut above just about everyone else. And his astrological chart shows why.

Super Aspects for Professional Athletes

From the standpoint of proving that astrology really works, it would be best if all of the 12 Super Aspects also helped athletes to become super-successful. Here again, the Magi Society's wish has come true. The 12 Super Aspects do work on athletes.

It appears that each of the 12 Super Aspects provides something that is very helpful to the athlete. But the Magi Society has found in its research that in addition to needing Super Aspects in their birth charts, athletes also require enhancements to Mars or Pluto in order to become a superstar athlete. Over 75 percent of superstar athletes have at least one Super Aspect and at least one enhancement to Mars or Pluto. This percentage gets higher as the qualifications for superstar status increases.

The following enhancements to Mars are Sports Champion Aspects:

- Mars-Sun enhancement;
- Mars-Mercury enhancement;
- Mars-Jupiter enhancement;
- Mars-Uranus enhancement;
- Mars-Neptune enhancement; and
- Saturn trine Mars.

The Super Sports Champion Aspects are:

- Mars-Venus enhancement;
- Mars-Pluto enhancement; and
- Venus-Pluto enhancement.

The Pluto-Sun enhancement is also a Super Sports Champion Aspect. The reason is that Pluto rules competitive sports, and Pluto is sub-ruler of energy.

Also, the Jupiter-Pluto enhancement is a Super Sports Champion Aspect. Since this is the Super Success Aspect and it works in so many professions, it makes sense that it also applies to sports, especially if you take into consideration the symbolism of the planets. Pluto rules sports because sports is competitive, and Pluto rules competition. Therefore, Jupiter enhancement of Pluto symbolizes success (Jupiter) at sports (Pluto).

And the Super Fame Aspect is also a Super Sports Champion Aspect. It makes sense that any aspect that helps someone become famous will also help athletes achieve renown. For this reason, the Jupiter-Uranus enhancement is a Super Sports Champion Aspect.

In chapter 8, we pointed out that the bidirectional quincunx of the Sun and Jupiter, or the Sun and Uranus, or the Sun and Pluto, were the equivalent of Super Aspects. These aspects are also Sports Champion Aspects. In addition, the Pluto semi-sextile of the Sun is a Sports Champion Aspect.

And finally, Mars enhancement by EXDEK is a Super Sports Champion Aspect.

So, in total, there are 17 Sports Champion Aspects, and 10 of them are Super Sports Champion Aspects. Seven of these 17 Sports Champion Aspects are also Super Aspects. They are the Pluto-Sun enhancement, the Venus-Pluto enhancement, the Jupiter-Uranus enhancement, and the Jupiter enhancement of Pluto. In addition, bidirectional quincunxes of Jupiter and the Sun, or Uranus and the Sun, or Pluto and the Sun, are the equivalent of Super Aspects. Therefore, these seven aspects can overlap from sports to other professions providing fame and fortune, and they are the most common aspects of the super-successful.

The average superstar athlete has two Super Aspects plus two Sports Champion Aspects.

Aspect Integration

Earlier in this book, we discussed the concept of aspect integration, or combining and integrating the symbolism of all important aspects in a single birth chart to produce an integrated and accurate interpretation of the chart. In this chapter, we have had 16 great examples of this.

Now, we are not trying to prove that astrology really works by merely listing a number of aspects that work. We are also proving the validity of astrology because the symbolism of astrology works. And the more good aspects a person has in his or her natal chart, the more likely it is that the person will be extraordinarily successful. The 16 superstar athletes in this chapter have a total of 48 Super Aspects. In addition, they all have the best possible enhancements to Mars. On the whole, the better the birth chart, the better the athlete.

***

FOURTH CHALLENGE TO SKEPTICS

If astrology did not work, it should be easy for skeptics to list superstar athletes who do not have any of the 17 Sports Champion Aspects. We challenge skeptics to name a greater number of superstars who *do not* than we can list superstars who *do*. However, skeptics cannot include anyone who has more than one Super Aspect. We must choose athletes who have at least one Super Aspect and at least one Sports Champion Aspect.

The fact of the matter is, the Magi Society has examined the birth charts of EVERY superstar of American sports, and we know skeptics cannot meet this challenge. We are limiting our challenge to American sports because we do not want skeptics to choose people no American has ever heard of from a country that is insignificant. The American public will know immediately who is or is not a superstar of American sports. And there are more professional athletes in America than in any other country. If the skeptics cannot meet our challenge

using athletes in American sports, they will not be able to do it elsewhere using foreign athletes either.

🪐　🪐　🪐

Champion chart 1: January 31, 1947
Birth date of Nolan Ryan

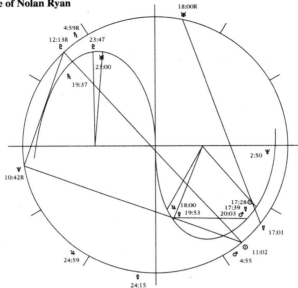

Champion chart 2: December 30, 1935
Birth date of Sandy Koufax

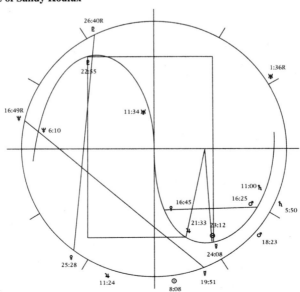

Champion chart 3: April 23, 1921
Birth date of Warren Spahn

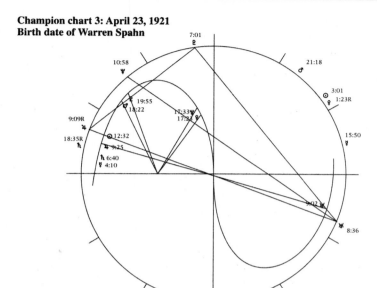

Champion chart 4: October 5, 1965
Birth date of Mario Lemieux

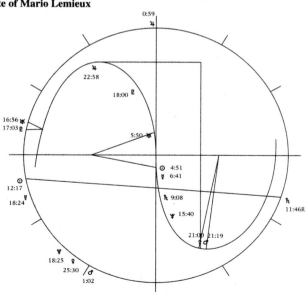

Champion chart 5: August 14, 1959
Birth date of Magic Johnson

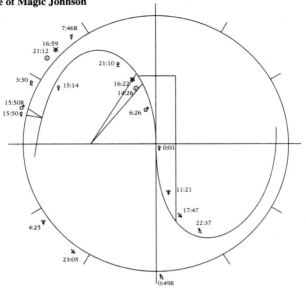

Champion chart 6: May 6, 1931
Birth date of Willie Mays

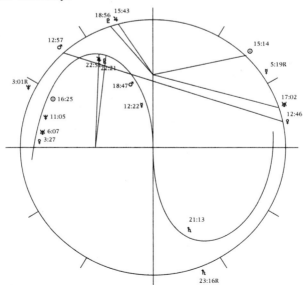

Champion chart 7: November 25, 1914
Birth date of Joe DiMaggio

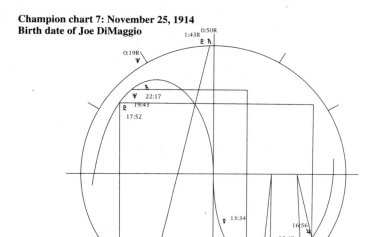

Champion chart 8: April 14, 1966
Birth date of Greg Maddux

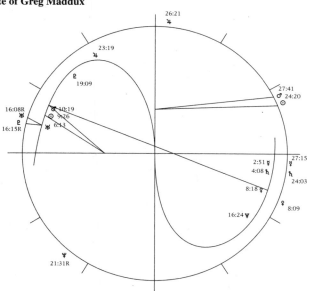

Champion chart 9: March 20, 1948
Birth date of Bobby Orr

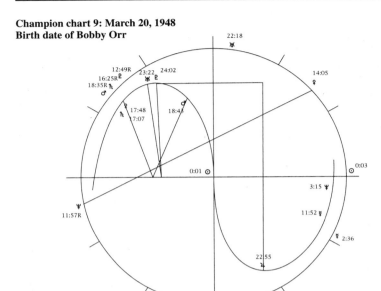

Champion chart 10: February 12, 1934
Birth date of Bill Russell

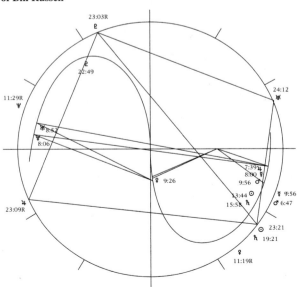

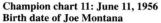

Champion chart 11: June 11, 1956
Birth date of Joe Montana

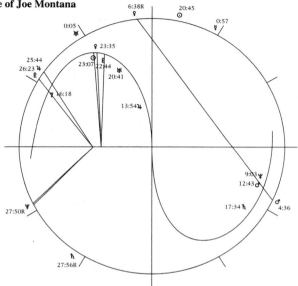

Champion chart 12: March 7, 1950
Birth date of Franco Harris

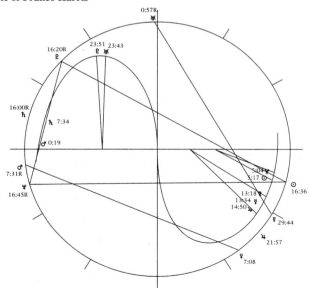

Champion chart 13: May 15, 1969
Birth date of Emmitt Smith

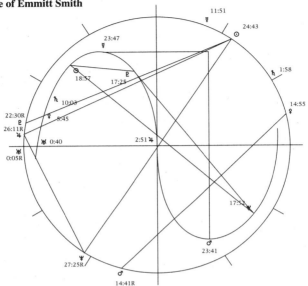

Champion chart 14: July 25, 1954
Birth date of Walter Payton

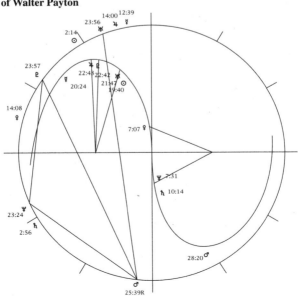

Champion chart 15: January 26, 1961
Birth date of Wayne Gretzky

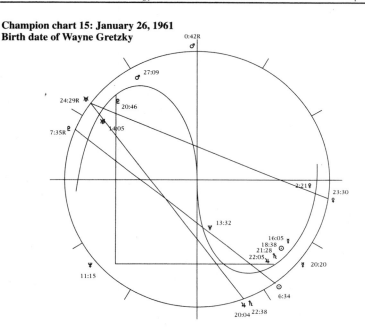

Champion chart 16: February 17, 1963
Birth date of Michael Jordan

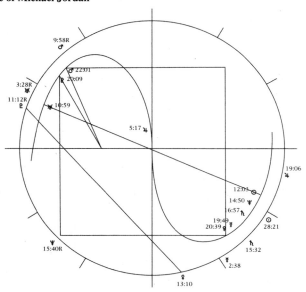

ASTROLOGY RISES! EVOLUTION FALLS!

While you have been reading parts of this book, especially the last chapter, you may have been thinking that if astrology really works and the most athletic people are those with certain astrological aspects rather than people with certain genes, how does this affect the theory of evolution? Our answer is that by proving that astrology really works, we have also proven that evolution is not the origin of all species.

The Magi Society states with complete confidence that because astrology works, the theory that evolution is the origin of species will fall. Darwinism, neo-Darwinism, punctuated equilibrium (a recent variation of neo-Darwinism), and similar evolution-based theories will all have to be discarded.

Hallelujah!

We must point out here that the general public does not realize that there is a difference between Darwinism and evolution. Evolution within a species is a scientific fact. For example, horses may grow bigger from one millennium to the next, and humans' brains may become larger over thousands of years, and we may find that we have less hair and smaller little toes as time marches on. These are examples of evolution within a species, but they are not examples of Darwinism. Instead, **they show how a species evolves within itself.** Such intra-species changes are facts. Just to confuse us, scientists call this process of gradual change within a species *evolution,* and they also refer to Darwinism as *evolution.* But Darwinism refers to changes from one species to another. Scientists would like us to believe that proof of the existence of intra-species evolution is in itself also proof of the theory of Darwinism. But the existence of intra-species evolution does not in any way prove Darwinism.

Why is this the case? Well, it's because gradual change within a species always occurs without any changes to the structure of the chromosomes and the number of genes of that species. On the other hand, Darwinism talks about processes that create new species, and such processes virtually always require changes in the number of genes, and changes in the structure of the chromosomes. The simple fact is that no one has come up with a viable theory to explain any genetic mechanism that allows for the addition or subtraction of a gene, let alone a chromosome. Genes can be replaced by another gene, or a group of genes can be rearranged. But there is no explanation, whatsoever, for how a chromosome of 300 genes can become a chromosome of 301 genes. And the mystery is far greater in trying to explain how 24 pairs of chromosomes can become 23 pairs of chromosomes. Human beings have 23 pairs. All apes, gorillas, chimpanzees, monkeys, and orangutans have 24 pairs.

It is a fact that **Darwinism has never been proven** despite monumental efforts by scientists to do so. To rephrase what we just wrote, nobody has proven that evolution is the actual reason that all new species were formed. It has never been proven that the gradual evolution that exists within a species is the cause and origin of the approximately 1.75 million different species on Earth.

The huge difference between intra-species evolution and Darwinism is something that scientists who support Darwinism do not want to publicize. They generally point to examples of extremely slow evolution within a species and extrapolate such evidence to support Darwinism. For example, scientists point to changes in the size of teeth, skulls, tails, and so on, within a species and infer that over millions of years, such changes "must have" resulted in the formation of new species. But this inference has never been proven. Therefore, Darwinism has never been proven. That is why they still call it just a theory, not a law. Literally millions of scientists have tried to prove Darwinism, and all have failed.

One reason so much effort has been expended in trying to prove Darwinism is that whoever proves it would probably receive the Nobel Prize. What do you think should be given to anyone who disproves Darwinism?

What the Magi Society has proven about astrology completely disproves the fundamental premise of Darwinism and every other theory that concludes that all species evolved from "natural selection." This is because all such theories are based on the false premise that says that the members of a species who are most fit to survive will do so, and will pass on their ability to survive to their offspring through genes, so that their offspring will also have a survivability advantage over other members of the same species. To put it another way, the fittest survive because of something in their genes, and they pass their genes on to their offspring who will also be more fit to survive than other members of the same species.

Surprise, surprise: **Astrology proves that the fittest are not those who have the best genes, but they are those who have the most favorable astrological aspects in their natal charts**. And, of course, astrological aspects cannot be passed on to offspring or to anyone else. In other words, men like Rocky Marciano, Bill Russell, and Walter Payton would have been among the fittest humans in any generation, and would have survived better than almost any other humans because they were born with several Super Aspects. But none of their children would have any greater chance of inheriting these Super Aspects than anyone else. This fact breaks the chain that is necessary for any form of Darwinism to work.

The theory of Darwinism is totally dependent on the premise that an exceptionally fit member of a species is able to transmit and pass on to its offspring whatever survivability advantage it has. Scientists today agree that the only transmission mechanism for this linkage between parent and offspring are the genes of the genetic system. Advocates of Darwinism have tied their theory so closely to genetics that the very viability of Darwinism completely depends upon their premise that survivability advantages of the well-adapted members of a species are able to be transmitted to their offspring through genes. Magi Astrology has just disproved this premise.

Now, we know that there are genetically inherited traits. But the extensive study conducted by the Magi Society unequivocally proves that the traits that are most important to survival are astrologically acquired. The variable traits that are genetically inherited are very limited. All the important survival advantages such as intelligence, luck, beauty, stamina, strength, coordination, agility, longevity, and so on, are all astrologically predictable and astrologically derived. We even have evidence that such factors as good eyesight or poor respiratory capacity and asthma are astrologically predictable, and are therefore astrologically derived.

The Magi Society does agree with scientists to the extent that the science of genetics is indeed valid. But we also know that there is no known genetic mechanism that allows for the addition or subtraction of genes or chromosomes. And we also know that there are problems with unproven but accepted genetic theories that support Darwinism. The breeding of thoroughbred racehorses is an excellent example of some the many problems with some of the presently accepted theories of genetics.

The richest men and women have been breeding thoroughbreds for over 22 generations of horses. Every breeder has one primary goal: to breed faster racehorses. They have all failed to do so. After enormous amounts of money and over 22 generations of breeding the best sires to the best mares, the record book shows that thoroughbreds do not run any faster now than they used to. Of course, every once in a while a track record is broken. But this is very rare. Presently, generally accepted theories of genetics would lead us to assume that the continual breeding of the fastest male horses (sires) to the fastest female horses (mares) would result in faster horses. This is not what has happened. The fact is that there is no general increase in the speed of the species, even though the condition and speed of the actual racetracks has improved. This is because the capability of a racehorse to win races is not only genetic, it is very much astrological. This is not to say that genes have absolutely no influence. Of course they do. But the extremes in racing prowess are astrologically influenced and astrologically predictable.

We do not want to use this book as a forum to prove this. We wish to do so by challenging skeptics to a contest.

***

FIFTH CHALLENGE TO SKEPTICS

The Magi Society invites skeptics of astrology to recruit experts on the breeding of thoroughbred racehorses to join them on their side. Afterwards, the skeptics (with the help of as many experts as they would like) and the Magi Society would each choose an equal number of two-year old horses who have not yet raced. Shall we each choose 100 horses? Let us see whose horses win the most money during the next two years. The rule is that the skeptics may not choose any horse that has any of the 17 Sports Champion Aspects, and may not choose a horse with any significant planetary synchronization involving Mars. Skeptics may choose horses that have no more than one Super Aspect. But the Super Aspect cannot be the Uranus-Sun enhancement, Jupiter-Uranus enhancement, or the Jupiter-Pluto enhancement. This is fair because most horses fit this criteria, and we do not want skeptics to secretly use astrology in order to make their selections. The Magi Society must choose only horses that have at least one Sports Champion Aspect, or horses that have more than one Super Aspect.

The Magi Society will win this challenge even though none of us are experts on thoroughbreds. But we *are* experts on astrology, and that will prove to be the winning difference.

***

Astrology, Not Genes, Controls Survivability

Every theory that concludes that evolution is the origin of the species is based on the premise that the viability of every member of any species depends primarily on the genes of that individual. So far in this book, we have proven that astrological aspects have a significant influence on whether someone is likely to be super-successful as an athlete. Obviously, those who can be great athletes are also better able to survive than the average person. The super-athletes can run faster and longer, and they are stronger than the average person. Classic Darwinism uses such traits as examples of how natural selection works. But Darwinists did not know that astrology controls such traits. This is one of the reasons that proof of astrology is disproof of Darwinism.

We are not saying that astrology controls every trait and characteristic that influences survivability. But we know that astrology controls many of the most important ones. For example, the Magi Society knows from its research that just as astrological aspects control the extremes of physical prowess, astrological aspects also control the extremes of mental prowess. By this we mean that the most intelligent persons are those with the most beneficial enhancements of Mercury, Jupiter, and the Sun. Super intelligence is astrologically derived; it is not genetically derived. Since Darwinists have placed so much emphasis on humankind's intelligence as the key to its domination over all other species, they will do everything possible to discredit this book. But everyone should make up their own minds by analyzing birth charts using Magi Astrology. Proof of astrology comes from just checking it out and applying common sense.

To go a little further, it's necessary to point out that Mercury rules communication and intelligence, and Jupiter rules good judgment and wisdom. This means that a Jupiter enhancement of Mercury is a very powerful and beneficial aspect, and individuals fortunate enough to have Jupiter-Mercury enhancements are considerably more intelligent than average. To a lesser extent, the Venus enhancement of Mercury works in the same way. However, any enhancement of Mercury by any planet will improve a person's chances of possessing the highest levels of intelligence. This includes an enhancement aspect of Mercury by Saturn. Saturn provides the ability to concentrate, and it increases a person's ability to focus on a problem; but this occurs only if the aspect by Saturn to Mercury is an enhancement aspect.

But intelligence is often evaluated and judged from a subjective viewpoint. Is Fidel Castro intelligent? What about Vladimir Lenin or

Karl Marx? Or Mao Tse-Tung? You can see how subjective the evaluation of intelligence can be. For this reason, we will not present any birth charts of "very intelligent" individuals. But we suggest that you do your own exploration and learn the truth of what we have written.

However, we do want to support what we have written in another way. Psychologists have known for a very long time that even though both parents may be geniuses, their children are usually above average in intelligence but not nearly as gifted mentally as either parent. Conversely, psychologists know that if both parents are morons, their children are usually not morons; they are usually somewhat less intelligent than the average person but more intelligent than either parent. This phenomenon has been referred to as "the rule of the return to the norm" or "regression to the norm." And although it does not in and of itself prove astrology, it does have to be regarded as an example of a disproof of Darwinism.

If Darwinism were correct, geniuses should breed higher levels of geniuses. But they do not. And if Darwinism were correct, superstar athletes should breed super-superstar athletes. But they have not.

The reason for the rule of the return to normalcy is astrology. It is astrology that creates the bell curve of normal distribution. The bell curve does not shift in one direction from generation to generation the way Darwinism predicts. This is because astrological aspects govern the shape of the bell curve, and the extremes are created by the power of astrological aspects. You cannot have extremes unless you have astrological influences. We have proven this irrefutably in the last ten chapters.

This does not mean that genes have no bearing on energy levels or intelligence levels. They do have an influence on both. But astrological aspects have a greater influence than the genes whenever anyone is at the extreme levels. There are no genes of super energy—only astrological aspects of super energy.

For these reasons, Darwinism cannot possibly be true.

There Is No Genetic Mechanism for Darwinism to Work

As we mentioned earlier, only a small percentage of Americans are aware of the fact that man has a different number of chromosomes than the chimpanzee, gorilla, and orangutan. These other primates all have 24 pairs of chromosomes; humans only have 23 pairs of chromosomes. These are facts that advocates of Darwinism do not seem to want to publicize.

What we find interesting, and somewhat amusing, is that 136 years after the publication of *The Origin of Species*, no scientist has been able to find a mechanism to prove that Darwinism is consistent with genetics. Although Darwinists point to the existence of mutations as genetic validation for their theory, mutations have never been known to cause a new species because the number of genes and chromosomes remains the same.

Darwinism and neo-Darwinism require that every species in the theoretical evolutionary chain evolve from a less complex life form, and all species would have to have been descendants of single-cell organisms that had only one pair of chromosomes with very few genes. How is it possible for 10 genes to become 10,000 if there is no mechanism for 10 genes to become 11 genes? You see, the genetic system as we know it works to maintain the status quo. Living cells duplicate themselves with nearly perfect fidelity. If there are 10 genes, it will not become 11 genes because that would be abortive, and reproduction could not be concluded successfully. There is simply no genetic mechanism that anyone is aware of that would allow for new species to originate through any form of Darwinism.

The genetic system allows for the replacement of a gene, or the transposition or inversion of a number of genes, but not the addition or subtraction of any genes. Bio-technicians and geneticists could try to add a gene to a human chromosome forever and never have such a chromosome be a party to a successful fertilization.

Modern genetic discoveries are contrary to Darwinism and neo-Darwinism. This is why you never hear about any new genetic discoveries that verify Darwinism.

This is why today, 136 years after Darwin first published his theory, Darwinists trying to prove their theory are still pointing to a few skulls and bones, or saying how similar we act to monkeys. They completely avoid discussions of genetic mechanisms. Isn't it strange how in this era of scientific achievement and quantitative analysis, evolutionists are still pointing to old bones and behavior patterns to try to prove Darwinism? This is because they have nothing better to point to.

We, of the Magi Society, like the following analogy when comparing evolution theory to reality:

For about 100 years, man has been building automobiles. Now, all automobiles have a lot in common. They all have four wheels, a steering mechanism, a motor, windows, brakes, seats, and so on. We built these automobiles using dies and molds. When we created a new model, we first designed and produced a whole new set of dies and molds for the new model. Every model of automobiles has had a different set of dies and molds.

We liken the dies and molds to chromosomes and genes. Each species has its own, and each car model has its own. When new models of cars were built, they were not built from the molds and dies of another model. This is because there is no way to change the molds and dies. There is also no way to change chromosomes and genes. Although a Rolls Royce looks like it evolved from a Ford Model T, it really did not because the tools, dies, and molds used to make the Rolls Royce are different from those used to make the Ford.

Advocates of Darwinism or neo-Darwinism like to say that man and apes look and act alike, and we evolved from apes. But the Volkswagen Beetle and the Porsche 356 looked alike. They were even designed by some of the same engineers. But there was no way you could build the Porsche with the Volkswagen's tools and dies. The similarities between the two cars is not due to one having evolved from the other in the Darwinian sense, but because there are not too many different ways to build a car. In the same vein, the similarities between man and ape do not exist because one evolved from the other. Since there are 1.75 million different species on Earth, you are bound to have similarities. But there is also no way you can get a human being out of the chromosomes and genes of an ape.

A History of Misleading Statements

Many scientists have made very misleading statements about evolution-related information. For example, they have been claiming that the "genetic material" of apes and humans is 99 percent identical. This statement is confusing at best. We do not want to write a chapter on biochemistry. Suffice it to say that scientists are not telling us the whole story when they make such statements. It is based on their unproven belief that almost all of the material that makes up a chromosome is not "genetic material." But the fact is that the shape, length, and appearance of a human's chromosomes are so different from those of any of our supposed ancestors', that such a statement has to be regarded as absurd and purposely misleading.

In fact, supporters of Darwinism have had an undeniable history of misleading the public about the fact that Darwinism has never been proven. For example, when Darwinists were unable to provide the "missing link" between man and ape, some Englishmen in 1911–1912 simply perpetrated a fraud and claimed that they had found a skull of the missing link, and called it "Piltdown Man." Evolutionists hailed this fake skull as proof of Darwinism. This fake skull also helped supporters of Darwinism overcome their critics. It was not until 1953 that it was revealed that the skull was a hoax. By that time, anthropologists believed they had better fossil evidence of ancestral man. We do not agree. Even to this day, there are so few fossils of ancestral man that all such fossils ever found can be fit into a car. In fact, all such fossils will fit into just the *trunk* of a car. Compare that to the enormous number of fossils of dinosaurs that lived 100 million years earlier, and one has to wonder if a few fossils mean anything at all—especially since there is a clear history of mistakes in the analysis of such fossils. Another example of such mistakes is that in 1932, the jaw of an orangutan was mistakenly claimed to be that of ancestral man. It took the usual decades before the mistake was "discovered."

Until the early 1970s, anthropologists and paleontologists had consciously misled the public into believing that the fossil record contained ample evidence that supports Darwinism. In point of fact, the exact opposite was and still is true. Even though there are about a quarter million different species of fossil life forms known today, there is no real evidence of transitional forms between major groups of animal life. Nearly always, there are no links whatsoever. In a very few instances, there exists a particular fossil that some say is a link, but other paleontologists disagree. In other words, the fossil record disproves Darwinism. But paleontologists actually kept this fact from the public.

There was no publicity about the fact that fossil links were missing until two American paleontologists proposed a new theory of evolution in the early 1970s, called "punctuated equilibrium." This theory proposes that new species are formed quickly rather than gradually, the way Darwinism claims. If new species are formed quickly, there would be no transitional forms. The punctuated equilibrium theory is designed to overcome the fact that the fossil record has no links. To support the new theory, the paleontologists pointed to the fact that the fossil record had no transitional forms. But what the theory really did was to make more people aware of the absence of transitional forms in the fossil record, and realize that paleontologists had misled the public.

This is an example of the tyranny of science. It highlights one of the most egregious problems confronting the public in the search for the truth. Many scientists will be less than truthful when dealing with evolution or astrology. Even worse, when it comes to scientific evidence, they want to be in complete control of the choosing and testing of the samples. In other words, they want to be the prosecutor, the judge, and the defense attorney. And no one outside of their own circle is allowed to evaluate or criticize their conclusions. The public should not accept this. People with Ph.D.'s who have based their whole lives on Darwinism are not going to change by themselves. If ever confronted with the choice of accepting that they have been wrong their whole lives, or attacking what is actually true, almost all will believe that the truth is not true.

Fortunately, we now know better.

Status of Present Theories of Evolution

The general public is not aware of the fact that since the early 1970s, scientists have begun to seriously question the gradualism doctrine of Darwinism. One problem that Darwinism could never overcome was that evolution had to occur faster than changes in the environment; but there is a great deal of evidence that environments change faster than any conceivable form of gradual evolution. This is just one of the many reasons most scientists now believe that some kind of abrupt changes to species must be part of the evolution process. A number of new theories espousing abrupt evolutionary change have been proposed. The absence of transitional forms in the fossil record is only one of the reasons behind these newer theories. There are other facts that are contrary to Darwinism, which are forcing a rewrite of evolution theory. Chief among these is the fact that Darwinism has never been able to satisfactorily explain how complex organs could have evolved gradually.

Darwin himself was so concerned about the "complex organ" that he admitted in *The Origin of Species* that his theory would "absolutely break down" if it could be demonstrated that any existing complex organ "could not possibly have been formed by numerous successive slight modifications." Darwin was right in this regard. His theory does break down because there are many complex organs that could not have possibly evolved slowly.

The complex organ that Darwin himself seems to have been most worried about was the eye. The eye is so complex, and all its parts so interactive and interrelated that it is inconceivable that it could have developed one step at a time. In the eye, the lens, the pupil, the tear glands, and muscles, the retina, and light-sensitive rods and cones, as well as the transmitting nerves to the brain, all have to work together perfectly or the eye will not function at all. It is impossible that each evolved separately and gradually. But this is exactly what Darwinism proposes.

If Darwin was worried about trying to explain the eye, think about how worried he would be if he were alive now and knew about the complexity and perfection of organs and systems he had no knowledge of in his time (such as the immune system). It is the existence and complexity of such systems and organs that have forced many scientists to accept the fact that gradual evolution cannot explain the observed facts. But no one has been able to propose any theory that can reasonably account for the evolutionary development of such bodily functions and organs. So at the present time, there really is no scientific theory that successfully explains the presence of so many life forms with their complex and near-perfect organs and biological systems. But scientists do not want to admit this fact. They continue to cling to some form of Darwinism, even though they admit that the gradualism principle of Darwinism is now unlikely to be valid.

Why Astrology Is a Benevolent Design

Astrology is the great equalizer. It gives every parent a chance to have an exceptionally gifted child. We believe that this is a wonderful blessing from Divine Providence. Imagine what a horrible world it would be if Darwinism really worked. No underprivileged family would ever have a chance of bearing someone such as Michael Jordan, Bill Cosby, Bill Gates, and so on. It would not be possible because if Darwinism were valid, the children of such families would have the same disadvantageous genes that their parents had and would have to follow their parents' footsteps into failure. If Darwinism worked, children of the super-rich and super-successful would almost all become super-successful themselves because they would not only have the advantages of their parents' supposed super genes, but they would also have the help of their parents' influence and money. Such a world would be a horrible one with no hope for the poor and deprived. But, thank God it is not the case!

Through the miracle of astrology, which we believe is designed by Divine Providence, the poor have just as good a chance of having an exceptionally gifted child as the rich. And this has always been the case throughout history. This is one reason why the power of astrology is a great gift from Providence.

The Existence of God Is More Probable than That of Human Beings

Most scientists believe that human beings evolved by chance. They say that in the infinity of time, and with literally billions of galaxies, each having hundreds of millions of stars, the evolution of man is a certainty. There are enough stars, they say, and there is enough time for humans to have evolved by chance.

In fact, given enough time and enough stars, these scientists can readily accept the evolution of anything—anything, that is, except the evolution of something like God. God is the one thing that these scientists cannot conceive could ever evolve or exist. Yet the existence of humans is much less likely than that of God because humans are much less survivable than almost anything else. We get sick too easily, need clean water too regularly, bleed and die too readily, and we are even crazy enough to kill each other. Our babies are so unfit to survive that we have to nurture them with constant attention for a dozen years before they can truly survive on their own. Pregnant women are significantly incapacitated during a large part of pregnancy and are much too vulnerable. And the process of childbirth is dangerous and painful. Are all of these characteristics those of the most highly survivable species?

The evolution of humans is less likely than the evolution of God. In fact, if evolution does work, then God must have evolved long before humans did. God, or a life force being who does not need food or water, does not get sick, does not die, and does not bleed or need shelter, is perfectly evolved. Once God exists, It is forever. If humans exist, they could still perish forever for any number of reasons. So if scientists think that humans evolved, why not also God? If Darwinism actually worked, God would have been the first to evolve. The fact is that many scientists do not want there to be a power greater than their own; they do not want God to exist. This is the real reason they do not acknowledge the existence of God.

The Earth Was Designed to Benefit Humans

Humans owe their existence to the beneficence of Divine Providence and bountiful Earth, which the Magi Society believes is designed by Providence. For example, humans could not have survived without trees, which provide us shade from the Sun, recycle our carbon dioxide into oxygen, allow us to have fire, the wheel, tools, boats, spears and arrows for hunting, and a myriad of other useful things we have come to take for granted (such as paper). This Earth also provides us with wheat and rice and other grains that are, miraculously, storable, and that do not perish or degrade until we cook them, so long as they do not get wet. Could we have survived without such nonperishable foods? We believe that trees and grains were provided to humans as gifts from Providence.

In this world, we have been provided with everything we have ever needed for advancement. For example, rubber comes from trees; we could not harness electricity without rubber for insulating the electrical wires. Glass comes from sand and the use of fire; we could not have had light bulbs without glass. And water! Not only is it absolutely necessary for any form of life on Earth, water also puts out fires, allows us to wash things, and is a necessity in so many other areas of life, from the making of paper to cooling our automobiles. Can you imagine a world where we could not wash ourselves or wash our food? It must be a benevolent design that our need for enormous amounts of clean water is fulfilled automatically by water's own evaporation, condensation, and natural property of falling back down to the ground in the form of clean, drinkable rain. If the Earth were not just the right temperature, and if the air on Earth were not just the right density, this cycle of water to vapor to clouds back to water would not exist. And neither would life.

So much of what we find naturally on Earth has never been improved upon by human beings. Cotton, wool, silk, and leather are all better than any synthetics. And they can all be recycled.

We bring all this up to make one simple point: there is an enormous amount of evidence for Providence. Atheists and agnostics not only do not believe in this evidence, they do not even acknowledge its existence. But it is not because there is no evidence of Providence. Rather, it is because they do not want Providence to exist because they do not want there to be a power greater than themselves. Their beliefs are steeped in the enormity of their own egos as opposed to the observed facts of this world, so they refuse to see. And this is the main reason that scientists prefer to believe in evolution as the origin of species.

☄   ☄   ☄

ASTROLOGY IS AN ALLY OF RELIGION

Astrology is definitely an ally of religion. In particular, astrology is an ally of Judaism and Christianity.

In the Old Testament, the Book of Numbers predicted that a Messiah would be born, and the sign for the Messiah is a Star; God would let man know the Messiah was here by the appearance of a star. The Gospel of Matthew clearly states that wise men (Magi) came from the east to Jerusalem seeking the newborn Messiah because they had seen his star in the east. Christian tradition has given a name to the star that the wise men saw. It is called the Star of Bethlehem.

The simple fact of the matter is, both the Old Testament and the New Testament contain many references to astrology. But unfortunately, interpretation of these references varies greatly. We cannot say that we are experts on Biblical interpretation. But in our opinion, there is a great deal of evidence that at least some of the original writers of the Bible were believers in astrology; therefore; there is no valid reason to believe that astrology is condemned by God. To the contrary, the Bible specifically says that God uses the stars to give us signs and knowledge. This is not to say that there are not some verses that could be interpreted as being against stargazing. But there are certainly more Biblical verses that approve of astrology, or tell us that the stars are messages from God, than there are verses that could be interpreted to the contrary. We believe that the verses that are somewhat negative towards astrology were in fact not meant to be so in the original language of the scriptures. They were directed not at astrologers of the Magi mold, but rather against pagan oracles and the like.

Besides the fact that astrologers from the East were the ones who foresaw the birth of Christ and they are referred to as "wise men" by Matthew, the New Testament has some unmistakable references to astrology that can only mean that the writers were very knowledgeable about it; perhaps they were even practitioners. And why should they not be practitioners if Matthew referred to the Magi, who were astrologers, as "wise men"?

We should discuss a few of the astrological references in the Bible. The first one that is very important is in the Book of Genesis. It says: "And God said, Let there be lights in the firmament of the heaven to divide the day from the night; and let them be for signs, and for seasons, and for the days and years:" (Genesis 1:14).

"Let (the lights) be for **signs**"—some scholars have told us that the actual Aramaic translation literally is "let them be for signs of things which in the ordinary course shall come to pass." Whether or not this is true, it is highly significant that the first purpose of the "lights" (planets and stars) was for "signs"; then after that, the purposes of the "lights" were for the "seasons, and for the days and years.

King David is attributed authorship of Psalm 19. We believe he was referring to astrology when he wrote "The heavens declare the glory of God....Day unto day uttereth speech, and night unto night sheweth **knowledge**." What knowledge could you possibly get at night other than knowledge derived from the stars and astrology? Especially since night "sheweth" the knowledge. The only things that are shown at night are the planets and stars.

There are 12 signs of the zodiac. Christ had 12 disciples. Twelve is the number of tribes of Israel. And 12 is a number used very often in the Bible—not 10, which is the number of fingers on our hands and a more logical number to use.

In the Book of Revelations, there is this amazing verse: "And there appeared a great wonder in heaven; a woman clothed with the Sun, and the moon under her feet, and upon her head a crown of twelve stars...and the woman fled into the wilderness, where she hath a place prepared by God, that they should feed her there a thousand two hundred and threescore days." (Revelations 12:1-6) The last phrase refers to a time period that is 1,260 days long. That is an incredibly odd number of days to refer to. It is our opinion that the author of Revelations was referring to the solar eclipse cycle of 1,260 years. Every solar eclipse repeats itself in the exact degree of the same sign every 1,260 years. The Bible often equates a day for a year, which is another astrological reference because of the "day for year" calculation of astrological progressions.

Where does the Bible say a "day for a year"? In Ezekiel 4:6. God says: "I have appointed thee each day for a year." This could be the reason why astrologers use the day for a year calculation for progressions. And it works.

There are hundreds of references to astrology in the Bible although some are obscure, except to biblical scholars. For example, "Mazzaroth" in Job 38:32, means *signs of the Zodiac*. Very few people know that. And electional astrology and the transits appear to be the background message when Ecclesiastes 3:1-8 says: "To every thing there is a season, and a time to every purpose under the heaven: A time to be born, and a time to die; a time to plant, and a time to pluck up that which is planted; A time to kill, and a time to heal; a time to break down, and a time to build up;...a time to get, and a time to lose; a time to keep and a time to cast away;...A time to love, and a time to hate; a time of war, and a time of peace." These verses seem to say that there is a correct time to do everything and if you choose the wrong time, you will not be successful. This is the rule of electional astrology (see Chapter 13).

Astrology and the transits are also the likely background when Ecclesiastes continues in chapter 9:11 with: "I returned, and saw under the Sun, that the race is not to the swift, nor the battle to the strong, neither yet bread to the wise, nor riches to men of understanding, nor yet favor to men of skill; but time and chance happeneth to them all. For man also knoweth not his time: as the fishes that are taken in an evil net..." These verses seem to say that everyone can have bad transits, and when they occur, you will not have the same abilities as when you did not have such transits; for example, if you were the swiftest runner normally, you will not be so swift when you have negative transits.

This leads us to the interesting thought that the world would be completely different if there were no fluctuations in our abilities from day to day. Martina Navratilova would never lose a tennis match, and Sandy Koufax would always pitch a shutout. Such a world would not only be boring, but it would be unfair. You would never have a chance at beating someone who was better than you. But this is not the case. We have all defeated persons who were better. And we have all been beaten at something by a person who has inferior skills. The world is much better off with these ups and downs. It gives everyone a fighting chance and keeps almost everyone on top from getting too egotistical. We all get a chance to learn from our disappointments. The Magi Society believes astrology was designed to do this. It is a wise design.

The Star of Bethlehem

Was there really a Star of Bethlehem? Skeptics say that it is totally apocryphal. However, historians and Biblical scholars have recently discovered interesting new evidence that there really could have been a star very similar to what Matthew described.

Christ's year of birth has now been calculated to be between 8 B.C. and 4 B.C. This is because Christ must have been born after the tax census of 8 B.C., and before the death of Herod in 4 B.C. We now know from records kept by Chinese astrologers that there was both a comet and a new star in 5 B.C. We have also learned that Magi astrologers paid close attention to the rare conjunctions of Saturn and Jupiter, which occurred three times in 7 B.C. These conjunctions occurred in Pisces, the sign that the Magi associated with the Hebrews. The Magi knew that Jupiter conjunction Saturn was a good event because they knew that Jupiter overpowered Saturn. The Magi would have interpreted the Jupiter-Saturn triple conjunction in Pisces as a positive occurrence for the Hebrews. Perhaps this encouraged them to be on the lookout for a new star that would be the sign for the birth of the King of the Jews. Two years later, the Magi would have seen the same new star that the Chinese astrologers recorded. When the Magi saw the new star, they could have then set out on the journey to the land of David, as written in Matthew. And it is possible that when they arrived, the comet pointed the way to Christ because the tail of the comet would create a guide as to direction and would have appeared to stand over Christ's position.

Good Transits Are the Blessings of Providence

The principles of Magi Astrology are not contrary to the Old and New Testaments. And there is evidence in the Bible that God designed astrology.

Why are there bad transits and negative progressions if astrology was designed by a Benevolent Providence? The answer lies in the nature of human beings and their needs.

Let us think about the way we teach little babies to walk. In the beginning, we need to hold them up by both arms, and we help them take tiny steps. From time to time, it is necessary for us to let go of the baby's hands and let the baby try to walk by itself or else it will neither learn as quickly nor as well. But we need to keep lifting it back up by both arms, again and again, until it eventually learns.

This is how transits and progressions work. When we have good ones, God has lifted us up by both arms. When we have bad ones, He has let go of our arms. But He is always there watching us, rooting for us, and will help us when we call out for Him, just the way that parents do who are watching their babies when they let go of their arms. That is what good and bad transits and progressions really are.

And without good and bad transits, the world would not be as pleasant to live in. Can you imagine how annoying and depressing it would be if you always lost your tennis matches to a player who is a little better than you? But this is not the case. When your transits are very good or your opponent's is a little bad, you will win. This gives you hope and encouragement to become better. And it teaches you humility and gives you a reason to work harder. The world is more enjoyable because of transits. And every once in a while, the transits get so good that you accomplish something very meaningful. But to keep you from becoming too egotistical, some bad transits will occur to keep everything in perspective as we realize that we are not as great as we thought, after all.

Transits and progressions will even create times of danger. With danger, we can learn courage. In times of struggle, we are meant to attain wisdom, learn self-sacrifice, and selfless love. And if we have learned enough, we also learn how wonderfully designed this world really is. And what a perfectly benevolent design astrology is, one that could only be created by Providence.

Astrological Knowledge Increases Our Free Will

Free will is one of the most important principles of most religions. Contrary to what skeptics claim, astrology enhances free will. To be more precise, knowledge of astrology will provide us with more free will than we have ever had before.

Prudent use of astrological knowledge provides us with an insight into the timing of when we have the best chances of success at any endeavor. Too often, people who fail at a project abandon the dream forever. The abandonment is often forced upon us due to the enormous cost of the failed project. The failure also impairs our ability to succeed in other endeavors. It may require a great deal of healing before we can embark on anything else new. This is true whether the cost of failure is financial or emotional. The fact is, any failure will reduce our free will; and one failure can restrict us from other accomplishments.

We repeat these verses from Ecclesiastes: "To every thing there is a season, and a time to every purpose under the heaven..." Knowledge of astrology and prudent use of it will increase our free will. We are not always able to accomplish what we want at the time that we most want it. But wise application of astrology can help us succeed at endeavors at the time when we are most able to succeed. And this increases our free will, because without astrology we would have failed altogether and given up.

Now, it is true that problematic transits can force us into circumstances we do not want to be in. Whenever God gives us a chance to learn and be on our own, we will never be able to do as well as when we are carried by Him. But by applying our knowledge of astrology, we will be better able to handle any difficult circumstances, and our problems will not seem as drastic, especially since we will be more prepared to deal with them.

Ecclesiastes also says "For man also knoweth not his time: as fishes that are taken in an evil net..." But prudent use of astrology will reduce the number of times we are in an evil net and will also make the net easier to get out of. And together, this judicious use of astrology gives us much more free will to accomplish what we hope for.

Astrology Points to God's Existence

Proof of astrology is proof of Providential design, and also is proof of Providence. So far in this book, we have provided some reasons why astrology is a benevolent design. In particular, astrology helps to maintain as much equality as possible in the world. Because every parent, no matter how poor or rich, has an equal chance of having a super-successful child, the world is a much better place to be.

But there are other astrological proofs of God.

An enhancement transit of Jupiter to your Sun provides good fortune and health, vitality and wisdom, and sound judgment. At the same time, in the experience of the Magi Society's founders, the positive Jupiter transit also brings the native closer to God. By this we mean that if you are usually able to believe in God, but there are times that you have some doubts, the doubts disappear when you are having a favorable transit by Jupiter (the planet that represents good judgment and wisdom). On the other hand, the doubts about God are powerful when you have a problematic transit by Saturn to your natal Sun or Jupiter! Such negative Saturn transits also increase negative attitudes and varying degrees of depression. When negative transits by Saturn to your natal Sun or Jupiter occur, you have the most doubts about God. But it is these same transits that inflict you with your worst judgment. Therefore, it makes sense that what you believe during unfavorable Saturn transits is less accurate, and what you believe during the helpful Jupiter enhancement transits is more accurate. Since a person's faith in God is greatest during positive Jupiter transits, it makes sense that all of this information gives us very strong evidence of the existence of God.

In the future, when you have one of these transits, take note of how you feel and what you believe. Make sure that such a transit is applying and within 0:45 degrees longitude or 0:20 degrees declination. You will be amazed at the difference in the way you view the world and your life during these two types of transits.

There is more astrological proof of God.

When astrology is generally accepted, scientists will be seeking to discover how it works. Are there astrological forces similar to the gravitational force or the electromagnetic force?

We would like to save scientists the trouble of looking for them. We do not believe that they will find any astrological force even though there are certainly astrological influences. Scientists will want to explain astrology's influences through their language of physics and other sciences. But astrological influences cannot ever be explained in such ways; neither can they be physically detected. The planets' positions and movements do not actually influence us actively; the planets' astrological positions are "signs" of what is actually influencing us. (Referring back to the Bible, Genesis refers to the planets and stars as "signs.") And since we believe that favorable transits are really God's gifts to us, it will not be possible to detect such gifts in a physical way.

The fact that astrology works, but is not detectable or explainable, will be the closest thing to proof of God. It is not conclusive proof. But God does not want to provide us conclusive proof of His being, because once there is proof of God, we would have less free will since we could no longer ignore Him. Preservation of our free will is very important to Him.

Science and Religion

Scientists love to say that it is necessary for science to ignore any influences of God because such influences are not able to be subjected to scientific investigation. But the Magi Society states that all the laws of physical matter are created and maintained by God. That is why there is order rather than chaos. Without Providence, there would be no order. And it is important to take this fact into consideration in scientific research because science would make monumental strides if it did. Science would also save itself a great deal of wasted effort if it took into account the fact that Providence designed the world.

For example, not too long ago, scientists thought that there were micro-organisms that would be able to survive on any substance. Any substance at all. The theory was that microbes mutate so rapidly and there were so many "zillions" of microbes, that there must be some microbes that could live off anything, including salt. The reason that salt was an important example is that scientists were looking for a way to efficiently desalinate salt water. This would help solve the water shortage problem in many areas of the world. Just throw in the microbes, and let them eat salt; when the microbes were through, you could just filter them out, and presto!—you have desalinated water. Cheap.

Guess what? There are absolutely no microbes that can live on salt. If there were, they would infest the oceans and kill off all the life in the seas. And this is exactly the reason why there are no "salt-eating" microbes: God designed this world such that there could never be microbes mutating into having the ability to live on salt, thereby threatening life in the oceans.

Now, if scientists looked at the world from the standpoint of having been benevolently designed, they would not have wasted their time and effort looking for salt-eating microbes. Also, they might have realized that Darwinism and survival of the fittest would not have been the way God would have designed the world because it would lead to the loss of the self-sacrificing qualities of humankind. Self-sacrificing people would die earlier than the selfish ones. If Darwinism worked, we would only be left with the very aggressive, selfish traits. But this is not the case. And looking at the world from the viewpoint of a benevolent design would have allowed scientists to realize that Darwinism was wrong, and scientists would have looked for the ways that God preserved the finer characteristics of humankind. One such way is astrology. If scientists had discovered and proven astrology a long time ago, that would have been quite a scientific achievement—maybe the greatest one yet!

To sum up, it pays to look for God's designs and take Him into account in scientific research.

ELECTIONAL ASTROLOGY WORKS

W e have presented what we consider to be conclusive evidence that the symbolism and aspects of astrology really work when studying the birth charts of individuals. Astrology is extremely worthwhile because it gives us the edge in knowing more about people. But it would be even better if we could use astrology to help ourselves be more successful—at work, at home, in our married lives, and so on. In the next three chapters, we will learn how to apply electional astrology to accomplish just that.

ELECTIONAL ASTROLOGY is that part of astrology dealing with choosing the most favorable times to do anything. It is invaluable for the planning of engagements and weddings; the purchase or sale of businesses, homes, and automobiles; the signing of important documents such as contracts, agreements, lawsuits and proposals; and much more. It has been our experience, and the evidence in this chapter will serve as verification, that every endeavor you commence has a birth chart, and this birth chart represents the project from start to finish. The date that is used for such birth charts is the date that you begin your endeavor. The more favorable the astrological aspects of the birth chart of the project, the more successful the project will be.

Electional Astrology Works for Business

Some excellent examples of the way in which electional astrology can work in the business world are reflected by some of America's top companies, such as the 30 corporations that comprise the Dow Jones

Industrial Average (DJIA). They were all founded on extraordinarily favorable astrological days. Every single one of them.

The birth charts of these giants of U.S. industry are the astrological charts of the days that these companies were incorporated. In order to form a corporation, it is necessary to file papers of incorporation with the Secretary of State of one of the 50 states in this country. Most companies have chosen to incorporate in the state of Delaware because of favorable laws for corporations in that state. For example, Chevron, Texaco, McDonald's, and J.P. Morgan are all incorporated in Delaware even though they conduct almost all of their business outside of that state. Each of the 50 states has its own Secretary of State, and each of them keeps very accurate records about the dates of incorporation of all the companies that are incorporated in their states, even when such dates are over a hundred years old. There can be no dispute over the accuracy of dates of incorporation.

In chapter 3, we had decided that we will only do the birth charts of the most successful entities. Just as there can be no dispute about dates of incorporation, there can also be no dispute about which are the most successful corporations, as this success can be measured easily through their earnings, as well as by the market values of the companies. These statistics are public information, with the earnings being certified by major accounting firms. For these reasons, incorporation dates are an ideal way to prove that both astrology and electional astrology work.

Since we expect astrology to work on the birth charts of corporations, we would also expect that what holds true for the birth charts of individuals such as Bill Gates, Harrison Ford, and Joe Montana will also be true for corporations. In other words, the symbolism for birth charts of corporations is expected to be consistent with the symbolism for birth charts of people. Therefore, when we are dealing with the birth charts of America's most successful corporations, we would expect strong enhancements of Pluto, because the key symbolisms of Pluto are big business and power. All successful companies would have to be able to deal in big business, and they have to be able to attain power. In fact, we would assume that the same 12

Super Aspects of enhancement that we found to be prevalent in the charts of the super-successful men and women earlier in this book will also be dominant in the charts of the 30 corporations that make up the DJIA. This turned out to be the case, so we found that astrology is just as provable using the birth charts of corporations as it was using birth charts of people and events.

In chapter 5, we listed the 30 companies that comprise the DJIA. Fourteen of them have Sun-Pluto enhancements in their birth charts. We chose 5 of these 14 companies and have provided you with their birth charts at the end of this chapter. These five companies are American Telephone and Telegraph (AT&T), Procter and Gamble, General Electric, Eastman Kodak, and Boeing. As you can see from these five examples, the Sun-Pluto enhancement is a dominant aspect in the charts of super-successful corporations. And unlike many of the birth charts in the last chapter, the Sun-Pluto declinational enhancements were not in the extreme degrees of declination. Because all five birth charts had Pluto well away from the extremes of declination, or the enhancement to Pluto was also in the longitudes, these corporations' Sun-Pluto enhancements were much rarer an occurrence. It happens only about once every 15 days. But it's statistically significant to note that 14 of the 30 companies have the Sun-Pluto enhancement.

These 30 corporations also had other enhancements to Pluto. Eleven of the 30 have the Jupiter-Pluto enhancement. The Uranus-Pluto enhancement occurred six times, and there were eight Venus-Pluto enhancements. A total of 26 of the companies had at least one of these four strongest of the Pluto enhancements. That is more than 85 percent. This is all statistically significant.

It is interesting to note that Boeing was incorporated on a day that had a Sun-Pluto planetary eclipse. This is the strongest possible aspect to the Sun for success in big business, competition, and power. It is also the rarest of all planetary eclipses involving the Sun. Using an orb of five degrees for the longitudes and an orb of three degrees for the declinations, a planetary eclipse of the Sun and Pluto occurs so rarely that it has not occurred at all since 1940; and will not occur again until 2016. It is such a powerful influence and so beneficial for corporations that, besides Boeing, there is another company in the DJIA that has it. United Technologies was incorporated just two days later than Boeing. Companies incorporated within a few days of each other are often in similar businesses. Both Boeing and United Technologies are heavily involved in air transportation. Boeing is the world leader in passenger planes, while United Technologies has a commanding position in the helicopter and jet engine field. But Boeing has the stronger aspects; in fact, Boeing is so powerful and successful as a competitor, that for many years its export of commercial aircraft accounted for over half of all the nondefense-related exports of this country. Such is the enormous power of the Sun-Pluto planetary eclipse.

Another fiercely competitive and successful exporter is Honda, the Japanese auto manufacturer. Automobile-related products account for about two-thirds of the entire trade deficit between our country and Japan. Honda is Japan's largest automobile exporter to our country, and was incorporated with Jupiter parallel Pluto and Venus conjunct Pluto. Therefore, Honda has the Super Success Aspect; it has two of the strongest Pluto enhancements. No wonder it is so successful.

At this point, we have another challenge to skeptics of astrology.

***

Sixth Challenge to Skeptics

The Magi Society knows that the most successful corporations in America have two or more Super Aspects. We challenge skeptics to find super-successful corporations without any Super Aspects in their birth charts. We will find many more super-successful corporations that have two or more Super Aspects. If skeptics do not meet this challenge, we have the right to say that astrology is proven.

***

It should be obvious by now to all of you who have always known that astrology works that it will be well worth your while to learn all you can about electional astrology. Not all of us will need to form corporations, but electional astrology works just as well on wedding dates and engagement dates, the purchase of homes and automobiles, the starting of a bank or brokerage account, beginning new jobs and getting together with someone new (like a blind date or a meeting with a prospective business associate or client). Do not let the schedule of a wedding caterer determine when you will get married. You should learn to choose your own favorable dates. Here are more examples of electional astrology.

Coronations and Countries

It is much, much easier for most people to accept that astrology works on living persons than to accept the validity of astrology when it comes to corporations. The astrology of the birth charts of individuals is substantially less metaphysical than the astrology of non-living entities, such as corporations. And that, in turn, is still easier to accept than the idea that every action has an astrological chart.

Did you ever see the movie *Alexander the Great* starring Richard Burton? Most people do not know that Aristotle was Alexander's tutor. This was the very same Aristotle that we all learned about in history class. What we did not learn in school is that he was the most respected astrologer of his time. As noted in chapter 8, Aristotle erred with respect to some of what he taught, but he was very right in many of his ideas about astrology. In the movie, there is a scene where Alexander disembarks a ship onto Asia Minor; he throws a spear into the sand and then declares in effect, "I now claim the whole of Asia, land won by the spear." Alexander the Great actually did this. He did it because Aristotle taught him that if you make such a proclamation on a very favorable astrological day, you will succeed in your declaration. In other words, Alexander the Great used electional astrology by making declarations. It is the same idea as having a birth chart for weddings. When you say "I do," and you are pronounced husband and wife, that is the time used for the birth chart of weddings. Alexander made many declarations; he also conquered more square miles per year than anyone else.

Similarly, kings and emperors used astrologers to help them choose a favorable astrological day for a coronation. You probably know that most coronations, even today, are held at noon. This is because the Sun is conjunct to the midheaven around noon, and such a conjunction is considered very favorable. The most successful coronation in history is that of William the Conqueror as King of England on noon, Christmas Day, 1066. Astrologers have generally used the chart of this coronation as the chart of the country of England. (The birth chart of this historic coronation is at the end of this chapter.) History tells us that this date for the coronation was selected by William's astrologers. This is another great example of the success of electional astrology.

After examining the birth chart of England, you can see that it looks like the chart of a super-successful corporation in that it has three of the four strongest enhancements to Pluto. It has the Sun-Pluto parallel, Uranus-Pluto parallel, and the Venus-Pluto parallel. It also has Jupiter trine Sun, which is one of the other eight Super Aspects. It is the Jupiter trine Sun that William's astrologers chose for the coronation. All told, this chart has 4 of the 12 Super Aspects.

This is such a strong chart that in spite of the fact that Europe was at war almost nonstop since that coronation, enemy armies have never set foot on British soil. Neither Napoleon nor Hitler managed to invade England. And the Spanish armada failed. Remember when we said that astrology is the science of what is nonphysical, such as good and bad luck? Well, England is very fortunate. At one time we would hear the words, "The Sun never sets on the British Empire," because it had possessions all over the world. At one time, England owned Canada, Australia, New Zealand, India, South Africa, Egypt, and other areas around the world. Even today it is fortunate. It is the only industrial country in the world that is self-sufficient in oil. This is due to its North Sea oil wells. England's birth chart is so strong that it is the second strongest chart for countries. We all know that the United States must have the strongest chart, so we have included its birth chart at the end of this chapter.

(These two last charts are the only charts in this book that are not cast for 1:00 P.M. EST. Much historical research has been done by astrologers into these charts, and they are cast for the times that make the most sense historically and astrologically. The differences in opinion among historians and astrologers about the Declaration of Independence can be two full days. However, there are no changes in the most important aspects during those two days; all of the important aspects that exist on July 2 also exist for July 3 and July 4.)

The birth chart of the Declaration of Independence is the strongest chart we have ever seen. And the United States is the strongest country in the history of the world. We won the Cold War, and the important hot wars. America has everything; our natural resources are overshadowed only by our human resources.

Whether the Declaration was on July 2, 3, or 4, 1776, that birth chart is the only one that has all four of the most powerful enhancements to Pluto. That is correct—all four. This chart has Jupiter contra-parallel Pluto; and Pluto contra-parallel to the Sun, to Venus, and to Uranus. The Jupiter-Pluto and Venus-Pluto enhancements are particularly tight and are, therefore, enhanced by proximity. In addition to the four Pluto enhancements, the U.S. chart has five of the other eight Super Aspects. It has the Sun-Jupiter parallel, Venus-Jupiter parallel, Jupiter-Uranus parallel, Uranus-Sun parallel, and the Uranus-Venus parallel. This means that the chart of the U.S. has nine of the twelve Super Aspects.

But wait—we are not finished with favorable astrological influences in this birth chart. It was also born with a Venus-Jupiter planetary eclipse, one of the most beneficial of the planetary eclipses. This means that America also has the Venus-Jupiter conjunction Super Aspect, giving it a total of ten Super Aspects. It is even possible, if the July 2 date is the correct date, that the country has the Sun-Jupiter planetary eclipse in addition to the Venus-Jupiter planetary eclipse. On top of that, the American birth chart has a Super Sports Champion's Aspect, Venus parallel Mars in virtual exact aspect and in high declination. Therefore, this aspect is enhanced by extreme declination and also by proximity enhancement. All of the above provides the country itself with boundless energy. Is it any wonder, then, that America the Beautiful is also the envy of the world?

It is widely accepted that the coronation date of King William the Conqueror was selected by astrologers. Even skeptics realize that in those days, astrologer-priests were consulted by most kings. But most skeptics will not accept that the United States is an example of the success of electional astrology. However, in our opinion, it is the best example. And we are proud to now provide proof that this country's founding fathers deferred to astrology.

We all know that Benjamin Franklin played a key role in the founding of our country. We also know that he was the publisher of *Poor Richard's Almanac*. What most Americans do not know is that *Poor Richard's Almanac* was an astrological publication. In those days, all almanacs were astrological. They were published to advise the public, particularly the farmer, on matters such as when to plant certain crops (for example, when "Mars trines Jupiter"). Almanacs also used astrology to predict the weather. For these reasons, there can be no question that Benjamin Franklin was an astrologer. We do not believe that it is possible that he presented astrological advice in his almanacs without believing in the information himself. We are sure he was a man of integrity. Besides, there is even more proof that America's Founding Fathers believed in astrology. And it is written right in the Constitution of the United States.

Our Founding Fathers established the tradition that the inaugural date of Presidents would be March 4. What does this have to do with astrology? As we have learned in this book, astrologers believe that the trine aspect, which is 120 degrees, is the best aspect. Remember that the most important days for peace have been days with Jupiter trine Sun. On March 4, the Sun is 120 degrees away from the Sun's position on July 4. This is because the Sun is the only planet that is in the same degree of longitude and declination on the same day each year, give or take a fraction of a degree. It is reasonable to assume that this country's Founding Fathers were influenced by astrology in picking March 4 for inaugurations. The March 4 inaugural date was subsequently changed through an amendment to the Constitution in this century during Franklin Delano Roosevelt's time.

The same is true regarding Election Day, which used to be November 4 until it was changed to the first Tuesday of November, unless the first Tuesday is November 1, in which case Election Day is the second Tuesday of November. America's Founding Fathers had established traditions such that the Sun's locations on Election Day and Inaugural Day would create a grand trine when added to the Sun's location on July 4, the birth date of the Declaration of Independence. This is all very interesting and also strong evidence that America's Founding Fathers used astrology and that they believed in electional astrology. But beginning more than a hundred years ago, people started to forget why Election Day and Inauguration Day were set up the way they were. So now, virtually no one knows why (except the readers of this book, of course).

Now, all of the information presented above is strong evidence that our country was founded by men and women who believed in astrology. But they did not know about the new planets. And they may not have known about the declinations. So why did they choose to sign the Declaration of Independence on the day that they did? The reasoning is simple: without the outer planets, they correctly believed that the two best aspects were Jupiter conjunct the Sun, and Jupiter conjunct Venus. In this book, we use a very tight orb of only three degrees for the aspects in the longitudes. But if you use the orb customarily employed by astrologers both then and now, the days June 29 through July 5, 1776, had both of these aspects. We believe that this is why our country's Founding Fathers chose to hold the Continental Congress at the time that they did, and why they signed the Declaration of Independence when they did.

Starting a New Job

The day that you start a job with a new company or organization will have a profound effect on whether or not you will be successful in that position. The date will also determine how far you might rise in that company or organization.

It is not easy to find out the date that the CEOs of America's top companies began their employment. But the most high-profile success story that has a verifiable starting date is that of Pope John Paul II. He was ordained on November 1, 1946. That is the date of his association, and employment, so to speak, with the Catholic Church. (The birth chart of this day is the last one in this chapter.)

The key astrological aspect of this date was the Sun-Jupiter planetary eclipse, which signifies a day of success, good fortune, peace, and Christianity. The orbs of the two conjoining aspects that make up this eclipse are so close that such days occur only once in 250 days. Add this to the fact that there was also a Uranus-Pluto parallel with proximity enhancement, and you know that any person ordained on such a day had an excellent chance of great success within the Catholic Church. Obviously, the Pope was as successful as anyone could possibly be.

Another example of success associated with an astrologically favorable starting date at a job is the presidency of Ronald Reagan. The so-called Reagan Revolution confounded and mystified Democrats. During Reagan's first term in office, his popularity was higher than that of any President before him, since such polls were taken. We attribute this fact to the birth chart of his inauguration, which is the starting date for his Presidency. It had the best possible Super Aspect for a Presidency—Uranus parallel the Sun. Uranus is the ruler of popularity and political success. Reagan's first term was popular enough so that for his second term, he won by the second biggest landslide in the history of American Presidential politics. It also helped that he was born with the Magi Pyramid of Jupiter, Pluto, and the Sun.

Before we go on to the next chapter, we want everyone to understand that we fully realize that using just two examples of starting dates for "jobs" is nowhere near enough to prove that electional astrology works on employment dates, even if they involve the Papacy and the U.S. Presidency. But as we explained in chapter 7, parts of this book are designed to teach astrology to those who wish to learn it, as opposed to serving as "proof" of astrology. This is one such part of this book.

On the other hand, we do believe that we have proven that astrology works on incorporation dates. Even though we have only been discussing 30 corporations, these *are* 30 of the most successful corporations in our country. As we explained in chapter 3, by choosing the most successful individuals or corporations, we can prove astrology without having to do hundreds of thousands of birth charts. This methodology has been perfectly acceptable to scientists for centuries although now that we have proven astrology using this method, scientists will probably declare this methodology invalid. But we know better. Do not let them fool you.

Chart 58: April 15, 1892
Birth date of General Electric

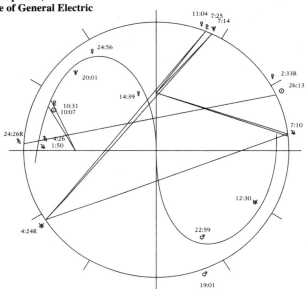

Chart 59: May 5, 1905
Birth date of Procter & Gamble

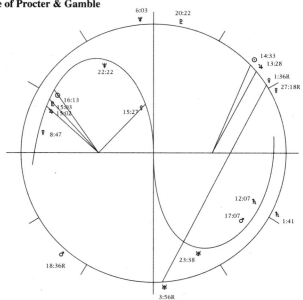

Chart 60: July 19, 1934
Birth date of Boeing

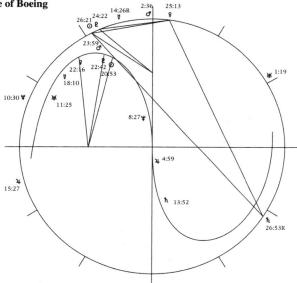

Chart 61: October 25, 1901
Birth date of Eastman Kodak

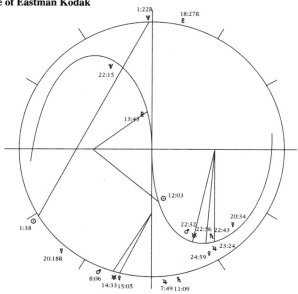

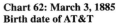

Chart 62: March 3, 1885
Birth date of AT&T

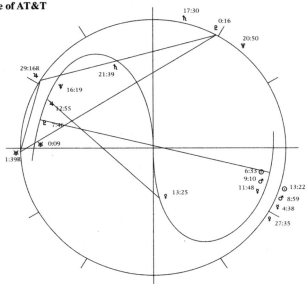

Chart 63: December 25, 1066
Coronation of William the Conqueror

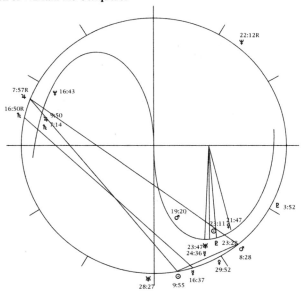

Chart 64: July 4, 1776
Declaration of Independence

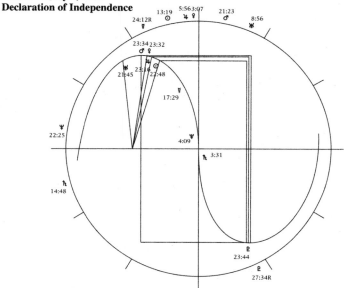

Chart 65: November 1, 1946
Pope John Paul II (ordained)

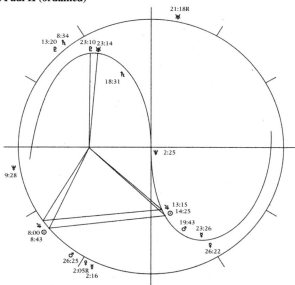

APPLYING ASTROLOGY
TO LOVE AND MARRIAGE

Now let's do something very exciting. Let's learn how to harness the power of astrology to choose a wedding date for yourself or for anyone else.

As we explained earlier, it is possible to use astrology to improve your chances of success at absolutely every type of endeavor you may want to engage in. Such undertakings could include the purchase of homes or businesses; the signing of legal documents, including contracts, loan agreements, partnership and incorporation papers, lawsuits and responses to lawsuits; having any medical procedures done, including plastic surgery, implants, dentistry, and even testing; and just about anything and everything that has a definable starting time.

The natal chart of any undertaking is the chart of the starting date of the act that signals the onset of the event. The exact time of day and the place are also very important because they are necessary in order to determine the calculated points. But in this book, we will continue to ignore the 12 houses, and other calculated points, for electional astrology. We will soon publish another book that will reveal some of the Magi Society's secrets about the longitudinal houses, as well as declinational houses. But in this book, the chapters on electional astrology will be limited to providing you with broad rules on what astrological aspects to avoid and what aspects to seek in the natal chart of an electional day for various forms of endeavors and enterprises.

The single most important electional date you can choose in your whole life is your wedding date. It is a chance to reshape your whole life because the birth chart of your wedding date will have a profound effect on your married life, including how much success and fame you will have.

The Astrology of Wedding Dates

Weddings have natal charts that have such a powerful influence on the participants' lives that the chart of the wedding is almost as important as the birth charts of the individuals involved. If there is no money in the wedding chart, the couple will find it very difficult to amass money while they are married. If there is no power in the wedding chart, the spouses are unlikely to achieve positions of power during their marriage. In addition, the transits and progressions to the wedding chart greatly influence the lives of any children.

Half of America's marriages end in divorce. Other marriages break up due to the early death of one of the spouses. In our opinion, both types of unfortunate occurrences are avoidable through astrological planning. Evidence for this concept is not as unimpeachable as the evidence already presented in proof of astrology. Yet the evidence is still very, very strong. But it is not our purpose to prove the astrology of weddings. This chapter is not written to prove anything. It is written as a guide for those who believe in astrology. However, since astrology works so well, the more you learn about astrology and the more you research it, the more you will believe in it.

This chapter will examine some of the most famous weddings of recent times. We will show that these natal charts are astrologically compatible with the way these marriages turned out, thus giving us very strong evidence of the importance of astrology as applied to marriages. Then we will learn what aspects are good and bad for successful weddings.

These are the weddings that we will examine:

1) Queen Elizabeth II and Prince Philip;
2) Prince Charles and Lady Diana;
3) Prince Andrew and Sarah Ferguson;
4) John F. Kennedy and Jacqueline Bouvier;

5) Aristotle Onassis and Jacqueline Kennedy;
6) Robert Kennedy and Ethel;
7) Edward Kennedy and Joan;
8) Joseph Kennedy and Rose;
9) O.J. Simpson and Nicole Brown;
10) Grace Kelly and Prince Rainier; and
11) Hillary Rodham and Bill Clinton.

(The Magi Astrocharts of all 11 weddings can be found at the back of this chapter.)

It's interesting to note that eight of these marriages have ended in divorce, early separation, or premature death of a spouse. Only three of the weddings could be considered successful. These three are the marriages of Joe Kennedy, father of the Kennedy clan; Queen Elizabeth II; and the Clintons. Remarkably, **all three had Jupiter enhancement of the Sun.** These three astrological charts confirm our belief that it is the aspects to the Sun that are the most important in determining the essence of anything because the Sun represents the actual entity; in these cases, the Sun represents the marriages. The more favorable the aspects to the Sun, the better the marriage is able to survive bad transits when they occur. Therefore, it is not a coincidence that of the 11 super high-profile marriages we are investigating, the only 3 lasting marriages are those that have natal Suns enhanced by Jupiter. Jupiter seems to provide whatever is necessary to hold a marriage together.

What we have learned from this is to never let the schedule of the wedding caterer or the availability of a church interfere with your choice of an astrologically favorable wedding date. **Make certain that your wedding date has a strong enhancement of Jupiter to the Sun.** This is the number-one priority. Do not settle for Pluto enhancement of the Sun in the wedding chart. Remember what the symbolisms mean. Jupiter enhancement of the Sun signifies good fortune, peace, and success in the marriage. Pluto enhancement of the Sun, on the other hand, gives the marriage and its participants power. Of the 11 weddings we are examining in this chapter, 3 have Pluto enhancement of the Sun. They are the weddings of Robert Kennedy, Edward Kennedy, and Grace Kelly. Each had power, but each ended sadly. So, although the Sun-Pluto enhancements are favorable for individuals, it is not as beneficial for weddings.

Another example of the very strong effect of the aspects of wedding charts is the Jupiter-Uranus enhancement. It cannot be just a coincidence that the wedding charts of all three Kennedy sons who were in politics had this rare astrological aspect. Bill Clinton, Al Gore, and' Newt Gingrich have this same aspect in their natal charts. For this reason, we will sometimes call this aspect the ASPECT OF POLITICAL POWER, and other times we will call it the SUPER FAME ASPECT because so many of Hollywood's superstars have this aspect as well.

Astrologically speaking, most marriages are destroyed and dissolved by bad progressions and bad transits. This means that when you choose a wedding date, besides choosing a date that has the Sun well aspected by Jupiter, it is imperative to choose a date that does not contain negative progressions by Saturn to any planet. To learn what to avoid in wedding charts, we need to learn about the astrological influences of each of the eight failed marriages. This should be compared to the aspects and progressions of the three successful weddings. This knowledge will help us better understand how to choose wedding dates.

Let us now analyze these 11 weddings from an astrological perspective. As you do so, take note of how closely the aspects of a wedding date actually depict the real marriages.

1) Marriage of Queen Elizabeth and Prince Philip:

This is regarded as a successful marriage even though none of the children have had a successful marriage. The Queen's own marriage seems to have never been in turmoil or at risk of ending in separation or divorce. The couple seem to get along with each other royally.

Super Aspects: Jupiter parallel the Sun (fortunate and blessed marriage); Uranus parallel Pluto (power from the masses); Pluto trine Venus (money from power and power from money; the Queen is the richest woman in the world); Uranus contra-parallel Venus (famous amount of money). Astrology is amazing, isn't it?

Major progressions: *Negative:* none. No progression by Saturn. This is unusual and is one of the main reasons the marriage has been very successful even though there are always problems in their children's marriages. *Positive:* A beneficial Jupiter trine Pluto peaked in 1986; Prince Charles and Di separated the next year after the favorable progression left. A beneficial Pluto parallel Uranus peaked in 1992; Prince Andrew and Fergie separated after this good progression left.

A beneficial Jupiter conjunction to Venus peaks in the year 2000; this is a fabulous progression to have. A beneficial Pluto parallel Venus peaks in 2006; this is also a great progression.

Notice how the progressions of the marriage chart can time key events in the lives of the children. A positive progression will protect the marriage, the spouses and the children until the progression peaks, after which time problems can crystallize. A negative progression can force any problems to culminate before the negative progression peaks.

2) Marriage of Joe Kennedy and Rose:

Super Aspects: Jupiter trine Sun (fortunate and blessed wedding); Jupiter parallel Uranus (famous wedding); Jupiter contra-parallel Pluto (successful wedding and a wedding with strong financial resources derived from big business); Uranus contra-parallel Pluto (powerful wedding with power coming from the masses); Jupiter contra-parallel Neptune (long-lasting financial security); Neptune trine Venus (a wedding with money from long-lasting sources).

This wedding of Joe Kennedy's had six Super Aspects. No wonder it built the Kennedy clan! The heartbreaks are probably related at least in part to the Saturn-Pluto conjunction.

Major progressions: *Negative:* Saturn conjuncted Pluto around 1932; Edward Kennedy was born that year, but it could be just after the progression peaked. Saturn semi-sextile to Neptune peaked in 1971;

Robert Kennedy died in 1968, before the negative left. Note that here, as in the case of Ron Goldman, a negative progression of Saturn to Neptune times the death of an individual. *Positive:* Jupiter parallel Pluto 1932; Edward Kennedy born; here too as in the case of progressed Saturn conjunction of Pluto peaking in 1932, this progression could also have passed at Edward's birth. We would need to calculate the progressions from the exact time of the wedding in order to assess this.

Jupiter trine Sun peaked around 1943; Joe Kennedy was appointed Ambassador to the Court of St. James (England) by President Roosevelt in 1937; after this favorable progression left, the first son, Joe Jr., was killed in 1944 during World War II. Here is another example of a positive progression (Jupiter trine the natal Sun of the wedding) protecting the marriage from disaster until the progression leaves.

3) Marriage of Prince Charles of Windsor and Diana:

Super Aspects: Uranus contra-parallel the Sun (this aspect means famous marriage, we kid you not); no other Super Aspects

Major progressions: *Negative:* Saturn conjunction of Jupiter peaked in 1987; Prince Charles and Di began to lead separate lives in 1987. Saturn was semi-sextile Venus about 1991; the couple are formally separated in 1992. Saturn was sextile the Sun about 1994; Prince Charles says publicly that he never loved Di. There were so many negative progressions by Saturn, and each one took its toll.

There are no positive progressions of any significance. The Saturn conjunction Jupiter and Saturn parallel to Jupiter are very damaging negative progressions. This is why so many palace watchers believe that the marriage may turn into one of the most famous divorces in history.

4) Marriage of Prince Andrew and Sarah Ferguson:

Super Aspects: Jupiter contra-parallel Pluto (no problems with money); Jupiter contra-parallel Venus (this is traditionally regarded as a very good aspect for weddings, and it is, but it is not related to the Sun, which is the key planet of all electional birth charts).

Major progressions: *Negative:* Saturn contra-parallel the Sun is in play for 90 years. This is a very negative progression to have for so long. The Magi Society calls such a long-lasting progression a PER-PETUAL PROGRESSION. Obviously, a favorable perpetual progression is great, and a bad one is horrible. This is a bad one. Saturn will begin to be semi-sextile Neptune, and applying in the year 2002. Saturn is in trine to the Sun applying until 2001

The fact that this wedding is on the rocks in spite of the presence of the Jupiter-Venus enhancement underscores the fact that it is the aspects to the Sun of the wedding chart that are most important. Although the Jupiter-Venus enhancement is very helpful, there are no positive aspects to the Sun. Instead there are negative progressions to the Sun. This is another wedding that royal watchers say will end up in divorce.

5) The wedding of John F. Kennedy and Jacqueline Bouvier:

Super Aspects: Jupiter parallel Uranus (famous marriage and one with power); Uranus parallel Pluto (more power); Jupiter parallel Pluto (the Super Success Aspect); Jupiter trine Neptune (again, no problems with financial security). But no Super Aspects to the Sun.

Major progressions: There was one significant favorable progression. This was the Jupiter trine Saturn, which ended in 1960, the year Kennedy was elected President. This is the strongest of the 12 Super Progressions. We believe that this progression helped Kennedy win the Presidency, since it peaked when he won the election. Aren't the progressions amazing?

There are no significant negative progressions by Saturn. But there are also no positive aspects to the Sun of the wedding chart, and the Sun is the lifeline. This marriage only lasted ten years and two months before Kennedy was assassinated. The assassination of a U.S. President obviously is related to the transits and progressions of more than just the President's wedding; it is also very much influenced by the transits and progressions of the natal chart of this country, as well as that of Kennedy himself, the inauguration date, and that of the people closest to him. However, the fact that there were no favorable aspects at all to the natal Sun of the wedding chart is a clear indication that the marriage was not going to be long-lasting.

6) The wedding of Robert Kennedy and Ethel:

Super Aspects: Pluto parallel the Sun (marriage of power); Uranus parallel Pluto (more power from the masses); Jupiter trine Uranus (fame and power); Uranus parallel the Sun (and more fame). With four Super Aspects, one would normally expect a good marriage. And it was good while it lasted. But without a Jupiter enhancement to the Sun, this birth chart is missing the good fortune needed to overcome the negative progressions of Saturn.

Major progressions: *Negative:* Saturn semi-sextile Neptune peaked in 1967. Once again, the timing of tragedy coincides closely with the progressions of a wedding chart. Robert Kennedy made the decision to run for the Presidency during the few years leading to 1967; he was assassinated a year later. Note that we had earlier pointed out that there was a negative Saturn-Neptune progression in the wedding chart of Joe and Rose Kennedy peaking in 1971, which also put negative pressure on Robert's wedding chart during this period.

There were no beneficial progressions of importance.

The symbolisms of the aspects of this marriage correctly foretold that this would be a marriage of fame and power. But without the protection of Jupiter to the natal Sun of the marriage, it succumbed to the negative Saturn progressions.

7) The marriage of Edward Kennedy and Joan:

Super Aspects: Pluto parallel the Sun (another marriage of power); Jupiter parallel Uranus (power and fame).

Major progressions: There are no significant negative progressions by Saturn.

A beneficial contra-parallel of Jupiter to Uranus peaked in 1966; this helped protect Edward Kennedy's brother, Robert, until after its peak. Robert Kennedy was assassinated in 1968. This marriage lasted 22 years. Joan stood by Ted Kennedy through a number of crises, including the famous 1969 Chappaquiddick disaster where Ted left the scene of an auto accident with a dead woman in the car. In the late 1970s, Joan and Ted were leading separate lives but attempted a reconciliation to aid Ted's presidential candidacy in 1980. Shortly after his bid for the Democratic Party's nomination failed, they agreed to a divorce.

Again, the symbolisms of the aspects of this marriage correctly foretold it would be a marriage of power and fame. But again, unfortunately for the spouses, there was no Jupiter enhancement of the natal Sun of the wedding chart.

8) The marriage of Aristotle Onassis and Jacqueline Kennedy:

Super Aspects: Jupiter and Pluto in conjunction (another marriage with no financial problems).

Major progressions: No significant progressions by Saturn. No significant beneficial progressions. Except for the Super Success Aspect, this was a very weak chart. Unlike the three Kennedy weddings already discussed, this wedding's natal chart did not have any aspects of fame or power. There were no enhancements at all to the natal Sun. After the wedding, neither Jackie nor Aristotle gained any fame or power that they did not already have prior to the marriage. The couple began to lead separate lives early in their marriage but remained married until Aristotle's death in 1975.

9) The marriage of O.J. Simpson and Nicole Brown:

Super Aspects: Pluto parallel Venus (no problems with money); Jupiter parallel Neptune (again no financial problems)

Major progressions: *Negative:* Saturn was moving towards negative progressions to Jupiter, Mars, Venus, Mercury, Neptune, and Pluto.

Some of these bad progressions were close to being perpetual. It is hard to find a worse day. There were no beneficial progressions.

The only aspect to the natal Sun was Saturn parallel the Sun, which is the opposite of Jupiter parallel the Sun. We strongly suggest that you do not get married on a day with such an aspect.

10) The marriage of Grace Kelly and Prince Rainier:

Super Aspects: Pluto trine Sun (another marriage of power)

Major progressions: *Negative:* Using our usual orb of about 1 degree for progressions, there were no negative progressions at the beginning. But Saturn formed progressions to Neptune, Pluto, the Sun, and Uranus beginning in 1980, when progressing Saturn was within one degree of natal Neptune. Grace Kelly died in an automobile accident in 1982. Just as was the case in the charts of Ron Goldman, and the weddings of Joe Kennedy and Robert Kennedy, the Saturn progression to Neptune appeared to time a tragedy.

There were no significant positive progressions.

Although the marriage was successful in many ways, we believe that the onslaught of four negative progressions coming into force in 1980 had a lot to do with Princess Grace's untimely death. This is another example of how important the progressions are, and how important it is to astrologically plan a wedding date.

11) The marriage of Hillary Rodham and Bill Clinton:

Super Aspects: Jupiter contra-parallel the Sun (blessed marriage); Jupiter parallel Venus (more blessings); Uranus contra-parallel Pluto (this adds power to the marriage).

Major progressions: No significant ones. Now we know why the Gennifer Flowers problem did not hurt Bill's marriage. His marriage chart has Jupiter enhancement of the Sun and Venus. Lucky him!

Jupiter Is the Key to Successful Marriages

If you want to have a successful marriage that will last for life, you must make certain that you are married on a day that has a strong Jupiter enhancement of the Sun. As you can see from our analysis of the 11 most famous weddings, such an aspect is the key to the successful ones.

Also, from our analysis, it is obvious that the marriage takes on a life of its own. Participants of a wedding that has a birth chart with Pluto enhancements are more likely to have power. The same is true for money; enhancements of Pluto provide money, and so do enhancements of Venus. Obviously, then, it is a good idea to have as many Super Aspects as possible in the wedding chart.

Make certain that you choose a date that will not have negative transits or progressions by Saturn. And choose a day on which both you and your spouse-to-be will have positive transits and progressions. By doing so, you will have an excellent chance of enjoying a long-lasting, successful marriage.

Is This Person Your Soul Mate?

Astrology can help us answer age-old questions relating to personal relationships. In an ideal world, there is supposed to be a soul mate for each of us. And some of us are blessed enough to be married to our soul mates on a very favorable astrological day. From an astrological perspective, there is no question that certain aspects made between the natal planets of two persons will create much more favorable bonds than others.

Fortunately, the laws of astrology are consistent in all of its applications. In other words, the symbolism of astrology and the interpretation of the aspects do not ever change, no matter what the application is.

For example, if one person's natal Jupiter is in trine to another person's natal Sun, this creates a Jupiter trine Sun and is very good for both individuals, particularly the Sun person. The Jupiter person will look at the Sun person with rose-colored glasses that filter out the faults and mistakes of the Sun person. The Jupiter person will forgive the Sun person for almost anything, and will almost always be supportive. An example of this is Hillary and Bill Clinton. Hillary's natal Jupiter is in nearly exact trine to Bill's natal Sun. Hillary, normally very demanding and a very difficult person to please, will look at Bill differently and forgive almost anything.

During the course of our lives, all of us have met many couples who make us wonder what in the world keeps them together—or, for that matter, how on Earth they got together in the first place. The answer is always in the stars. It is rare that a long-term couple does not have a number of strong equal-degree aspects created by their joint natal planets. Most often they involve Venus, Mars, the Sun, Neptune, or Pluto. Venus rules the love instinct. Mars rules the sex instinct. Since the Sun represents the person, the aspect of Venus conjunct the Sun means love (Venus) of the person (the Sun). The Venus person does the loving, not vice versa.

Pluto is the planet of obsessions and rules the reproductive organs. If your Venus or Mars makes a strong equal-degree aspect to someone's natal Pluto, especially an enhancement, you could become obsessed with that person.

Neptune is the planet of eternal bonding. If your Sun or Venus makes a strong equal-degree aspect to someone's natal Neptune, especially an enhancement aspect, you will feel as if you have known the person long before you ever met. It is as if you have known each other in another life.

The midpoints of the planets are also very powerful in creating bonds between two persons. Declinational midpoints seem to be slightly more important than longitudinal ones. For example, if your Neptune-Pluto midpoint enhances someone else's Mars, that person will be much more likely to have a sexual attraction to you. But if your Saturn-Pluto midpoint aspects someone's Mars, you do not have much of a chance. This is all part of what everyone has been calling "chemistry." It really is the stars! Different strokes for different folks.

The Magi Society will soon publish a book that will detail the likely interaction of two persons depending on all important aspects created by the natal planets of the two birth charts. We will not do it here because it is beyond the scope of this book and would require 100 additional pages. Besides, it is not provable in the eyes of a skeptic because **you can never prove anything that involves judgments**, and everything about interpersonal relationships is a judgment.

***

Now that you have learned about the declinations, check the birth charts of everyone who has been important to you in your life and see what the planetary bonds have been. You will be amazed. Remember that Hay House, the publisher of this book, publishes an ephemeris that not only includes the declinations, but also has the midpoints of both the longitudes and declinations, as well as highlighting the planetary eclipses. No other ephemeris has them. (This ephemeris is copyrighted.)

***

The Birth Chart of a Personal Relationship

The very first instant that you meet someone is the time that should be used for the birth chart of your personal relationship. There are two areas of consideration to determine if any relationship will be good or not so good. The first, and obvious one, is the strength of the aspects and progressions of the birth chart of the relationship, which is the natal chart of the day you first met. But you must also take into consideration your own transits and progressions, as well as the other person's transits and progressions, at the time of the initial meeting.

In fact, your transits and progressions are more important than the aspects of the relationship birth chart. The worst of all possible worlds would be to have a lasting relationship that is negative to you. If your transits are bad on the day the relationship was born, odds are very high that the relationship will be one that you would want to avoid. But sometimes the birth chart of the relationship has some very powerful aspects that make it long-lasting without giving it good fortune. For example, the Mars-Sun enhancement is the worst one. This aspect will strengthen the bonds and give energy (Mars) to the relationship (the Sun), but it will be combative (Mars). And if you were having bad transits when you first met, it will be a really problematic relationship—the kind that can lead to spousal abuse.

Again, the Magi Society will discuss this subject in great detail in a future book, which will include everything you need to know about judging whether you are having good or bad transits and progressions. But for now, a word to the wise: if your transits are negative when you meet someone, run in the other direction. Unfortunately, until you read one of our subsequent books, you will not know how to correctly evaluate your transits and progressions. So we hope that you will use the following hints to guide you in the meantime: if you are sick, your transits are bad; and if you are depressed or if you've just lost a lot of money, your transits are also negative.

Of course, there is a chance you will not be able to wait until our next books are published. If you need help from the Magi Society, or you would simply like to know more about us, you may contact us at: (212) 867-2905.

☄   ☄   ☄

Chart 66: June 17, 1950
Marriage of Robert
Kennedy & Ethel

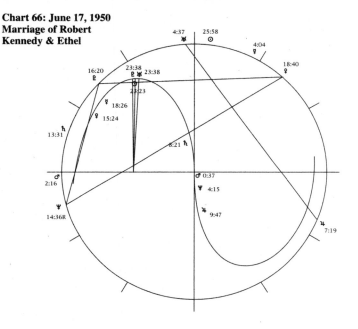

Chart 67: September 12, 1953
Marriage of John F. Kennedy
& Jackie Bouvier

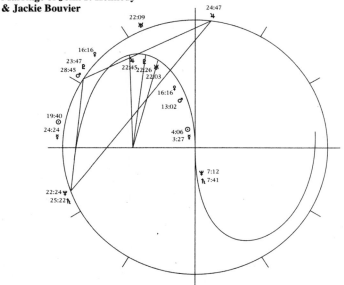

Chart 68: July 23, 1986
Marriage of Prince Andrew
& Sarah Ferguson

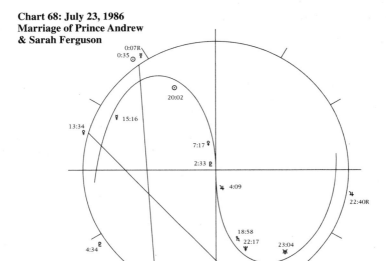

Chart 69: July 29, 1981
Marriage of Prince Charles & Diana

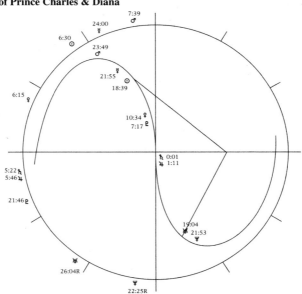

Chart 70: October 7, 1914
Marriage of
Joe Kennedy & Rose

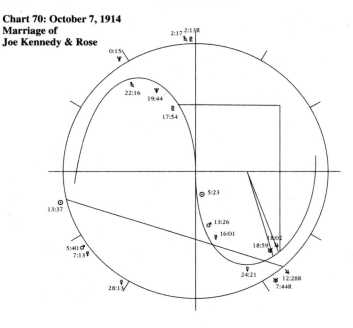

Chart 71: November 20, 1947
Marriage of Queen Elizabeth
& Prince Philip

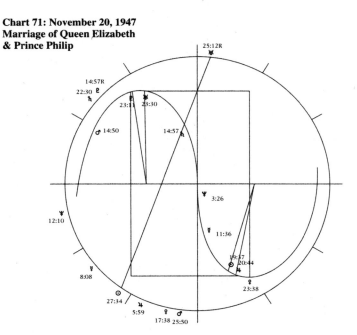

Chart 72: November 29, 1958
Marriage of Ted Kennedy & Joan

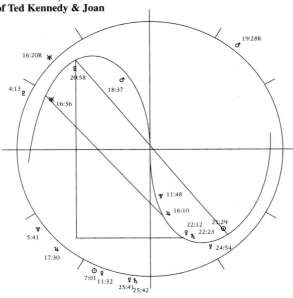

Chart 73: October 20, 1968
Marriage of Jacqueline Kennedy
& Aristotle Onassis

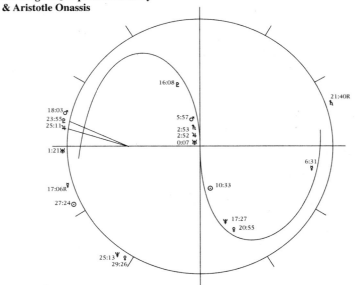

Chart 74: February 2, 1985
Marriage of O.J. Simpson
& Nicole Brown

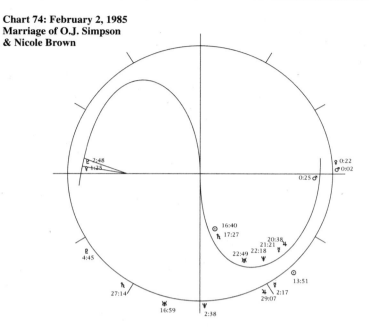

Chart 75: April 18, 1956
Marriage of Prince Rainier
& Grace Kelly

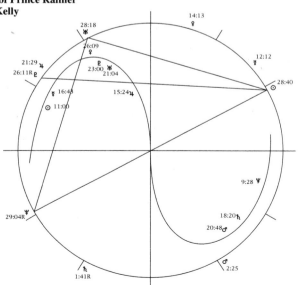

Chart 76: October 11, 1975
Marriage of the Clintons

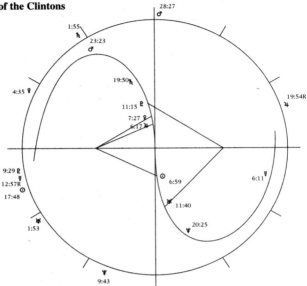

USING ELECTIONAL ASTROLOGY
IN FINANCIAL MATTERS

In the last chapter, we hope that you learned the importance of using astrology to plan your wedding date, and to use it to assess the day that you meet new people. These are two of the many ways in which the power of astrology can be harnessed to your advantage.

As we mentioned previously, you can also use electional astrology to help you plan the day you purchase a home, or the day you start a job or a business.

Last chapter's analysis of the 11 most famous weddings teaches us that aspects to the Sun are the most important aspects in a wedding chart because the Sun represents the marriage itself. The same principle is valid for all of electional astrology. The aspects to the Sun of an electional chart are always the most important aspects. The importance of aspects to the other planets will vary depending on what you are trying to accomplish. In this regard, you must again use the symbolism of the planets as your guide. The symbolism of astrology is consistent with all areas of astrology. What holds true for natal charts of individuals is also valid for all electional charts, whether we are talking about weddings, corporations, contracts, or anything else. In this chapter, we will focus on using astrology to help us become more successful in affairs of money, including our jobs.

Let us begin with using astrology in starting new businesses. For example, if you are trying to start a business that deals in motorcycles, it is imperative that you choose a day that has an enhancement of Mercury. Preferably, the enhancement should be by Pluto because Pluto enhancement of Mercury means big business (Pluto) in Mercury-related endeavors, which include all modes of transportation. The Harley-Davidson Company has just such an aspect. (Please refer to the birth chart of the Harley-Davidson Company at the end of this chapter.)

Harley-Davidson is the most successful U.S. company with respect to competing with Honda and other Japanese auto and recreational vehicle manufacturers. The Harley-Davidson Company is the only surviving U.S. motorcycle manufacturer. Honda, Suzuki, and other foreign companies have put all other U.S. motorcycle manufacturers out of business. Notice that the date of this incorporation was in 1991, yet the Harley-Davidson name has been around for decades. This is because the company was re-incorporated in 1991. The previous corporation had a strong chart, but not as strong as this new one. The previous corporation had just enough favorable astrological aspects to hold its own against the foreign invaders because it had a wide Sun-Pluto parallel and a wide Venus-Pluto parallel. But since the new corporation took over, Harley-Davidson has been able to gain market share and has become a well-known success story on Wall Street.

This new Harley-Davidson incorporation date has the only birth chart we have seen that has both a Sun-Pluto trine and a Sun-Pluto parallel; it means that the company has a Magi bilevel enhancement of Pluto and Sun. That makes Harley Davidson an absolutely fierce competitor. The birth chart is also so perfectly suited for the business that it is in. There is a Pluto-Mercury trine and a Pluto-Mercury parallel. This means that the company has two Magi bilevel enhancements involving Pluto. The two Pluto-Mercury aspects provide Harley with the ability to succeed in the big business of Mercury-related businesses. Mercury symbolizes transportation, the messenger, automobiles, and motorcycles. Honest, it does. It even says so in other astrology books published years ago. So what more could a motorcycle company ask for in its birth chart?

Venus Rules Money

Venus really does rule money. Since you cannot succeed in business without money, if you are starting a business, it is very important that the starting date has an enhancement of Venus. But it is also important that it is the right enhancement. For example, if you are going to sell to the public, you should choose the Uranus enhancement of Venus. But if you are starting an investment bank and hope to make money in investment banking, the Venus enhancement should be by Pluto. Another example would be drug companies—their Venus enhancements are usually by Neptune, which rules drugs.

Motorola is another good example. (Its birth chart is at the end of this chapter.) Motorola is the largest American manufacturer of hand-held communications equipment, such as cellular phones and pagers. It has been dominant in this area; Motorola made a profit of a billion dollars in 1994, and its stock was worth over $33 billion.

For the birth chart of Motorola:

Super Aspects: Jupiter trine Pluto; Jupiter parallel Neptune; Uranus parallel Venus

Midpoint enhancements: Jupiter-Uranus conjunct Saturn; Venus-Pluto trine Uranus; Jupiter-Uranus contra-parallel Pluto; Jupiter-Venus contra-parallel Pluto; Neptune-Uranus contra-parallel Pluto; Jupiter-Pluto contra-parallel Mercury; Jupiter-Venus trine Uranus

Uranus is the planet that rules broadcasting and communications equipment. Uranus also rules the public and mass merchandising. Motorola's chart has the Super Aspect Uranus parallel Venus. This aspect means that it will make money (Venus) from broadcasting and communications (Uranus). It also signifies the making of money from mass merchandising, which makes sense since the general public buys cellular phones.

Success in this area is further emphasized by two midpoint enhancements of Uranus: Venus-Pluto trine to Uranus, and Jupiter-Venus trine Uranus. Both enhancements help Motorola succeed in Uranus-related businesses. In this case, we are referring to mass merchandising, communications, broadcasting, and technology.

Motorola's success in competition comes from having the Super Success Aspect, Jupiter trine Pluto, and three midpoint enhancements of Pluto. In Motorola, America has a company we can be very proud of.

An example of another company that America can be proud of is Amgen, Inc. Amgen is the world's most successful biotechnology company. If you invested $30,000 in Amgen stock in 1986, you would have made over one million dollars just six years later. (Its birth chart is at end of chapter.)

For the birth chart of Amgen:

Super Aspects: Pluto conjunction the Sun; Jupiter trine Venus; Neptune parallel Venus; Uranus parallel Venus

Midpoint enhancements: Jupiter-Saturn parallel the Sun; Pluto-Uranus conjunction Mercury; Jupiter-Neptune trine Saturn

Amgen has a Super Aspect of Neptune parallel Venus. Neptune rules drugs, so this aspect means that Amgen will make money (Venus) from drugs (Neptune). The Neptune-Venus enhancement is common to successful drug companies. For example, Merck, the world's largest drug company, has Neptune trine Venus; Ely Lilly has Neptune contra-parallel Venus; Abbot Labs has Neptune sextile Venus. In Amgen's case, the Neptune-Venus enhancement is also a hundred-year progression and is therefore what we have called a perpetual progression. This progression is the ruling astrological influence of the natal chart and is the key to Amgen's phenomenal success. Perpetual progressions are so powerful that it is impossible to overstate their importance.

The Sun-Pluto conjunction and Jupiter trine Venus also add greatly to Amgen's ability to compete successfully and make money.

The Sun-Pluto Enhancement Is a Must for a Business

Besides an enhanced Venus, it is imperative that a new business begin with a Sun-Pluto enhancement. Obviously, this is because Pluto rules big business. Jupiter rules good fortune and happiness, which are necessary for marriages. Pluto enhancements are not necessary for marriages but are essential for businesses. Of course, it would be ideal if you could have both. But days with both enhancements are so rare that you usually cannot wait that long to begin a new business. Given the choice of the Jupiter-Sun enhancement or the Pluto-Sun enhancement for a business, do not even hesitate. Take the Pluto-Sun enhancement for businesses and jobs. Remember that 14 of the 30 Dow Jones Industrial Average companies have this aspect. However, since most of those companies originated long ago, you might be interested in two of the more recently formed super-success stories with Sun-Pluto enhancement, that of Microsoft and MCI.

The Microsoft Corporation is by far the world's most successful computer software company. Microsoft's software runs 70 percent of the personal computers in the world.

For the birth chart of Microsoft:

Super Aspect: Sun parallel Pluto; perpetual progression of Pluto to Venus

Midpoint enhancements: Jupiter-Pluto trine Venus; Mars-Jupiter trine Uranus; Jupiter-Saturn trine Sun; Jupiter-Uranus trine Saturn; Neptune-Pluto conjunct Saturn; Jupiter-Pluto parallel Mercury; Pluto-Uranus trine Sun

Amgen is the most successful biotech company in the world, and Microsoft is the most successful computer software company in the world. The similarities between Amgen and Microsoft are very interesting to study. Both have very precise Sun-Pluto enhancements. Both have the midpoint enhancement of Jupiter-Saturn to the Sun. Both have a hundred-year perpetual progression involving Venus. Microsoft has a wide conjunction of Pluto and Venus; the Pluto conjunction Venus progression lasts over a hundred years, meaning Microsoft can make money (Venus) from big business (Pluto) for over a hundred years. Microsoft's money-making power is further enhanced by the Jupiter-Pluto midpoint in trine to Venus. The company's ability to handle problems (Saturn) is very positive because of the two midpoint enhancements to Saturn.

MCI Corporation is the only company to ever compete successfully against AT&T. It sued Ma Bell on antitrust grounds and won by forcing the breakup of Ma Bell into seven "Baby Bells." MCI is now the second largest telecommunications company in the United States, but AT&T is still number one (it has a fabulous natal chart, also).

For the birth chart of MCI:

Super Aspects: Pluto parallel the Sun; Neptune contra-parallel the Sun

Midpoint enhancements: Jupiter-Neptune trine the Sun and Mercury; Jupiter-Pluto parallel Venus; Pluto-Uranus parallel Jupiter; Mars-Venus conjunct to the Sun and Mercury; Mars-Venus parallel to Pluto, Mercury, and the Sun, and contra-parallel to Neptune

Synchronization: Pluto, Neptune, and Mercury within 0:13 degree of declination; Pluto, Neptune, Mercury, and the Sun within 1:15 degree of declination

MCI, Amgen, Microsoft, and Harley-Davidson are four of the greatest success stories of the last ten years. They all have Pluto enhancement of the Sun. MCI's successful lawsuit against AT&T changed the face of telephone service in this country. For a hundred years before MCI, AT&T had always been able to either outwit and outmaneuver or buy out its competitors. By forcing AT&T to be dismembered, MCI was able to grab a big enough share of the telecommunications market to earn $1 billion in 1994. This is $1 billion right out of Ma Bell's purse.

MCI's success in business was predictable from its astrological chart. The astrological key to its natal chart is the quadruple declinational enhancement of the Sun, Pluto, Mercury, and Neptune. Pluto parallels the Sun and Mercury, and all three are contra-parallel to Neptune. This is logically interpreted as big business (Pluto) for MCI (the Sun) in electrical (Neptune) communications (Mercury). Obviously, telephones are electrical communication devices. The likelihood of success in this area for MCI is improved by the Jupiter-Neptune trine Sun and Mercury, meaning long-term (Neptune) success (Jupiter) in communications (Mercury) for MCI (the Sun). And similar to Microsoft, the Jupiter-Pluto enhancement of Venus provides MCI with the ability to succeed (Jupiter) in big business (Pluto) to make money (Venus).

The Aspects Will Limit How a Business Can Make Money

Have you ever wondered why some very successful corporations are complete failures in certain enterprises?

For example, International Business Machines (IBM) lost an enormous amount of money in the 1970s when it failed in its attempt to market copying machines. Almost everyone assumed that IBM would be able to successfully compete with Xerox in this field. After all, IBM already had a well-trained top-notch sales force that sold computers and typewriters to the same clients who were big users and buyers of copying equipment. IBM had a great reputation for quality, reliability, and service, as well as having AAA financial resources. At the time they embarked on their copying equipment venture, IBM had made a profit every year that they were in business since their inception in 1911. With all this going for IBM, its failure in the copying machine business is incomprehensible to most.

IBM employees have told us that the company lost close to $2 billion before pulling out of the copying machine business. This is in 1975 dollars, which would be about $6 billion 1995 dollars. That is a lot of money to lose and get nothing, absolutely nothing, in return (except a black eye).

As it turned out, Canon, the Japanese camera manufacturer, did what IBM could not do: it became successful at selling copying machines in this country. On the face of it, this was an incredible feat. Canon had no sales force or market presence in the American offices where the copiers were bought. Yet they beat out IBM, and they gained a significant market share from Xerox.

Many business school professors gave lectures trying to explain what happened. But nobody had a good explanation. This is because the answer, my friend, is in the stars.

As we tried to show you earlier in this chapter, certain types of businesses require specific astrological aspects. A corporation cannot succeed in a business for which it is not astrologically suited. Canon was a manufacturer of cameras, which means it was in a very similar business to that of copying machines. Both businesses require taking images of something, and reproducing these images. Because Canon is so successful in the camera business, it must have an astrological aspect that helps it to be successful in that business. And because the copying machine business is so closely related to the camera business, Canon was also well suited astrologically to enter and succeed in both businesses.

On the other hand, IBM was not in any business that was related to the replication of images when it entered the copying machine business. In our opinion, IBM could not succeed in that type of business. It did not have the astrological aspects to do so.

There are thousands of examples similar to what happened to IBM. For instance, way back in the 1950s and '60s, General Electric tried and failed in the computer business. The reason we use this example is because GE, like IBM, is one of the most successful corporations in the world. It is one of the handful of companies that still has an AAA credit rating. It failed in the computer business because it was not astrologically suited for it.

Another giant of U.S. industry that failed in a business you would expect it to succeed in is AT&T. Ma Bell also lost billions in the computer business. GE failed before there were personal computers. Ma Bell failed after personal computers became popular. But just think about it. Ma Bell, with all its name recognition and resources, fails in a business that start-up companies like Compaq make billions from. Compaq started from ground zero on February 16, 1982. In 1994, Compaq shipped more personal computers than any other company in the world. Ma Bell, during that time, gave up trying to sell computers by itself and ended up buying NCR to maintain a presence in the business. The Magi Society emphatically declares that the basis for these phenomena lies in the stars.

What astrological aspects are important for the computer business? Neptune and Uranus are the duo-keys to computers. Astrologers associate Uranus with technology and computers. The Magi Society's studies agree with this assessment, but we also know that Neptune rules all electrical devices. Therefore, computers have Neptune and Uranus as co-rulers. IBM and Compaq were incorporated 71 years apart. When IBM was incorporated in 1911, Uranus was 20:59 degrees south declination. During the next 71 years, Uranus made a full declinational cycle and came back to 20:52 degrees south declination when Compaq was incorporated. In the birth chart of both corporations, Neptune enhanced natal Uranus in the declination. (Please see their charts at the end of this chapter.)

For the birth chart of **IBM**:

Super Aspects: The Sun-Neptune parallel; Neptune parallel Venus; Uranus contra-parallel Venus

Magi Triangle of Pluto, Uranus, and the Sun; Magi Pyramid of Uranus, Neptune, and Venus

For the birth chart of **Compaq**:

Super Aspects: Pluto trine the Sun; Jupiter parallel the Sun; Jupiter parallel Venus

Magi Triangle of Pluto, Neptune, and the Sun; Magi Pyramid of Jupiter, the Sun, and Venus.

IBM sells the most mainframe computers in the world. Compaq sells the most personal computers in the world.

There are remarkable astrological similarities between these two companies. In particular, Compaq has Uranus parallel Neptune, and IBM has Uranus contra-parallel Neptune. We interpret this aspect in these two ways: long-term financial security (Neptune) from technology and computers (Uranus), and also mass merchandising (Uranus) of electrical devices (Neptune).

Notice that IBM has three bi-directional quincunxes. Uranus is quincunx to Pluto and the Sun; Jupiter is quincunx to Mercury. As we have been saying, bi-directional equal-degree aspects are very positive and powerful.

Our point is that if you are forming a company, it is wise to choose a day that is astrologically favorable for big business and making money, and also for the type of business the company will be engaged in. You need all three types of aspects to be truly successful in a particular business.

The following aspects are most favorable for big business:

- Sun-Pluto enhancement;
- Jupiter-Pluto enhancement;
- Venus-Pluto enhancement;
- Uranus Pluto enhancement;
- Enhancement of the Sun by the midpoint of Jupiter-Pluto;
- Enhancement of Venus by the midpoint of Jupiter-Pluto;
- Enhancement of the Sun by the midpoint of Venus-Pluto;
- Enhancement of Mars by the midpoint of Jupiter-Pluto; and
- Enhancement of Mars by the midpoint of Venus-Pluto.

The nine enhancements above are all very powerful. The more of these aspects that you can get in your start-up day, the more successful your company will be in big business. And if you are successful in business, you will automatically make money. But it is also very important that your company has additional enhancements that specifically involve Venus, the ruler of money. The following enhancements are most favorable for making money:

- Venus-Pluto enhancement (which was also listed above);
- Venus-Neptune enhancement;
- Venus-Uranus enhancement;
- Venus-Jupiter enhancement;
- Venus-Mars enhancement;
- Enhancement of Venus by the midpoint of Jupiter-Pluto (also listed above);
- Enhancement of Venus by the Jupiter-Neptune midpoint;
- Enhancement of Venus by the Jupiter-Uranus midpoint; and
- Enhancement of Venus by extreme declination.

All of the above enhancements to Venus will help your company make money. But we must again emphasize that each one has a particular bias as to the type of business you can make money in. You need to refer to the symbolism of the planet making the enhancement to Venus. For example, if the enhancement of Venus is by Uranus, the company is most suited to make money in areas that are ruled by Uranus. If the enhancement to Venus is by a midpoint, the company is most suited to make money in areas that most closely combine the symbolism of the two planets making the midpoint. It will help your understanding of what we mean if we provide you with the following examples:

- Alcoa has Neptune parallel Venus. Neptune rules minerals and anything that comes from the ground. Alcoa is the nation's largest aluminum company.

- AT&T has Jupiter contra-parallel Venus. Jupiter's influence is less specific than that of the other planets; it provides good luck. AT&T essentially had a monopoly on telecommunications. That requires a great deal of good luck.

- Boeing has Venus-Pluto parallel. This means money from big business, and success in competition and investments.

- BankAmerica has Venus-Pluto contra-parallel. Remember that Pluto rules debt and investments. So BankAmerica makes its money from debt and investing, including the purchase of other banks. In the last five years, BankAmerica has bought more banks than any other company.

- Bankers Trust Company also has Venus-Pluto parallel. In this case, the Venus-Pluto enhancement manifests itself in investing for itself. It makes the vast majority of its money from investing its own money in currencies and from derivatives.

- Wells Fargo Bank has three enhancements to Venus. Neptune and Uranus are contra-parallel, and Mars is parallel. This gives Wells Fargo many avenues to accumulate money. It does so through mortgages (Neptune, because it rules land), mass banking (Uranus), and Wells Fargo has the energy (Mars) to make money.

- Chrysler is one of the most famous turnaround stories in American business. It was once in bankruptcy. Now it makes billions. Guess what? It was reincorporated March 4, 1986 and has been a miracle ever since. It now has Pluto enhancement of Venus. Astrology could have told you it would make tons of money. Chrysler now has one of the same aspects that Honda has: the Venus-Pluto enhancement. Chrysler has been able to give Honda a run for its money since its re-incorporation in 1986.

- Disney has a triple parallel of Venus, Mars, and Mercury. It makes money from efforts (Mars) in Mercury-related ways, including communications. Disney was reincorporated on November 24, 1986. The original Walt Disney Company had a birth chart with Jupiter contra-parallel Pluto, and both Mars and Neptune were contra-parallel Venus. These aspects gave the old Disney company ability to make money in their Disneyland theme parks. The new corporation does not have this ability. Perhaps this is why Euro-Disney is a disaster.

- Exxon has Venus enhanced by extreme declination. Venus is 24:59 degrees. This aspect means great amounts of assets.

- Eastman Kodak has Uranus conjunct to Venus. Kodak is our country's largest seller of film, which means it sells to the general public, which is ruled by Uranus. Uranus also rules inventions, and Kodak invented color film. Although Eastman Kodak invested in drug companies, such investments have been regarded as unsuccessful. They sold their Sterling Drug Division in 1994, and did not do well with it. The company has Neptune trine Sun in its birth chart so it likes to be in the drug business; Neptune rules drugs. But it has no strong aspects of making money from drugs (Neptune enhancement of Venus), or from buying businesses (Pluto enhancement of Venus).

- Polaroid has Uranus enhancement of Venus, just like Eastman Kodak. And like Eastman Kodak, Polaroid makes most of its money through the mass merchandising of film-related products At one time. Polaroid was the darling of Wall Street. In the 1960s, every investment manager was looking for the next Polaroid or Xerox. The shares of both companies were selling at price earnings multiples so high they are unheard of today. Kodak sells more film than any other company. Polaroid sells more instant film than any other company. Isn't it interesting that the two U.S. companies most successful in selling film both have Uranus enhancement of Venus?

- General Electric has Venus enhanced by extreme declination. Venus is 24:56 degrees. This aspect does not restrict GE from making money in any particular area.

- International Paper is the largest paper company in the world. It has Pluto parallel Venus, meaning money from big business as opposed to the general public, and as opposed to money from inventions and technology.

- Merck is the largest drug company in the world. It has Neptune trine Venus, just as you would expect because Neptune rules drugs.

- Minnesota Mining and Manufacturing has Venus-Mars parallel and Pluto sextile Venus. These aspects mean money from efforts (Mars) and from big business.

- Procter & Gamble has a triple parallel of Venus, Jupiter, and Pluto. How lucky can you get? This gives the company a number of ways from which it can make money, and it does so.

- Sears has a quintuple parallel of Venus, Jupiter, Neptune, Uranus, and Mars. This is another example of a company with many ways of making money. Sears has been in the insurance business through its ownership of Allstate; it has also owned businesses in real estate brokerage and securities brokerage. Its retail businesses also expanded into the production and sales of automotive equipment and services.

As you can see, Venus enhancements delineate the areas in which a company is most suited to make money. So far, we have not done any midpoint enhancements of Venus. This is because it will require dozens of pages for a thorough analysis, and the Magi Society will soon publish another book that will provide the details of all enhancements to Venus. The purpose of this present book is limited to helping you understand the principle of Venus enhancements, and to help you realize how important they are to money-making efforts.

All Aspects Have an Effect

Finally, we want to briefly discuss the astrological principle that all the aspects are important when choosing a day to begin a business. Besides the Sun-Pluto enhancement, the aspects to Pluto and Venus are the most important. But all aspects are important and will have a hand in determining the viability of a business plan.

Here is a very good example. When we discussed the aspects of the Harley-Davidson Company, the motorcycle manufacturer, we mentioned that it had an enhancement of Mercury by Pluto. We pointed out that this was very fortunate for the company because such an aspect imparts ability to succeed in big business in the area of transportation vehicles, including motorcycles. Well, Chrysler has the same enhancement. Pluto is parallel Mercury in Chrysler's natal chart. It is not a coincidence. Astrology really works.

We hope that it is not necessary to remind you that no matter what, avoid progressions by Saturn. We understand that it is sometimes difficult to avoid all negative progressions, but there is a rule of Magi Astrology: the good progressions overpower the bad ones. If you have no choice and cannot avoid a bad progression by Saturn, be absolutely certain that you have a number of good progressions at the same time. Otherwise, do not begin the project. It would mean it was not meant to be, and you will save yourself money, time, and anguish.

Using Astrology for New Job Opportunities

Not everyone starts a new business, but almost everyone has the occasion to start a new job. If you are very happy with your job, stay with it; don't fix something that's not broken. But if you are looking for a new opportunity, it is imperative that you pay attention to the stars. Both the day you first interview for a job, as well as the actual day you start a job, will have an incredible bearing on whether or not you will be successful.

The astrology of new jobs is essentially the same as the astrology of new businesses. But choosing a new job is even more complicated. You should somehow find out the starting date of the company or business you are contemplating working for so you can cast its birth chart. Even if your prospective employer is a major company, remember that all companies go through bad periods. Sometimes it's possible to tell if a company will enter hard times and lay off employees. A good portion of your own success at a job lies with the success of the entire company or, at the very least, your department.

Use the guidelines we have already provided in this chapter to help you elect a starting date for work, and for interviews. A good starting date will have some Super Aspects involving both the Sun and Venus. But the type of work you are interested in doing will have to be given some consideration. For example, Neptune rules artistry and artistic talent. If you want to be a dancer, singer, or musician, take this into account. A Neptune enhancement of Venus, Mercury, Mars, or the Sun will be helpful in this regard; so will a Jupiter enhancement of Neptune. We all know by now if you want to succeed in big business, choose enhancements involving Pluto and Venus. Our next book will go into all of this in great detail.

Buying a House

Buying a house is usually the largest and most important investment an American family makes. The day you sign a mortgage is the key astrological date. It is more important than the day you sign to purchase the house, but both are important.

The reason the mortgage signing is so important is that a mortgage is a continuing obligation for the lifetime of the mortgage, which is usually 15 to 30 years. If you sign a mortgage on a very unfavorable astrological day, and you are having bad transits at the time of the signing, it is going to be much more difficult for you to meet your mortgage obligations. On the other hand, if you sign a mortgage on a very favorable astrological day, and your transits are positive on that day, you will have improved your chances of fulfilling your obligations, and of making money on the house should you want to resell it.

Neptune rules real estate, and Pluto rules investments, so when you are signing a mortgage, choose a day that has enhancements to both planets, a day with Super Aspects, and a day without negative Saturn progressions. Also, choose a day when you will have good transits to your Pluto, Sun, Venus, and Neptune.

But most important of all, choose a day that has enhancements by Jupiter, especially to the Sun. In this regard, signing a mortgage is like a wedding. Jupiter enhancements will somehow help you through the bad transits. It is important to understand that when you sign a mortgage, you are making a financial promise. This is like a wedding where you are also making promises. Your ability to keep the promise will be dependent in large measure on the strength of the Sun on the day you make your commitments. Nothing helps you keep promises like Jupiter enhancements of the Sun.

The Importance of Your Transits and Progressions

Just as it is of utmost importance to get married when you are having good transits and progressions, it is equally important that you take into consideration your transits and progressions when you select any electional date. The trouble is, it is very complicated to calculate all of your progressions and transits. As we have been saying, the Magi Society will soon be releasing a book that deals with transits in detail. But we understand that you may have to make urgent decisions before that time. If you need to contact us, feel free to do so.

It has been the intention of the Magi Society to help all of our readers learn enough of the basics of electional astrology to be able to start harnessing the power of astrology. If you have learned everything we have so far disclosed about astrology, by the time you come to this part of this book, you will have a greater knowledge of the astrology of aspects than anyone who has not read this book. But it will probably be necessary for most of you to go back through this book and read it again to have a real understanding. We say this because we know that some of the concepts introduced in this book require time and study to fully understand. And we mention all of this now because we want to warn you not to throw away your marriage, your company or business, or your job just because you are disappointed with their birth charts. Even though the knowledge in this book is very powerful, it is not complete. There is much, much more to astrology. A little knowledge is a dangerous thing. If there is good in your marriage, job, and business, please keep them. Nothing is ever perfect.

In the future, we will be publishing more books. Please believe us when we say that there is more than 20 times as much astrological knowledge in future books and computer programs. In the meantime, if you would like to know more about the Magi Society, or if you have any astrological questions about anyone's birth chart, or about choosing an important date to initialize anything, you may contact us by telephone at (212) 867-2905.

We also have representatives and members abroad to whom we can refer you.

☄   ☄   ☄

Chart 77: March 8, 1991
Birth date of Harley-Davidson Company

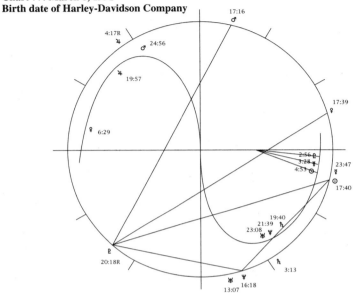

Chart 78: March 9, 1973
Birth date of Motorola Corp.

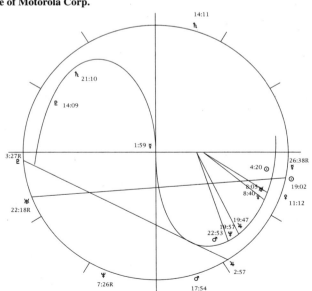

Chart 79: October 31, 1986
Birth date of Amgen

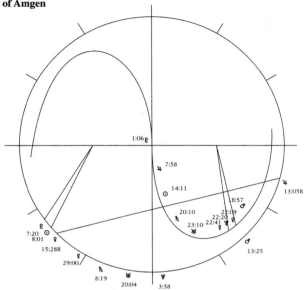

Chart 80: September 19, 1986
Birth date of Microsoft Corp.

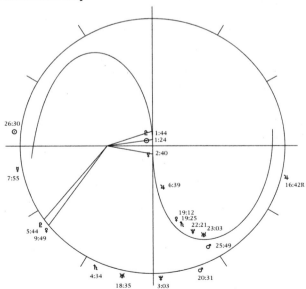

Chart 81: August 8, 1968
Birth date of MCI

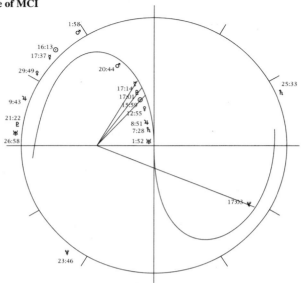

Chart 82: February 16, 1962
Birth date of COMPAQ

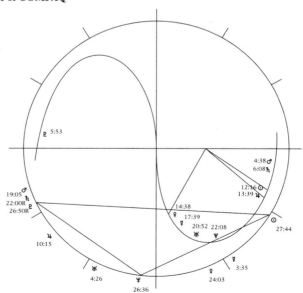

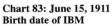

Chart 83: June 15, 1911
Birth date of IBM

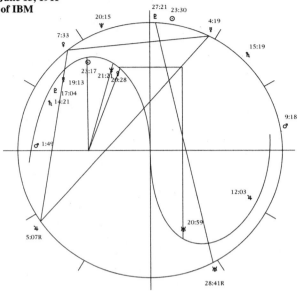

ADDITIONAL POINTS OF INTEREST

Why Is Science a Foe of Astrology?

On January 16, 1995, Japan's city of Kobe was devastated by an earthquake that left over 5,000 dead and literally hundreds of thousands of people homeless. On that day, there was an extremely rare alignment of planets. Uranus and the Sun, and the Earth and the Moon were all aligned in an exact straight line such that the Sun and Uranus were on one side of the Earth, and the Moon was on the exact opposite side. This means that the gravitational forces of Uranus and the Sun combined to pull the Earth one way, while the gravitational force of the Moon pulled the Earth in the exact opposite direction. There was a full Moon that day, and the Sun and Uranus were in 26 degrees Capricorn; the Moon was in opposition to both because it was in Cancer 26 degrees.

Isn't it strange that scientists never ever discuss the possibility that one of the catalysts of earthquakes might just be the gravitational effect of the Sun and Moon? After all, we know that the Sun and Moon cause high and low tides, which means they do move massive amounts of water. Certainly, the movement of water will also move land masses.

Obviously, the Sun and Moon can move land masses as well as water masses. So why don't scientists ever talk about it? There can only be one reason: scientists refute anything to do with astrology and the idea that any planet can influence life or this world. So intense is this repudiation of astrology that the public never hears any mention of the Moon's position in weather reports—even though we know the Moon has a strong influence on the weather. Scientists completely ignore the possible influences of the planets. Maybe this is one of the reasons why scientists have a horrible record of trying to predict the weather.

We, of the Magi Society, believe that we are not being too harsh on scientists. We are aware of a number of cases where otherwise reputable scientists have twisted the truth and employed chicanery to vilify astrology. An example of this occurred as recently as January of 1995. This time, the perpetrators were members of England's Royal Astronomical Society, also known as the RAS. In a carefully crafted news release in January of 1995, the RAS made it sound like it had just discovered that astrologers' horoscopes were all "wrong" because astrologers did not know about the precession of the equinoxes, which, according to the RAS meant that astrologers did not know what sign a planet was in. The RAS also claimed that astrologers goofed 3,000 years ago, because there are really 13 constellations instead of 12.

What this all means to us is that the Royal Astronomical Society did not take the trouble to learn enough astrology in order to be qualified enough to critique it. Or perhaps they simply decided to twist the truth.

Here is why the Royal Astronomical Society was utterly wrong:

Remember our discussion of the precession of the equinoxes in chapter 8? We explained that about 1,850 years ago, the ancient astrologer Ptolemy understood the precession of the equinoxes. Because of this, he developed the method of astrology that uses a TROPICAL ZODIAC where 0 degrees Aries is defined as the position of the Sun at the spring equinox. This position moves backwards along the constellations one degree every 71.5 years, and is the cause of the changes in the Ages, such as the Age of Aquarius after the Age of Pisces. Our point is that it was astrologers who discovered the precession of the equinoxes, and we did this 1,850 years ago. For almost 19 centuries, astrologers took it into account in their horoscopes. Apparently, the Royal Astronomical Society did not bother to learn enough about astrology to realize this, so they mistakenly thought astrologers did not know about the precession of the equinoxes. Or, the RAS knew that astrologers discovered the precession 1,850 years ago, but the RAS decided to twist the truth in order to vilify astrologers.

With regard to the Royal Astronomical Society's claim that there are really 13 constellations, the Magi Society says: "So what?" There are actually many more than 13 constellations, but only 12 were used by ancient astrologers as a guide in locating the planets. This book has provided ample evidence that ancient astrologers were literally prescient when they divided the Zodiac into 12 equal parts, thus allowing for the easy determination of the longitudinal equal-degree aspects, which we now know works.

So why do scientists revile astrology? Perhaps it is caused by a general unconsciousness among such people caused by aspects in their astrological charts. Perhaps it is extreme ego. Or it could be fear of having to throw away a lifetime of convictions. After all, with astrology proven, they have to eat much of what they have said during their professional years.

But there is something else at work here. Probably very few reputable scientists born this century have seriously looked into astrology. And almost certainly, few, if any, have checked into the declinations of astrology. And the primary blame for this state of affairs lies with the people who proclaim themselves to be astrologers. The Magi Society's members and associates know many self-proclaimed astrologers. Almost all of them are somewhat superstitious, exactly as scientists believe they are. And almost none of these so-called astrologers really *understand* astrology. We use the word *understand* here because we believe that if they did understand astrology, they would have naturally researched the declinations and enhanced their knowledge. But we also use the word *understand* because it has not been necessary for astrologers to "understand" astrology in order to provide a client with a fairly accurate astrological reading. Most astrologers can do so even though they do not "understand" astrology. And it is because they can provide accurate astrological readings without the declinations that many of them have not found it necessary to seek additional or new knowledge.

But because most astrologers are actually somewhat superstitious, and because they are not thirsty for new knowledge, and are unscientific, they have given scientists the impression that astrology itself is full of superstition, and is unscientific.

We hope that scientists and skeptics of astrology will examine the work of the Magi Society with an open mind. We hope that every skeptic and scientist will examine the birth charts of every superstar of sports, and every superstar of business, and every superstar of Hollywood and politics, and learn for themselves how incredibly valuable astrology really is. Only by doing birth charts the Magi Society's way can they learn for themselves the "scientific truths in astrology" that 47 percent of Americans believe in. And we hope they all join the Magi Society afterwards.

Statistical Validation of Astrology

The skeptic can view everything we have learned as coincidence. How many coincidences does it take to create a law? The odds are so great against all the "coincidences" in this book simultaneously occurring that to actually write down the odds against such an occurrence happening, the zeros would take up a whole page.

The Magi Society has subjected the 12 Super Aspects and the 17 Sports Champion Aspects to rigorous scientific statistical tests and have found that the principle of Super Aspects is validated. The positive influences of Super Aspects have been verified. Our statistical study is not published with this book because it is beyond the interest level of most of our readers. However, anyone who wishes to obtain the study can contact us.

But even the skeptic should realize that there are too many "coincidences" in this book for these occurrences to actually be coincidental. The symbolism of astrology is consistent for individuals, corporations, marriages, countries, and anything else that has a definable starting date. Rare aspects that help provide power, or money, or fame, or good fortune to one type of birth chart act the same way on all the other types. The Super Success Aspect helps bring success to individuals as well as marriages, corporations, and countries.

In this book, we have also presented the birth charts of, and analyzed the key astrological aspects of, many of the very best athletes in American sports. In our research, we analyzed all of them. In this book, we have covered the top athletes in tennis, hockey, baseball, and basketball, as well as the very best quarterbacks and running backs of football. We have shown that astrological aspects work with all of them.

In addition, we proved that the Super Aspects worked on the country's richest men, the world's most powerful men, Hollywood's most famous long-lasting superstars, and America's most successful corporations, as well as these companies' Chief Executive Officers.

The Super Aspects also work on the most famous weddings of recent times, and on the most powerful countries in the world. And they also work for the most powerful corporations.

Anyone who needs our statistical study to be convinced about the validity of astrology would have to have a very deep-rooted skepticism of astrology. In such a case, no amount of statistical validation may be enough.

Genetics and Astrology

The Magi Society knows that there is enormous validity to the science of genetics, but geneticists and other scientists have extrapolated too much from it. We suggest that everyone should avoid extrapolation and limit themselves to what is proven. What do we mean by *proven*? Scientists themselves agree that nothing in science is proven unless it can help us make predictions that are statistically valid.

But scientists have a habit of hiding behind the phrases "science does not at this time understand..." and "science cannot at this time accurately predict...." These phrases are always followed with "but scientists believe.... " If science cannot do something or cannot understand something, it should not pretend it can. Science should not be in the business of believing; it should stick to the facts. The propensity of scientists to proclaim their theories as facts is egotistical in light of the fact that over 90 percent of all scientific theories are eventually disproved.

We say all this because scientists have many unproven ideas about genetics. Geneticists have been unable to make accurate predictions except in cases where geneticists have isolated the function of a particular gene. For example, scientists cannot predict the intelligence of offspring. Nor can they predict the athletic prowess of offspring. They cannot even predict the body shape of offspring. Will your child be like you in body shape? Even if your spouse has the same body shape as you, no scientist can be accurate in predicting the shape of the body of your children.

The Magi Society believes that Magi Astrology is every bit as scientific as genetics. But contrary to the exclusionary principle of genetics, astrology is inclusive. By this we mean that genetics excludes the idea that there is another science that can be the equal of genetics; but Magi Astrology is inclusive of genetics; it combines astrology with genetics.

For example, Michael Jordan was born with a fabulous birth chart. But not everyone born on that same day is a great basketball player. In fact, Michael Jordan is the only great basketball player born that day. Why? First of all, Jordan has unique physical characteristics that are probably more genetic than astrological. Only a small percentage of the people born the same day as Michael Jordan will have hands as large as Jordan's. Extra-large hands are very important in basketball because anyone who can pick up a basketball with the palm of one hand turned down has a tremendous advantage in the game. Jordan's huge hands allow him to control the basketball with just one hand while he is in the air—hence, his nickname of "Air Jordan." Chalk one up for the effect of genetics. In addition, Michael is 6' 6". Not everyone born on his birthday is that tall. And perhaps Michael's peripheral vision is much wider than normal, a condition that may be primarily genetically governed.

Another reason there is only one Michael Jordan is that the life of Michael is very much related to the life of his parents and the wedding chart of his parents. Now you understand better why we painstakingly charted the progressions of all of the 11 super-famous weddings in chapter 14. The lives of the children that resulted from these marriages are influenced by them.

Our fundamental assertion is that both astrology and genetics influence the life of an individual. Which is more important? We believe that there is no question that astrology is much more important in determining if anyone has a jump start on fame and fortune. But genetics, like free will, paints in some of the details of everyone's life.

Another example of the influence of astrology is that of Charles
Barkley, the other great basketball player of the Jordan era. "Sir
Charles" Barkley was born three days after Michael Jordan. Both have
the same extraordinarily powerful triple declinational enhancement
of Mars, Pluto, and Venus, which gives both basketball superstars
three Super Sports Champion Aspects. (But remember that Michael
has a fourth one in the longitudes.)

During the peak of their basketball careers, these two men were the
two best basketball players. They are both about the same height, but
have very different body shapes. Jordan is streamlined; Barkley looks
much bulkier, and is built more like a football fullback. There are very
few basketball players with Barkley's body shape. Yet, Charles
Barkley is such a great basketball player that he is the shortest player
in the history of the NBA to win a rebounding title. He led the league
in rebounds in 1987. These two men, Jordan and Barkley, with very
similar astrological aspects, but with very different body shapes, are
two of the best athletes ever. This shows why astrology is more important than genetics, especially whenever we are dealing with an individual of extraordinary abilities.

We invite all skeptics to look into the birth charts of the super-successful. That is the only way any skeptic might be convinced that astrology really works. For example, when Jordan went into his initial
retirement (as of this writing, he is back with the Chicago Bulls), and
with Barkley getting older, the person who took their place as Most
Valuable Player was Hakeem Olajuwon, the center of the world-cham-
pion Houston Rockets. Does astrology also work on Olajuwon's birth
chart? What would the skeptics say if they knew that Olajuwon also
has the incredibly rare triple declinational enhancement of Mars, Pluto,
and Venus that Jordan and Barkley have?

We do not know what skeptics would say, but we do know that Olajuwon does, in fact, have this very rare triple enhancement!

You May Choose Your Own Arena

Michael Jordan and Charles Barkley were born just three days apart.
Both made the choice to excel in basketball. Mick Jagger and Sena-

tor Bill Bradley were born just two days apart. But in this case, the pair led almost completely different lives, except that they are both super-successful. You might recall that Mick Jagger was born with the best of all possible Magi Triangles. He has the Jupiter-Pluto-Sun Magi Triangle. So does Senator Bill Bradley. Bradley was a Rhodes Scholar and probably the best basketball player to come out of Princeton University. He helped the New York Knicks win two championships, and he is the only professional basketball player to become a U.S. Senator. What this means is that Jagger and Bradley each chose to use their abilities in different ways.

In the case of Senator Bradley, he was able to become a great athlete not only because he was born with the Super Aspects intrinsic to his Jupiter-Pluto-Sun Magi Triangle, but also because he has a Super Sports Champion Aspect. His ability to play basketball is in part explained by the fact that he has the Super Sports Champion Aspect of Venus trine Mars. Mick Jagger also has this aspect. But instead of directing the energy he gets from it into a sport, Jagger uses the energy to perform on stage. Anyone who has seen one of his concerts has to have been amazed by Mick Jagger's energy level. Some have incorrectly attributed the high energy level to drugs. But Jagger does not need drugs for energy. He has a Super Sports Champion Aspect.

What this all means is that it is a very good idea to know your own birth chart and analyze your aspects. You should do the same for your friends and loved ones. The aspects are a guide to what is most suitable for the native and what he or she is most likely to succeed in. The Magi Society believes that every person is able to do very well at something respectable and be very happy at it. The problem is, too many of us are pushed into trying to achieve something we are not astrologically suited for. Too often, we are in the wrong professions. For example, great singers would probably not be great investment bankers. And great investment bankers would probably not make great singers. And above all, far too much emphasis is placed on fame and fortune. Too many lifetimes are wasted trying to achieve the unattainable. Instead, a simpler life can produce much more happiness and ultimately, that is the greatest success. Through astrology and analyzing our own birth charts, we can have a much better idea at what we can excel in. And the world was designed so that if we do what we are best able to do, we will also be happiest when we do it.

A Safer and Happier Life Through Astrology

We cannot promise fame and fortune if you learn how to apply astrology to your life. But we do believe that everyone who wisely uses astrology will lead a more stable, safe, and happy life.

Magi Astrology will make your life more interesting; you will have insights you were never before privy to, and this will give you an edge.

For example, when Bill Clinton announced on October 3, 1991, that he was a candidate for the Presidency, you could have checked the birth chart of that day, and his *own* birth chart, and determined that there was a very good chance he would become the Democratic Party's Presidential nominee. Why? Because there was a Pluto parallel Sun on October 3, 1991, the date Clinton announced. It was a day of power. And on that day, Uranus was in contra-parallel and applying to Clinton's natal Pluto. This transit is awesome in providing power (Pluto) from the voting public (Uranus). The aspect was only 0:04 degrees away from being exact. If you then looked at George Bush's transits (as explained in chapter 7), you would have known that Bush's popularity was going to shrink dramatically by election day because Uranus would no longer be contra-parallel to his natal Sun. Add it all together, and you would have been the best political analyst of that Presidential campaign. Think of how smart your boss or friends would have thought you were if you had predicted that Clinton would win as early as October of 1991, when Bush's popularity rating was over 80 percent!

Or, take this other example. In August of 1987, there was a great deal of publicity about the Harmonic Convergence due to occur that month. The stock market roared ahead to record levels on August 24, just as the most Jupiter enhancements were occurring. What if you had noticed this and told all your friends to sell their stocks and bonds? And what if you followed your own advice, as well? You would have been a hero and saved yourself from losing money in the stock market crash of October, 1987.

Another example? Perhaps you are a football fan. In September of 1994, you are just as surprised as everyone else that the San Diego Chargers are off to a flying start and playing better than anyone expected. You check the birth charts of the Chargers' star quarterback Stan Humphries and you find out that he has three Super Aspects including the Super Success Aspect, as well as two Sports Champion Aspects. You also find out that the Chargers' star running back, Natrone Means, also has a very powerful astrological chart. His natal Sun is trined by Jupiter, and he has two Sports Champion Aspects including the most powerful one of all, the Venus-Mars enhancement. Ah ha!, you say. You bet on the Chargers to win the Super Bowl. But you lose because you forgot to note our warning that astrology does not promise you fame or fortune. You forgot to check the birth charts of the key players of the San Francisco 49ers. Quarterback Steve Young also has the Super Success Aspect, as well as two Sports Champion Aspects. And Deion Sanders chose to play for the 49ers even though he could have made millions more elsewhere because he wanted to play for a Super Bowl winner. Deion Sanders has one of the strongest birth charts in professional sports; he probably has the most fortunate birth chart in football today. He is likely to choose the right team to play for. The Chargers did not win the Super Bowl, but you had a very enjoyable season, and you were much more aware of what was really happening as the season progressed because of your knowledge of astrology.

Or, you love to ski and have been planning a ski trip with some friends. Before booking reservations for the trip, you check your ephemeris and find out that you have a transit of Saturn square your Pluto on the weekend you had planned to ski. You decide it might be dangerous to ski when you have such a transit. You pick another weekend and sit home during the Saturn transit. Because you knew about the Saturn transit, you were cautious and took prudent measures. You lived through the bad transit without enduring any mishaps.

It could also be that you are having problems at work. You were passed over for a promotion and are very disappointed. But you notice that you did start your job on a very good day. You check your ephemeris and find out you have been having a quincunx transit by Saturn to your natal Sun. You realize that it is hard to obtain a promotion during such a transit; even if you get one you may not want it because you are having a problematic transit and would not have wanted to make changes during such a transit. You reconcile yourself to waiting for another chance. But knowing about astrology makes not getting the promotion easier to handle. Besides, you notice that Jupiter will trine your Pluto in three months. You plan on asking for a promotion around that time.

Little by little, if you use astrology correctly, you gain just enough of an edge in life to make a big enough difference to really appreciate that knowledge of astrology is a gift of Providence. Without this knowledge, you have much less free will because you are not aware of what is happening and therefore cannot make an intelligent decision.

More Proof of Astrology

Throughout this book, the Magi Society has presented a total of six challenges to skeptics of astrology. Would you like a preview of how a challenge might play itself out?

Let us repeat our fourth challenge to skeptics:

FOURTH CHALLENGE TO SKEPTICS

If astrology does not work, it should be easy for skeptics to list superstar athletes who have none of the 17 Sports Champion Aspects. We challenge skeptics to list more such superstars than we can list superstars who do have Sports Champion Aspects. Skeptics cannot include anyone who has more than one Super Aspect. We must choose athletes who have at least one Super Aspect and at least one Sports Champion Aspect.

***

In this book, we have been using an orb of 3:00 degrees for the longitudes and 2:20 for the declinations. But we are so sure we will win this challenge that we are willing to tighten up the orb. Let us use an orb of only 2:20 degrees for the longitudes and only 1:50 degrees for the declinations. This means that the Super Aspects will occur less often, which means it will be harder for the Magi Society to find athletes who fit within the parameters of the challenge, and it will be easier for skeptics to find athletes who fit their parameters. But we are confident we will win anyway.

As a preview of how a challenge could go, let us look at basketball's very best players—those who have won the Most Valuable Player (MVP) awards in the NBA. A total of 18 players have been given this award since the first one was handed out in 1956; obviously, some have won the award more than once The following is a listing of every player who has been MVP, and their Super Aspects and Sports Champion Aspects:

Bob Petit: Born December 12, 1932
Sports Champion Aspects: Neptune parallel Mars, Neptune conjunction Mars
Super Aspects: Pluto contra-parallel the Sun; Uranus trine the Sun

Bob Cousy: Born August 9, 1928
Sports Champion Aspects: Mars parallel Mercury; Pluto semi-sextile the Sun
Super Aspects: Jupiter parallel Neptune; Neptune parallel Venus; Jupiter parallel Venus (Magi Pyramid)

Bill Russell: Born February 12, 1934
Sports Champion Aspects: Venus parallel Mars; Uranus contra-parallel Mars
Super Aspects: Jupiter trine Sun; Jupiter contra-parallel Neptune; Jupiter contra-parallel Uranus (Magi Pyramid); Uranus contra-parallel Venus; Neptune contra-parallel Venus

Wilt Chamberlain: Born August 21, 1936
Sports Champion Aspect: Jupiter contra-parallel Pluto (is also a Super Aspect)
Super Aspects: Neptune parallel Venus

Oscar Robertson: Born November 24, 1938
Sports Champion Aspect: Pluto trine Sun (also a Super Aspect)
Super Aspect: Jupiter contra-parallel Uranus

Wes Unseld: Born March 14, 1946
Sports Champion Aspect: Pluto parallel Mars
Super Aspects: Neptune parallel the Sun; Neptune parallel Venus (Magi Pyramid)

Willis Reed: Born June 25, 1942
Sports Champion Aspects: Uranus parallel Mars
Super Aspects: Jupiter parallel Pluto; Pluto parallel the Sun; Jupiter parallel the Sun (Magi Pyramid); Neptune trine Venus

Kareem Abdul-Jabbar: Born April 16, 1947
Sports Champion Aspect: Saturn trine Mars
Super Aspect: Jupiter in bidirectional quincunx of the Sun

Dave Cowens: Born October 25, 1948
Sports Champion Aspect: Jupiter parallel Mars; Pluto contra-parallel Mars; Uranus contra-parallel Mars
Super Aspects: Jupiter contra-parallel Pluto; Jupiter contra-parallel Uranus; Uranus parallel Pluto (Magi Pyramid); Uranus trine Sun; Neptune contra-parallel Venus

Bob McAdoo: Born September 15, 1951
Sports Champion Aspect: Pluto semi-sextile the Sun
Super Aspects: Jupiter parallel the Sun; Jupiter parallel Venus (Magi Pyramid); Uranus parallel Pluto

Bill Walton: Born November 5, 1952
Sports Champion Aspects: Venus parallel Mars; Mars parallel Mercury
Super Aspects: Jupiter contra-parallel the Sun; Uranus parallel Pluto.

Moses Malone: Born March 23, 1955
Sports Champion Aspect: Jupiter parallel Pluto (also a Super Aspect)
Super Aspect: Jupiter parallel Uranus (Magi Pyramid)

Julius Erving: Born February 22, 1950
Sports Champion Aspect: Mars trine Mercury
Super Aspects: Jupiter trine Neptune; Uranus parallel Pluto

Larry Bird: Born December 7, 1956
Sports Champion Aspect: Jupiter contra-parallel Mars
Super Aspects: Pluto contra-parallel the Sun

Magic Johnson: Born August 14, 1959
Sports Champion Aspect: Venus conjunct Mars
Super Aspect: Jupiter contra-parallel Uranus

Michael Jordan: Born February 17, 1963
Sports Champion Aspects: Venus contra-parallel Mars; Venus trine Pluto (also a Super Aspect)
Super Aspects: Pluto contra-parallel Venus; Uranus contra-parallel the Sun

Charles Barkley: Born February 20, 1963
Sports Champion Aspects: Venus contra-parallel Mars; Pluto contra-parallel Venus (also a Super Aspect)
Super Aspect: Uranus contra-parallel the Sun

Hakeem Olajuwan: Born January 21, 1963
Sports Champion Aspects: Venus contra-parallel Mars; Pluto parallel Mars
Super Aspects: Pluto contra-parallel the Sun; Pluto contra-parallel Venus

There! You have them all. Every Most Valuable Player in the National Basketball Association. Not a single one of them would have been able to fit the parameters of the skeptics. They all were born with at least one Sports Champion Aspect and at least one Super Aspect. That's 18 out of 18.

Astrology really works!

🪐   🪐   🪐

Consider this:

It is Christmas time and the wind is howling. In a tiny apartment of a tenement in a big northeastern city, a young couple do their best to keep their newborn child warm. The heat has not worked for weeks. The father, weakened by severe asthma and restricted by a poor education, has been unemployed for months. The mother has been able to work as a secretary from time to time but has very poor eyesight and cannot seem to hold onto a job. Neither parent possesses any special talent or employable skills, but both have enormous love for their child and each other. The world appears cruel to them now as they view their surroundings. They huddle in the corner, as far as possible from the icy window. Their greatest hope is that their child will have a much better life than their own.

Through the miracle of the benevolent design of astrology, the young couple's child *can* have a wonderful life. Unlike the world that Darwinists believe exists, the reality is that the child will not be saddled with the disadvantages of its parents' so-called inferior genes. Thank God!

Think about it: Henry Ford had only a grade school education. But he had four Super Aspects. Andrew Carnegie had to begin working at the age of 13; he earned $1.20 per week in a cotton factory. At age 67, Carnegie sold his Carnegie Steel Company for $500 million. He had four Super Aspects. Bill Cosby grew up in a housing project in Philadelphia. He shined shoes and delivered groceries. He has a Magi Pyramid of Jupiter, Sun, and Pluto. He is widely regarded as the wealthiest African-American entertainer in Hollywood. Considering that very successful parents usually use their power and influence to help their children, what chance would these men have had if they had actually been born with inferior genes? They would have had no chance. But Providence designed the world so that astrology is a benevolent design which overrules Darwinism.

As we explained in chapter 11, proof of Magi Astrology is the closest thing to proof of Providence because it verifies the existence of a very purposeful and benevolent design in the universe. Through the benevolent design of astrology, every parent has an equal chance of having an extraordinarily gifted child. And every parent has the realistic hope that their children's lives will be better than their own. Do not ever let the skeptics take that hope away.

Think how unfair the world would be without astrology. Those who are very successful could actually pass on their success to their children. They could and would use their own success, money, and influence to help their children obtain the best education, and use their connections and power to help their children. If genes were also a factor, what chance would the children of the poor have?

However, due to the benevolent design of astrology, no matter how disadvantaged certain parents may be, their children can be super-successful. Champion athletes have had parents who had no athletic talent. Geniuses came from nowhere. Do you know who Albert Einstein's parents were? Or Sir Isaac Newton's? Were any of them great intellects? And how come so many children of great men and women are themselves below average? Astrology was designed so that there would be no clans or families that could dominate for more than a few generations. This makes the world a more hopeful place for the underdog. After all, Christ did teach us that the meek shall inherit the Earth.

The Magi Society realizes that skeptics will not exactly embrace this book. But we did not write it for them. In part, we wrote it to challenge them. After they have read this book, only those skeptics who want to be unreasonable and do not want to accept the truth will continue to refute the validity of astrology. We know that they cannot meet our challenges. Nonetheless, we expect to be attacked and vilified by the most diehard of skeptics. What we have written will be misrepresented, taken out of context, and nitpicked. When skeptics find out that they cannot succeed in meeting our challenges, they will claim that it is not necessary to meet them. When they realize that they cannot successfully criticize what we have written, they will criticize what we are; we are certain many of them will be untruthful in that regard, also. Please do not let the skeptics fool you. Do not let them avoid the challenges. Astrology really works and is proven unless the skeptics can meet all of our challenges

But now that you, one of the 47 percent who believes astrology has scientific truths, realize the power of Magi Astrology, please do not run to your street-parlor astrologer asking for advice. Unfortunately, some of them are as superstitious as the skeptics say they are. There are only a handful of legitimate astrologers in the whole world. Take the time to learn about Magi astrology yourself, and the benevolent way it is designed. Let your mind be open to the order and fairness of it. Learn how beautiful it is. Enjoy it and be comforted in the knowledge that there is a higher power, one that is unimaginably benevolent, one that loves you and cares deeply about your welfare.

We hope that this book opens a new door for you, a door to a new and better life—a life in which you will be more knowledgeable and will have a far greater understanding of why events are occurring, how you will be affected by them, and what the long-term consequences of these occurrences will be. Please walk through the door and enter the Age of Aquarius. Bring your loved ones; bring your friends. Join us. Let us all help each other.

TO BE CONTINUED...

🪐   🪐   🪐

ABOUT THE MAGI SOCIETY

The Magi Society is an international association of men and women who know that astrology works and who are devoted to helping humankind in the Age of Aquarius. The founders include a statistician, a psychologist, a Wall Street money manager, an attorney, a computer expert, the world's best astrologers, and a number of very special private individuals.

If you would like information about the Magi Society, or if you want to become a member, or if you would just like to speak to one of our associates, you may contact us at: (212) 867-2905.

If this number changes for some reason, call Information in New York City, area code 212. We will be listed under "Magi Society."

APPARENT: The way that the planets look like they are moving, as opposed to what their actual motions are; in other words, what the eye sees rather than what is actually happening.

APPLYING: A term referring to the condition where a planet is moving towards another planet; but if, for example, Jupiter is moving away from another planet, Jupiter is separating. The term *applying* may also be used to describe an aspect where the two planets making the aspect are moving closer to each other.

APPLYING ENHANCEMENT: A term in Magi Astrology referring to the condition where an enhancement aspect is created by having at least one of the natal planets applying to the other, and the applying natal planet is Jupiter, Uranus, Neptune, or Pluto.

ASCENDANT: The degree and sign of the zodiac that is just rising at the eastern horizon at the time of a birth chart. The ascendant is one of the calculated points and is considered by most astrologers as very significant.

ASPECT INTEGRATION: A term in Magi Astrology referring to the process of blending and combining all the astrological aspects of a birth chart to create an integrated whole analysis that takes into account the force of all the aspects working simultaneously and continuously.

ASPECT OF POLITICAL POWER: Jupiter enhancement of Uranus. Bill Clinton, Albert Gore, and Newt Gingrich were all born with this aspect. It is also called the Super Fame Aspect because over half of the Hollywood megastars in this book have this aspect.

ASTROCHART: In this book, it refers to a natal chart with the declinations as well as the longitudes.

ASTROLOGICAL ASPECT: An alignment between two planets that is considered meaningful by astrologers. In the case of longitudes, all alignments between any two planets that create an angle that is a multiple of 30 degrees is an astrological aspect. There are also other angles that are considered to be meaningful by most astrologers but are not dealt with in this book because there is no proof at this time that they work. In the case of the declinations, an astrological aspect is an alignment between two planets where the two planets are in the same degree of declination, regardless of whether they are both in north or south declination, or one planet is in north declination while the other is in south declination.

BENEFIC: A planet that is considered by astrologers to provide beneficial influences; the influences can be either as a planet in aspect to another planet or as a planet in transit to a natal planet.

BIDIRECTIONAL ASPECT: A Magi Astrology term referring to any longitudinal aspect that is comprised of one planet in retrograde, while the other planet is in direct motion.

BI-LEVEL ENHANCEMENT: A Magi Astrology term referring to the very fortunate condition where a natal planet is enhanced in both the declinations and the longitudes, but where there is no planetary eclipse involving the natal planet. An example would be if the Sun is parallel Neptune, and at the same time Pluto is in trine to the Sun. Bi-levels are super-powerful.

BIRTH CHART: This is a two-dimensional representation of the longitudinal dimension of the locations of planets at the time of birth. (Please refer to one of the charts at the end of chapter 2.) The birth chart comprises a circle divided into 12 equal parts, each of which represents 30 degrees and is assigned one of the 12 constellations of the zodiac. The positions of the planets are drawn in symbolic form along the circle, and the degrees are notated alongside the symbol of a planet. The symbols of the planets and the twelve signs are listed on the first chart page at the end of the text section of chapter 2. Astrologers generally use a method of notating the degrees in a very confusing manner. Sometimes 23 degrees and 14 minutes is written as "23 (symbol for sign the planet is in) 14." But at other times the same 23 degrees and 14 minutes is written as "14 (symbol) 23." We find this absurd. If you are not familiar with this method and do not understand what we mean, do not worry about it. The Magi Society has minimized this confusion. In this book, we will always notate all degrees and minutes in the logical manner of always listing the degrees before the minutes, without the symbol of the sign in-between the numbers. That is, 23 degrees and 14 minutes will always be 23:14. It is customary for astrologers to draw lines connecting any planets that are in important aspects to each other. In Magi Astrology, a birth chart refers to an astrochart.

CALCULATED POINTS: An astrologically significant point in the birth chart that is not determined by the location and position of a planet. The midheaven, ascendant, and the 12 house cusps are examples.

CELESTIAL EQUATOR: The imaginary circle created by projecting the Earth's equator onto the backdrop of the sky.

CONFIGURATION: A pattern created by three or more planets.

CONJOIN: A term in Magi Astrology referring to the act of creating any of the following three aspects: conjunction, parallel, and contra-parallel.

CONJUNCT: Forming a conjunction.

CONJUNCTION: An aspect formed by two planets that are in the same sign and the same degree of longitude.

CONTRA-PARALLEL: An aspect in the declinations made between two planets that are in the same degree of declinations, but with the two planets on different sides of the celestial equator.

DECLINATIONAL BIAS: A term in Magi Astrology referring to the astrological phenomenon where planets always move more slowly through the extreme degrees of declinations, thus increasing the likelihood of creating aspects with each other.

DECLINATIONAL SYNCHRONIZATION: A Magi Astrology term for planets that are in planetary synchronization in the declinations.

DECLINATIONS: The vertical coordinate (or location) of the planets. The declination of a planet is the distance, in degrees, north or south of the Celestial Equator. The Sun's declination varies between about 23.5 degrees north to 23.5 degrees south declination. The change in declination is caused by the tilt of the Earth as it revolves around the Sun.

DIAGONALS: A term in Magi Astrology referring to the lines connecting the planets on a Magi Complete Astrochart, which is a two-dimensional map of the planets as they actually appear to the eye. Sometimes these lines, or diagonals, form powerful figures, such as isosceles or equilateral triangles. When planets align such that they can form such figures, the power of the planets is extraordinarily enhanced. We will deal with such matters in a later book.

DIRECT MOTION: Unlike retrograde motion, direct motion refers to the condition that exists when a planet appears to be moving forward.

ELECTIONAL ASTROLOGY: That part of astrology that deals with the selection of favorable days and times to begin an endeavor or a relationship. The theory is that every activity has a natal chart, and the astrological chart of a relationship or an endeavor is the chart of the commencement date of the activity. Just as is the case for natal charts of people, the natal charts of electional dates have aspects, progressions, and transits. The more favorable the natal chart of the time and date elected to begin the activity, the more successful the results will be.

EPHEMERIS: A book of astrological data that includes the astrological locations (at least the longitudes) of the planets on a periodic (usually daily) basis.

ENHANCEMENT: A term in Magi Astrology referring to a condition where any of the following four aspects exist: conjunction, trine, parallel, or contra-parallel.

ENHANCEMENT BY EXTREME DECLINATION: A concept in Magi Astrology referring to the very beneficial influences of a planet when it is at very extreme degrees of declination.

EQUAL DEGREE ASPECT: A term in Magi Astrology referring to a longitudinal astrological aspect formed by two planets such that the angle between the two planets is a multiple of 30 degrees. Examples are the 90-degree square aspect, or the 180-degree opposition aspect.

EXDEK: Abbreviation for enhancement by extreme declination.

EXTREME DEGREES: A term in Magi Astrology referring to the declinational degrees over 21 on either side of the celestial equator.

FALLOUT: A term in Magi Astrology referring to residual negative influences existing for a short duration after an exact negative transit or progression peaked and began to separate.

FOUNTAIN-OF-YOUTH ASPECT: A Magi Society discovery, this aspect is an enhancement of the Sun by Neptune; the aspect bestows youth and longevity to the native.

FOUR STRONGEST PLUTO ENHANCEMENTS: In Magi Astrology, this refers to the four enhancements to Pluto that are most helpful.

GRAND CROSS: A configuration of four planets aligned to each other in such a way that each is square to two of the other planets, and each planet is opposed to another.

GRAND TRINE: A configuration of three planets where each of the three are 120 degrees apart from the other two planets.

HOUSES: There are 12 houses in the usual longitudinal natal chart; each of the houses are said to rule different things. There are a number of different ways to divide the 360-degree longitudinal horoscope into 12 houses, but all these different ways of calculating the house do have one parameter in common: they all have six houses on each side of the horizon.

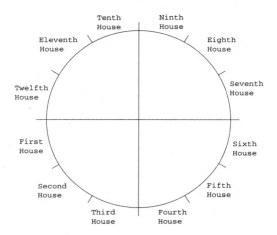

IN ASPECT: For the longitudes, a condition created by an alignment of two planets such that the angle between the two planets are in multiples of 30 degrees. For example, Mars is in aspect to Jupiter whenever the angle between these two planets is 30 degrees, or 60 degrees, or any other multiple of 30 degrees, including zero degrees.

For the declinations, "in aspect" is a condition created by an alignment of two planets such that the two planets are both in the same degree of declination, regardless of whether they are on the same or opposite sides of the celestial equator. For example, if Mars is in 20 degrees north or south declination, and Jupiter is in 20 degrees north or south declination, the two planets are in aspect to each other.

KEY WORDS: Words that accurately describe the influence, effect, or result of a planet or sign.

LONGITUDES: The commonly used dimension of astrology. When an astrologer says that the Sun is in 15 degrees Cancer, it means the longitude of the Sun is 15 degrees Cancer. The longitudes are the horizontal coordinate (or location) of a planet. It is measured in degrees eastward from 0 degrees of Aries.

LONGITUDINAL SYNCHRONIZATION: A Magi Astrology term for planetary synchronization of planets in the longitudes.

MAGI ASTROCHART: A birth chart drawn the Magi Astrology way. Normal birth charts depict the locations of only the longitudes of the planets. A Magi Astrochart includes the declinations. All planets that are in significant declinational aspect to each other are highlighted by connecting lines. The lines may directly connect the aspecting planets, or the lines may first touch at the S-curve, or at either the horizontal or vertical lines which run the length of the diameter and create a cross-hair.

MAGI ASTROLOGY: Astrological principles and rules of interpretation specifically developed by founders of the Magi Society.

MAGI PYRAMID: A term in Magi Astrology referring to the condition where in the declinations, at least three planets are each in aspect to one another. This usually occurs when three planets are all parallel to each other, but it is possible for it to occur when one planet is contra-parallel to two planets, which are, in turn, parallel to each other. To qualify for being a Magi Pyramid, the aligning planets can be any combination of the Sun, Venus, Jupiter, Uranus, Neptune, or Pluto.

MAGI TRIANGLE: A term in Magi Astrology referring to the condition where in the longitudes, at least three planets are each in equal-degree aspect to each other. The aspects can be any equal-degree aspects, but the largest configuration formed cannot be a T-Square or a square (cannot be a conjunction of two planets where both are in square to another planet). The aligning planets must be some combination of the Sun, Venus, Jupiter, Uranus, Neptune, or Pluto.

MALEFIC: A planet that is considered by astrologers to have negative influences; these influences can be either as a planet in aspect to another planet or as a planet in transit to a natal planet.

MIDHEAVEN: A calculated point in a natal chart, it refers to the degree and sign of the zodiac which is at the most elevated point at the instant of birth.

MIDPOINT: Usually refers to the unoccupied point in the zodiac that is exactly equidistant in longitudinal degrees to two planets. In Magi Astrology, the midpoint may be occupied and may be in the declinations.

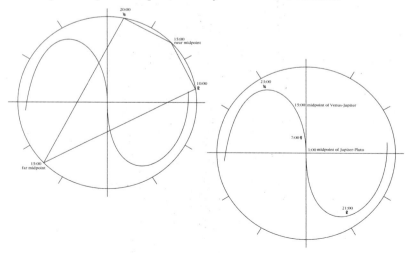

MONODIRECTIONAL ASPECT: A Magi term for an aspect that has both planets in retrograde, or both planets in direct motion.

NATAL: Refers to the planet at birth. The position of the natal Sun is the astrological position of the Sun at birth. In Magi Astrology, there are always two natal positions for each planet—one in the longitudes and the other in the declinations.

NATAL CHART: Same as birth chart.

NATAL PLANETS: The planets as represented in a natal chart.

NATAL POSITION: The position in longitude or declination of a planet at the time of birth.

NATIVE: The subject of the birth chart or the subject that has a particular aspect. For example, if we say that a Mars-Venus parallel provides the native with boundless energy, we mean that the person who has the Mars-Venus parallel aspect will have boundless energy.

OCCULTATION: The eclipsing of one planet by another planet.

ORB: The number of degrees within which an aspect is regarded as active and effective.

PARALLEL: An aspect in the declinations made between two planets that are in the same degree declination, and also on the same side of the celestial equator.

PERPETUAL PROGRESSION: A concept in Magi Astrology referring to the condition where a progression lasts many years.

PLANETARY ECLIPSE: Two planets creating an eclipse.

PLANETARY SYNCHRONIZATION: A concept of Magi Astrology, it refers to the condition where at least three planets are within orb to all make aspects to each other. This can occur in the longitudes or declinations.

PRECESSION OF THE EQUINOXES: The astronomic phenomenon where the backdrop of the fixed stars move backwards about one degree every 71.5 years.

PROGRESSION: In this book, and in Magi Astrology, progressions are transits that begin occurring immediately after birth and projected to influence the native in the future on the basis of a whole year of influence for each day of transit. For example, the transits that occur on the 50th day after birth will influence the native for the entire 50th year of the native's life.

PROXIMITY ENHANCEMENT: A term in Magi Astrology referring to the condition where any two planets (except Saturn) are in equal-degree aspect to each other, and the aspect is closer than 0:30 degrees. Such proximity of two planets in aspect to each other is considerably more favorable than a wide aspect of the same two planets. This is equally true for longitudinal and declinational aspects.

REFERENCE PLANE: Most planets revolve around the Sun on approximately the same plane; the reference plane is the plane of the Earth's movement around the Sun.

RETROGRADE MOTION: A visual phenomenon where a planet appears to be moving backwards in the sky from day to day; a planet does not actually move backwards, but will appear to do so from time to time because of the rate of change of the angular relationship of the Earth and the planet.

RULED BY: Influenced and controlled by. Each part of our body is ruled by a different planet. Each type of profession is ruled by a different planet. Everything has a planet as the ruler and another planet as a sub-ruler.

RULER: The planet or sign that has primary control and influence over a particular thing; for example, Pluto is the ruler of big business; Mars is the ruler of energy.

RULING PROGRESSION: A term in Magi Astrology referring to a progression, which is so powerful that it is the primary influence on the native's life. Such progressions can be positive or negative.

SECONDARY PROGRESSIONS: This is the usual term for what Magi Astrology refers to as progressions; see "Progressions."

SECTOR: A portion of the natal chart; the size of sectors may vary depending on how an astrologer wishes to use sectors, but they are always greater than the size of a single house.

SEPARATING: A term referring to the condition where a planet is moving away from another planet; but if, for example, Jupiter is moving towards another planet, Jupiter is applying rather than separating. The term *separating* may also be used in reference to an aspect where the two planets making the aspect are moving farther apart.

SPORTS CHAMPION ASPECT: A term in Magi Astrology referring to one of the 17 aspects that have been found by the Magi Society to greatly enhance athletic ability. Most of these aspects involve Mars or Pluto.

SQUARE: An angle of 90 degrees between two planets in the longitudes.

STATISTICALLY VALID: A scientific term referring to validation through the use of statistical testing procedures.

SUB-RULER: A planet or sign that has a secondary, as opposed to primary, influence over a thing. For example, Mars is the ruler of energy and Pluto is the sub-ruler. The influence of Mars over energy is greater than that of Pluto, but both have influences.

SUPER ASPECT: In Magi Astrology, one of 12 aspects discovered by the Magi Society to bestow to the native a significant advantage in achieving fame and fortune, or success in general.

SUPER SPORTS CHAMPION ASPECT: One of the 17 strongest Super Champion Aspects.

SUPER SUCCESS ASPECT: An enhancement of Jupiter and Pluto.

SYMBOLISM: The astrological principle that different planets have different influences, and each planet represents, or rules, different things, professions, disciplines, ideas, parts of the body, etc.

TRANSIT: The passage of a planet in motion over a position such that the passing planet is in aspect to a natal planet.

TRANSITING ASPECT: The aspect made by a planet making a transit to a natal planet.

TRINE: An aspect between two planets where the planets are 120 degrees apart in longitude.

TROPICAL ZODIAC: The zodiac system devised by Claudius Ptolemy, around A.D.165, which is the standard method of western astrologers today. It takes into account the precession of the equinoxes and adjusts for it such that the starting point of a horoscope, zero degree Aries, is always where the Sun is at the Spring Equinox, as opposed to using the actual zero degree of the constellation of Aries. The zero degree of Aries in the Tropical Zodiac moves one degree backwards every 71.5 years because of the precession of the equinoxes.

TWELVE SUPER PROGRESSIONS: In Magi Astrology, similar to a Super Aspect, the 12 super progressions refer to the 12 progressions that the Magi Society has found to be most beneficial to the native in achieving fame and fortune.

UNEQUAL DEGREE ASPECT: A longitudinal astrological aspect formed by two planets where the angle between the two planets is not a multiple of 30 degrees. Examples are the 45-degree angle of a semi-square, or the 72-degree angle of a quintile. Such aspects are not used in this book because the Magi Society has found no statistically validated proof that they work.

🪐 🪐 🪐

We hope you enjoyed
this Hay House book.
If you would like to receive a free catalog featuring additional
Hay House books and products, or if you would like
information about the
Hay Foundation, please write to:

Hay House, Inc.
1154 E. Dominguez St.
P.O. Box 6204
Carson, CA 90749-6204
or call:

(800) 654-5126

🪐 🪐 🪐